"This book is a tour de force, a synthesis of technical and professional scholarship, yet easily understood by any intelligent reader. Barnes organizes his material tightly and writes clearly throughout, with lucid introductions to and summaries of each section."

Eugene C. Best
Marist College

"This is a graceful and engaging work, written with warmth and wit. It comprehensively treats human religiousness as one phenomenon, common to our race, yet all the while deftly describing and analyzing that phenomenon.... The comparison of religions, philosophical reasoning, and psychological perceptivity are neatly intertwined. An intensely human book."

Robert T. Fortna
Vassar College

"This is a very useful and competent account of the development of human religious consciousness and behavior encompassing the entire human race from pre-historic beginnings to the present age. It is not a book of spirituality or of theology or philosophy, though all of these play a role and can be helped by this book. Neither is it a history of religions. It is, as the subtitle indicates, the story of human religiousness. The book is free of jargon and reads easily. It is a very useful introduction to the phenomenon of religion."

Robert F. Harvanek, S.J.
Loyola University of Chicago
Review for Religious

"The college student will find in this book a well-defined context for religious reflection. The college teacher might well find it a good text for an introduction to religious studies."

Daniel Liderbach
Canisius College

"...the inclusion of illustrative anecdotes adds spice to the underlying themes."

Spiritual Life

"Teenagers as well as adults can use this book with profit."
The Living Church

Revised

In the Presence of Mystery
An Introduction to the
Story of Human Religiousness

Michael Horace Barnes

XXIII
TWENTY-THIRD PUBLICATIONS
Mystic, Connecticut

DEDICATION

To my parents
Horace and Corlin
with love and gratitude.

Fifth printing 1997
Revised Edition 1990

Twenty-Third Publications
185 Willow Street
P.O. Box 180
Mystic, CT 06355
(860) 536-2611
800-321-0411

ISBN 0-89622-425-2
Library of Congress Catalog Card Number 89-52153
Printed in the U.S.A.

Preface

After four years of classroom use as a textbook, *In the Presence of Mystery : An Introduction to the Story of Human Religiousness* had evoked enough questions and suggestions to call for a second edition. The majority of the changes have been minor ones, clearing up small errors, revising passages for greater clarity, adding dates of birth and death for major persons mentioned, changing some language. There are also some major changes, listed below, especially in the chapter on morality and in places that concern myth.

Religion and Culture Have Evolved

A number of comments I have received have been directed against the thesis on which the book is built, namely, the claim by Robert Bellah and others that there is an evolution of culture and religion. Among many of those trained in the history of religions there is a strong conviction that theories of cultural evolution have proved to be both false and invidious, discriminating unfairly against all cultures which do not share in the thought style and morality of European cultures.

There was in fact much that was wrong with earlier evolutionary interpretations of religion and culture. The famous scheme of Auguste Comte, for example, identified religion with primitive belief styles, philosophy with classical cultures, and science with modern culture. *In the Presence of Mystery*, following Bellah, claims instead that religion (as well as science and philosophy) has primitive, archaic, classical, and modern forms.

Religion does not belong only to a primitive style of thought. The 19th-century theories of cultural evolution were also used as a justification for colonialist imperialism, on the grounds that the superior cultures of Europe ought to dominate lesser cultures. I too consider this illegitimate. There were other problems with many of the 19th-century formulations, enough to provide grounds in the early part of this century for the anthropologist Franz Boas to lead the movement away from using such schemes to interpret the cultures of the world.

Nonetheless, in the last thirty years or so, there has been an accumulation of anthropological studies testing the degree to which changes in economic and social complexity (as from primitive foraging cultures to more advanced agricultural-trading cultures) produce parallel changes in notions about the spirits and gods and in the form of the stories about them. There are also various studies on how Piaget's theory about cognitive development and Kohlberg's formulations about the development of moral reasoning correlate with degrees of social complexity and differentiation in various cultures. The result of these studies has been to substantiate both the general idea of cultural evolution as well as Bellah's specific outline of religious evolution. There is much that is still unclear and much that is in dispute about cultural and religious evolution, so it is best to speak cautiously. But the general fact of it is well supported by numerous anthropological studies.

Because there are still disputes, let me mention a few recent sources that summarize and review other studies. David Levinson and Martin J. Malone, *Toward Explaining Human Culture* (HRAF Press, 1980), analyze and compare studies on a large number of different cultures. Other relevant works are those of

Pierre R. Dasen and Alastair Heron, "Cross-Cultural Tests of Piaget's Theory, *The Handbook of Cross-Cultural Psychology*, Vol. 4 "Developmental Psychology" (Boston" Allyn and Bacon, 1981), Ch. 7, pp. 295-341; John R. Snarey, "Cross-Cultural Universality of Social-Moral Development: A Critical Review of Kohlbergian Research," *Psychological Bulletin* 97/2, 1985), pp. 202-232; and Dean Sheils, "An Evolutionary Explanation of Supportive Monotheism," *International Journal of Comparative Sociology* XV/1-2, 1974, pp. 47-56.

A Debt to Rahner and Tillich

Comments on the book have attributed its underlying theme either to Paul Tillich or to Karl Rahner. Both estimates are correct. A constant theme of the book is Rahner's notion that our humanness is constituted by our relation to an endlessly moving horizon of being, a mystery or Mystery, the awareness of which is the fundamental religious question. Much is also borrowed from Tillich, including ideas about ultimacy, estrangement, and symbols.

Tillich is already mentioned at a number of points. It is good to acknowledge here also the influence of Rahner. The original reason for writing this book was to introduce first-year college students to Rahner's notion of infinite mystery as the ultimate context of human life. This notion is valuable both for understanding a major element in many contemporary theologies and for recognizing the peculiar character of us humans as beings with a capacity for open-ended reflection and choice. For first-year students the notion of mystery as it appears today in theologies and philosophies is rather sophisticated, hard to grasp and hard to appreciate as something valuable. My own teaching experience convinced me that it was a notion that I had to sneak up on very slowly with a lot of specific information, a lot of concrete instances and images. An early working title for this book, in fact, was "Sneaking Up on the Mystery."

The Use of Repetition

The structure of the book reflects my own teaching experience in another way. Even a long and clear exposition of any one aspect of religion gets lost among the many aspects and is readily forgotten. So the reader will find each major idea described once in the context of one chapter's topic, and then find it again in the context of one or more later chapters and their topics. The repetition of the same idea in different contexts helps to make the idea clearer by showing it from different angles, and also makes it a firmer part of the reader's memory as it becomes more familiar from the repetition.

Changes in the Text

Some of the changes are major ones. Chapter Eight, on forms of morality, has been revised a great deal. The former version linked each of the four types of morality named with one of the four different types of cultures. While that neat pairing of a morality with a culture type is simpler to understand, it sacrificed too much accuracy. Each type of culture is a field where many styles of morality are in conflict. The current form of Chapter Eight better represents the complexity of interplay among moral styles and forms of culture.

Wherever references to the role of myth in religion and culture already appeared in the first edition, some extra material has been added—though sometimes just a sentence or two—to coincide with current interest in myth. The titles of Chapters Nine and Ten have been changed to emphasize the role of tradition in religion. In Chapter Eleven the label "systematic theology" has replaced the awkward "sacred" theology, and "simple faith" is now called "traditional faith" or "unchallenged faith." Portions of the last chapter have been revised to provide more clarity about the positions of Feuerbach and Barth; and what was formerly called the "Lonergan-style" position is now labeled the "implicit-faith" position. Descriptions of forms of liberation theologies have been expanded somewhat.

Acknowledgments

Let me take the time here to extend words of thanks: to graduate assistant John Lay for research; to Mark Moorman and Mary Lou Baker Jones for careful readings of the manuscript; to Matthew Kohmescher and James Heft for their support as chairpersons; to Rita Bowen, who has taught me better how to use this book as a classroom text; to Pat and Neil Kluepfel, a wonderful couple to deal with as publishers and persons; to John van Bemmel as a supportive editor, with ongoing counsel and encouragement provided by Stephen Scharper, also of Twenty-Third Publications; and a special and emphatic thanks to both Jim Dunaway and Steve Ostovich for their many specific and very helpful suggestions for revisions based on their own classroom experience with the text.

Contents

Introduction

There is a tale told by Australian aborigines about the beginning. Once there was no death in the world. But one day Purukupali the hunter returned home to find his son Jinini dead from the heat of the sun. Grieving, he picked up the body of his child and walked into the sea to drown himself. As he stepped into the swirling waters, he shouted that because his son had died, so must everyone else from that day on. And so it has been ever since. Purukupali was one of the original people of the world. Just before him had been Mudungkala, the original mother who rose out of the ground with her children, crawled about making hills and rivers, and decreed that the bare ground should grow green things for food and for creatures to hide in. And so it has been ever since.

Stories such as these may represent the earliest human attempts to express and come to terms with the great mysteries of life such as where the grass and the rivers come from and why we must all die. For the last 50,000 years or so, we humans have been engaged in an adventure of self-discovery. Over and over again we have discerned a dimension of mystery in our existence, in the fact of life and death, in the patterns of love and indifference and anger, in the regularity of pain, and in the surprise of joy. In all this there is mystery—why it is so, what promise or threat it holds, how we can deal with it.

Few things reveal as much about us as the story of how we have responded to the dimension of mystery. That story, for the most part, is the story of religion.

Facing Mystery

Religion is a human response to mystery. A primitive tribesperson is uneasy about the mysterious forces that cause rain, bring good luck, and make strange emotions enter the heart. The primitive tribesperson names these forces, gives them faces and tells brief stories about them, in order to deal with them. Later cultures develop greater and more complex myths, describing some of the mysterious forces of nature as gods and families of gods. With symbol, ritual, and elaborate story, humankind gives mystery concrete forms in order to tame it and make it less threatening.

Eventually, we humans discover that mystery is endless. About 2500 years ago, the major cultures of the earth stumbled onto the realization that beyond all the specific forms and faces we give to the mysterious forces that exist, there is an ultimate and infinite context of our lives that is an all-embracing mystery. There are various religious ways to label the mystery. In the West it is usually called "God." Buddhists call it nirvana. Other cultures have other names for it.

Even when we are not consciously aware of it, ideas about the ultimate mystery of life may be influencing us. When you have lunch, for example, you may decide what to eat on the basis of the social consequences, such as sharing a meal with a friend. Your friendship in turn will be based on various things, such as who is easiest to laugh with, who seems to like you more, who shares your values, or even who can help you socially. All of these criteria in turn are related to your basic feelings about which values are most important in your life, whether it be your own social success or having a friend to rely on in life's troubles or being able to take some satisfaction in your helpfulness toward others. And each of these in turn may rest on an even more fundamental sense of what life is finally all about. Are we but solitary strangers in a dog-eat-dog world? Or are we children of God awaiting another life? Or are we brothers and sisters on an adventure of life?

Without knowing it at times, we carry in us ideas about such things, ideas that are our implicit answers to life's mysteries. At a certain point in our thoughts we shrug our shoulders and say to ourselves that we will not try to ask some of these questions because we cannot see how to answer them. That is the point at which we have discovered mystery. We may then choose to ignore it, but it is still there. And the way we deal with it affects our lives one way or another.

We can deal with it in non-religious ways. Some people have formally declared the dimension of mystery to be simply the unknowable and therefore to be ignored. This is the position taken by agnostics. Others have said that the mystery that surrounds us is just endless possibility, empty in itself with no direction or meaning. This is the position taken by atheists. Agnostics and atheists alike find no *ultimate* meaningfulness in the mystery. They turn instead to the projects at hand, that of making a living, learning to love, preparing the way for future generations, finding some joy in great art and pleasant picnics and the laughter of a child.

All of these are treasures of life, but they have not satisfied everyone in history. Beyond living and loving and laughing, there still remains the "more," the mystery, the endless possible questions about who we really are, what we ultimately come from, whether there is any lasting purpose to our lives. Is it possible that we come from randomness, are accidents of nature, have no purpose in the end? A good-hearted paleontologist, Stephen Jay Gould, has proposed this in his book on evolution, *Wonderful Life*. Such ideas have haunted the great civilizations of humankind. Each of them has usually found religious ways to deal with the mystery, treating it not as a deadly emptiness but somehow as a fullness in which lies the meaning of human existence, naming that fullness "God," or in India "Brahman" or perhaps "nirvana," or in China calling it the Tao.

We will see more about the ways in which great classical religions of history such as Judaism, Christianity, Islam, Hinduism, Buddhism, and Taoism give a name to the ultimate Mystery. Some religions do not worry explicitly about whatever it is that is "ultimate" in reality. That is a fairly sophisticated idea, as we will see in Chapters Three and Four. But they do worry about the aspects of life that would be mysteries outside the realm of their understanding were it not for the ways in which their religious ideas give some name to these mysteries and explain them.

A Basic Human Faith

Most people in history have been religious in some way or another in the face of mystery. This reveals aspects of our human character that are sometimes hidden from us. First of all, we are stubbornly courageous beings. The religions of humankind are all manifestations of a kind of courageous faith in the meaningfulness of life in the face of the mystery that surrounds us. Facing mystery, we could wander in confusion, feel great fear, or even despair. Instead, we find the faith to see it as somehow valuable or intelligible. By naming it, embracing it, building a life in relation to it, we show a trust that ultimately mystery does not destroy but upholds the worthwhileness of our lives. This is what Jews, Christians, and Muslims do when they describe God as the ultimate mystery. This also, as we will see, is what Buddhists do by calling the mystery "nirvana," and Hindus by calling it "Brahman" or "Atman."

Beneath this stubborn and bold faith in the ultimate meaningfulness of life is something else especially human, which is that we are the strange being, the peculiar animal, that can be aware of mystery at all. We have the kind of consciousness that can ask questions, can wonder why things are as they are, and can become insecure as a result. We can think about ourselves, our identities, our place in the scheme of things. Because of that, we can worry about whether it all really does make sense.

Most questions can be turned into problems-to-be-solved so that they are no longer threatening, but there is always some genuine mystery left over that remains a question without an answer. The horizon of mystery always remains there in front of us no matter how far we travel. We find ourselves always able to ask one more question about what is worth living (or dying) for, about what sort of person we should be, about what our destiny is. Even when we ignore such questions, we remain an animal with an endless capacity for them.

Another way of saying this is that we are beings who are open to the infinite. We are beings who are related to whatever is the ultimate foundation or goal of all things (if there is such a foundation or goal, as religions claim), because our kind of consciousness is an openness to what is always beyond: the endless mystery.

As the religions of the world have been our usual way of dealing with mystery, it is a study of these religions that can show us the most about our own nature as beings who are open to infinite mystery. Most of the time our religions provide very specific beliefs, values, and behavior rather than general talk about mystery and the infinite. Religions provide symbols, rituals, moral codes, community life, and personal identity patterns. Each of these many and varied aspects of religion will be explored in some detail in the following chapters. But it is good not to forget that each of these specific forms of religion is significant for us humans precisely because each is one of the ways we bring our lives into a coherent and worthwhile focus in relation to the mystery around us.

The Development of Religion

There are so many specific aspects of religion that it is very difficult to make a coherent story out of it. One way is to follow a particular theory, that of the sociologist Robert Bellah, that claims that religion has passed through certain stages of development. Not all the scholars who study religion agree with this developmental theory. It is wise to be wary of theories; they are not always fully accurate. But Bellah's theory does a great deal to illumine and make sense out of the story of religion and the human capacity for the infinite that religion expresses. This theory has found growing support in the evidence gathered by anthropologists in recent decades.

Bellah's theory claims that religions generally pass through a progression of forms, from primitive and archaic to historic and modern. It also appears that each of us repeats this developmental pattern in our own lives. We are born primitive, and then we grow into archaic and eventually historic and even modern modes of thought. Descriptions of primitive tribespeople around a fire working their magic and invoking the spirits are also descriptions of something buried in your life's story and mine, in ways we do not easily recognize. What the whole human race has experienced is still within us.

Human culture and individual lives expand gradually into broader visions of life. Primitive culture lives in a relatively small world populated by various spirits and magical powers. Archaic cultures perceive a larger and more complicated world with powerful gods at work. Historic cultures conceive of a universal power or Being that exerts its influence everywhere. Finally, the mystics of history and now a modern religiousness emphasize the infiniteness of the Mystery, called by such a name as "God."

Likewise, each of us today may go through stages of understanding. Those raised to believe in God, for example, will begin by thinking of God as an invisible person, like grandpa perhaps, except bigger. At some point in life they may picture God as a cosmic power, clearly and obviously intervening in history and nature. Later yet, they may reflect more on God as infinite and mysterious, always present in a subtle and not obvious way. To abandon one way of thinking of God is not to cease to be religious; it is only a change in the way of being religious.

The cultural developmental process is still just struggling into the most recent stage in Bellah's outline, the modern stage. It has been emerging only in the last couple of centuries, a brief time on the scale of history. Modern religiousness has often been taken to be antireligious, especially by those who are most conservative in their religious feelings because it lets go of or reinterprets some older beliefs and practices. But modern religiousness is also a religious way of facing the mystery of our existence. To understand this modern mode of religion and culture, it is necessary to start at the beginning, with primitive and archaic religion.

The Study of Religion

A later chapter will introduce you to the study of theology. Theology is usually defined as rational reflection about the meaning and coherence of a religious tradition. Theology is most often done by those who accept and support the religious tradition they are reflecting on. Theologians are "insiders" for the most part. This book in general is not theology but is the study of religion. Such study is done, as it were, from the outside. That does not mean that it is necessarily done from a position of disbelief or skepticism, though it can be. You will find most of what is written here to be sympathetic to religion. But the perspective taken is that of looking in on our own human religious life, as though from the outside.

Another way of saying this is to note that some people study a religion to find out more about God and the supernatural and so forth. That is theology. Others study religion in order to find out about us human beings through our religiousness, to find in religious beliefs and practices and symbols clear insights or at least good clues to our own inner selfhood. We human beings are hard to figure out. The study of religion is a great help for learning more about us. That is the purpose and the approach of this book.

In the course of the next fourteen chapters you will find a great deal of information about specific aspects of religion, about spirits, magic, gods, God, Brahman, paradise and hell, heaven, belonging, identity, moral values, leaders and sacred texts, rituals and symbols, faith and reason, skepticism and modern beliefs. But throughout these chapters you will also keep meeting a strange side of ourselves: the capacity for the infinite that our mode of consciousness possesses that keeps us always on the edge of mystery. It is the capacity for reflection and freedom, for hope and despair, for responsibility and commitment. It is our humanness.

FOR FURTHER REFLECTION

1. Which seems more accurate: to think of religion as a set of answers or to think of it as an awareness of unanswered mysteries? Explain.
2. What would you say is life's ultimate meaning? Express as best you can why this is a difficult question to deal with.
3. Can most people get along quite well without any active concern for what is mysterious and uncertain about life? Explain.
4. In what ways do you think of human culture as a long, ongoing process of development? Explain what you believe about whether our culture is developing in a positive way.
5. What purpose do you have in mind for studying human religiousness? Is there anything about studying religion from an "outsider's" viewpoint that bothers you? If so, what?

SUGGESTED READINGS

Theodore Roszak, *Unfinished Animal*, 1975; on the religious impulse and a sense of mystery.

W. Richard Comstock, *The Study of Religion and Primitive Religion*, 1971; chapter 2 offers a compact summary of various ways of studying religion.

James L. Peacocke and A. Thomas Kirsch, *The Human Direction*, 1970; a general presentation of cultural evolution.

Robert Bellah, "Religious Evolution," *American Sociological Review*, Vol. 39 #3 (June 1964), pp. 348-374.

John Hick, *An Interpretation of Religion: Human Responses to the Transcendent*, 1989; a religious person's description of the human side of religion.

C. Daniel Batson and W. Larry Ventis, *The Religious Experience*, 1982; an analysis of a wide range of studies by psychologists about religiousness

STAGES OF
CULTURAL AND RELIGIOUS DEVELOPMENT

MODERN   complex civilization, most aware of the ultimate mysteriousness of the universe and life; approaches ultimacy with hope and openness; symbolic and tentative theology; a concern for the worldly well-being of others and trust in the future; basic value morality.

> **HISTORIC**   highly complex civilizations in which people search for the ultimate single Power of Being that encompasses all else; comprehensive and dogmatic theology; hope for a perfect other-worldly existence; universal laws morality.
>
> > **ARCHAIC**   towns with class structure in a larger world, with great and distant gods demanding worship; grand myths; dreams of idealized earthly life; acceptance (and taboo) morality.
> >
> > > **PRIMITIVE**   small groups living in a one-possibility local world, with magic and spirits at hand all around; folk tale-myths; a concern to live life happily; taboo (and acceptance) morality.

Each new stage incorporates previous ones in various ways, all building on the same basic human intelligence, moral capacity, and emotions. Individual development tends to follow patterns similar to these. Real life is much more irregular and complex than this neat schema.

PART I

THE NUMINOUS

One of the most difficult aspects of describing religion is that there is no single good word for what religions are concerned with. The best ordinary word is "sacred," but it has its limitations. It has to be stretched, for example, to cover the demonic forces many religions believe in. The sacred is also usually thought of as "holy," whereas most of the gods of ancient religions are not very holy at all, in the usual sense of the word. Other words are limited also. "Divine" will not quite cover magic and spirits. To many people, "supernatural" suggests only ghosts and not also an infinite God.

Rudolph Otto (1869-1937), a German theologian, used a more obscure word in his book, *The Idea of the Holy* (1917). He used the word "numinous" to refer to the "fascinating and awesome mystery" known as God. The word can serve a wider use here, to stand for the many ways that the mysterious dimension of existence has been encountered and given some religious name by the generations of humankind. Stage by stage, from primitive to modern, the numinous has taken on new names and faces. Descriptions of each of those stages in the next chapters will clarify the meaning of "numinous." The descriptions will also enable us to look again at ourselves as unusual beings who live with an orientation to mystery.

An Enchanted World

The Numinous in Primitive and Archaic Religion

PRIMITIVE RELIGION

If you were to awake some misty morning in the central high-lands of New Guinea, in the thatched and stilted home of a native tribal family, you would find yourself in a world alive with invisible powers and beings. Before dawn it would not be entirely safe to intrude upon the spirits who roam at night, so you would lie within the hut talking quietly, or begin to eat breakfast inside until sunlight made the outdoors more safe. When you went out you would have to know many special things, such as the need to respect the rights of certain snakes. To stare at them openly could provoke them to return as spirits when you slept again and make you ill. Perhaps, though, you were born with a special aura of power about you. If so, the snake might not be able to see you, so

11

you would be safe. At any rate, you would know some ritual techniques of your own to counteract the snake's power. In fact, you would know many kinds of magic to cause illness to your enemies and health to your pigs, and to deal with threatening spirits.

Until recently the daily life of mountain tribespeople of New Guinea provided a good example of what is meant by primitive religion. There are only a few places in the world where this has still been true, but in the mountains of New Guinea and Southeast Asia, in the Kalahari desert and the rain forests of Zaire, in the upper reaches of the Amazon and in the deserts of Australia, there are tribes not too far removed from the old ways. These people have been influenced by modern societies. The old ways are fading and being replaced by new modes of thought, for better or worse. But during the last one hundred years or so, anthropologists have learned to live among the tribes, to study their languages, to observe their customs carefully and sympathetically. These outsiders may never have fully seen life and reality as it appears to the tribespeople, but they have provided such thorough and complete descriptions of tribal life that we can form a picture of it that is probably close to the truth.

What anthropologists tell us about the primitive tribes gives us our best available basis to estimate what religion may have been like before there was any civilization on this planet. This is important information because it is not just information about the past; the study of primitive beliefs is also a study of ourselves. Primitive thought is woven into the greater complexities of later cultural forms, including our own. Primitive religion still lives in the niches of contemporary culture and in the corners of our personalities. We can begin to understand this by looking at the universe as primitive people see it, one full of numinous powers.

The Nonliving Numinous Forces: Luck, Magic, Mana, and Omens

Primitive people are conscious of many mysterious forces at work around them. Sometimes berries grow; sometimes they do not. Disease comes at unexpected times. A brother who is usually quiet and calm runs away screaming. For these and other events there must be causes, but often there are no visible causes. Sensibly enough, primitive people believe there must be invisible causes at work in the world, affecting people's lives. One category of invisible and mysterious causes is the category of nonliving numinous powers. There are many forms of it, and many names.

Luck is one form. This is not mere accidental luck, not chance or happenstance, but luck as a real force to make good things (or bad) take place. Some inanimate things have it, such as medallions that can ward off evil. Some once-living objects have it, such as rabbit's feet which bring good luck (though not to the rabbit, apparently). Some people have it. In every tribe or group someone is apparently born luckier than others, possessed of an inner power to succeed, be healthy, eat well, please people. Other people seem to be jinxed, afflicted by a power that attracts harm to them and those around them.

Magic is another name for this numinous power. Rituals have magical power to affect the weather, put snakes to sleep, insure pregnancy. Medicines in general are all full of magical power. (The English word "pharmacist" comes from an ancient Greek word meaning "magician.") Water from sacred streams has magical power to cure or to kill. Special signs made with the fingers can inflict harm or ward off demons.

For many primitive people names have a kind of magical power. To label something is to control it. Children experience this when they discover that by saying, "Mama," they can influence the large warm creature who holds them. In many tribes, people hide their true names so that no malicious spirit may control them by calling their name. The mere name of a spirit sometimes has power over other forces, a power to bless or a power to exorcise evil influences.

There is a magic in similarities. Pouring water on the ground from a gourd may stimulate further water on the ground from the sky in the form of rain. Painting a bison on the wall of the cave and hurling spears at it may help in tomorrow's hunt. There is magic in contact also. To touch a dead person without later purification can make a person ill. What belongs to you, your hair and saliva and food that has been in your stomach, has some relation to your whole self and can be used in magical ways to affect you. The magic connections in similarity and in contact can be used together in sorcery. If you construct a doll similar to a person you wish to harm and also use bits of hair or clothing from the person, that will make doubly certain that any harm done to the doll will affect the person it represents.

Some magic just seems to work. Those who believe in it do not claim to know what luck or magic or other such forces really are or why they really work. So often all a person can do is to memorize what does work. Notching the ears of cattle protects them from evil disease. Hex signs keep demons away. It is not necessary to understand why this works, so long as it does.

To make it easier to talk about this invisible non-living power, a name will help. One used commonly now by anthropologists is "mana." In 1891 a missionary named Codrington wrote to a colleague in London about the Southwest Pacific culture of the Melanesians. These tribes, Codrington reported, share a belief in an invisible power which is "the cause of all success in life that surpasses the ordinary." They called this power "mana." The name has stuck, as has its companion name "taboo" (or "tapu" or "tabu"). Mana-power can be good or bad, but because it is power it is often dangerous. Places, people, or objects with too much mana are therefore taboo—dangerous—and are to be avoided or handled with great care.

Mana-power may also make its presence known by peculiar effects on the environment. (Spirits do the same, as the next section will explain.) Such signs of numinous power are called "omens." The derivative word "ominous" suggests that omens are warnings about bad things to come. Vultures flocking over your house may be an ominous event. But there are also good omens and neutral ones. An itchy palm is an omen you will receive some money, it is said. A fire that flares up signifies that visitors are on their way, perhaps friendly, perhaps not. Primitive people live in a world where there may be numerous signs every day. Any odd occurrence is likely to foretell something. It is important to be alert to the signs.

Divination is a name for the practice of reading omens. For the most part anyone can read the signs that appear in nature and daily life. It is especially handy to have available some reliable method of divining. In some cultures bones or marked pebbles can be cast down on the ground to be read. In another, the shape of the clouds can be trusted to foretell the immediate future.

Numinous omen-power is useful in many ways. The English used to throw a murder suspect into a pond that had been blessed. If the suspect floated, the holy water was rejecting him. He was therefore guilty. (If he drowned, his innocence assured him of a good afterlife.) A New Guinea tribe discovers who is guilty by cutting off the head of a chicken and letting it loose to run around until it drops. Where it stops indicates who is guilty.

The numinous power in luck, magic, or omens can be good or bad, strong or weak, easily controlled or completely independent of human choice. It is a force residing in spirits, people, animals, inanimate objects, or daily events. It is a nonliving power, though some omens are signs given by spirits. It is unexplained in the sense that, by and large, it is just there in reality, affecting people even when no one can say why or explain what it is. Primitive people perceive such numinous power as relatively small and local. As we will see, archaic people believe in immensely powerful forms of it.

Living Numinous Beings: The Spirits

The world of the primitive is at least as crowded with spirits as it is with mana. However big the tribespeople conceive their universe to be, it is alive with invisible living beings, forces that are not only numinous powers but also conscious, with thoughts and feelings like those of a person.

There is a vast array of small nature spirits who live in different places and things. Each tree, river, field, rock, cove, cave, and mountaintop is likely to have its spirit. Often the spirit has a personality like the place where it lives: the spirit of a brook is talkative and lively; the spirit of the thunder is loud and angry.

There may be pests and demons, small invisible beings whose only interest is to cause trouble. They cause you to forget your stew on the fire until it burns. They make you trip and break a leg. They turn your milk sour and make your apples rot. Some of these are strong enough to cause major troubles such as disease, miscarriage, deformed children, and even death.

Many people have attendant spirits. When you are born, you have an invisible twin who will accompany you through life, or even two of them, one helpful and one harmful. Perhaps you have a spirit partner you must entertain and keep happy, lest it become angry with you. Or it may be more like a guardian angel, a protector, or source of luck.

The spirits of the dead are rarely very far away. Sometimes they live at the edges of the campsite or village. Other times they stay in the land of the dead, but might return to visit out of loneliness, or to cause trouble out of envy for the living, or to demand more remembrance and attention than has been given them, or to give advice in dreams, visions, or omens.

The original ancestors of the tribe may still be present. They established the tribe's customs, and sometimes they watch to punish anyone who violates them. Or they act as guardians and give warnings through omens.

You yourself are a spirit-being; your life is your spirit. It is even possible that within you are various spirits that together make up who you are. One tribe, for example, says each person has three spirits. Upon death one spirit dissolves, another remains to roam around on earth, the third goes to the sky to live. Another tribe believes that it is possible to capture one of the spirits of each person you kill in battle. A strong warrior grows in strength because each victory over another person allows the warrior to inhale the other person's spirit with its additional energy, to add its strength to that of the other spirits which the warrior already possesses. A person who has killed too often, though, may lose control of the many spirits within him and go mad.

Among all these numinous spirit-beings are other strange and numinous beings that are not spirits, yet not human either. There are elves, gnomes, trolls, leprechauns, and such. They are a little too solid to be spirits, yet they are in touch with the numinous in special ways. They can bless or curse a person or give warning signs, so it is worthwhile to be on good terms with them.

No single tribe is likely to see around them all of the forms of spirit-beings described here. Among the many spirits that a given tribe does believe in, only a few of them will have much importance. The spirits of the dead, a local nature spirit or two, an animal whose spirit is of special significance to this tribe, a few spirits who frequently produce omens to guide people—these and one or two others might be the only spirits a child learns much about. Yet no tribe is surprised to discover that the world is full of spirits, some of them the tribe had not known about before.

Dealing with Numinous Powers

Primitive existence is crowded with mana and spirits, so it is of obvious importance to know how to deal with them. A child growing up in a primitive culture learns about the various mana powers the way a modern child learns about household appliances. Each has its use. Some open cans; others toast bread. A child learns to use them, even without understanding how or why they work. It is the same with magical rituals, or "oracle" bones that foretell the future, or musical instruments that are taboo because they possess intense mana. A child in a primitive culture learns not to tread on taboo ground and not to dribble saliva where a sorcerer can get it and use it to do harm to the child. Magical potions can make someone fall in love with you or can make an enemy fall over dead. The proper song can attract the opossum close enough to hunt. The power-filled symbols on your chest can prevent spears from striking you. Mana-power is everywhere, to be used when possible, to be avoided when necessary.

Dealing with spirits also requires some care. Spirits are like people, with similar needs and feelings. Persuasive techniques can help. The spirits like attention and flattery. Kill a chicken occasionally to share with them; it will keep them happy (and you will have a nice meal). Pour a bit of beer on the ground now and then as a little gift. Be thoughtful toward the spirits and they may leave you in peace.

Some pest-like spirits can be threatened or driven away. Firecrackers at festivals, and loud gongs and clattering sticks at funerals may keep little demons or the spirits of the dead at a distance where they will do no harm. Some spirits are not too bright and can be tricked. When smallpox is spreading, leave a dummy image of yourself in front of your hut. The sickness spirit may mistake the dummy for you and curse it with smallpox, leaving you safe.

Magic can be handy in dealing with spirits. Certain signs or symbols can keep spirits away. A cross, a star, and a large variety of other signs have proved effective, according to different groups. Garlic has a noticeable mana, powerful enough to drive away evil spirits.

There are magical formulas, such as those for summoning spirits and for casting them out. The best magic is coercive magic, guaranteed to work provided only that the whole magical ritual is performed exactly right. Unfortunately, some demons also know magic and can cast contrary spells. Others will make you stumble in your speech and actions and thereby weaken the power of the magic. Some spirits are just too strong to be coerced by magic. Persuasion will have to be used instead.

Primitive Religion: Animism

Near the end of the 19th century, a British anthropologist named Edward Tylor (1832-1917) borrowed the name "aminism" as a label for primitive religion. It is based on the Latin word *anima,* meaning soul or spirit, and gave it a new form as the word "animism." People who believe that there are many and varied spirits invisibly roaming the world and affecting our lives are called animists; they also usually believe in some form of mana-powers.

Primitive tribes are all animistic to some extent. On this basis Tylor made the guess that animism is the origin of all religion. Many people were offended by this conclusion because it seemed to imply that all religious belief is fundamentally primitive. In defense of religion some pointed out that no one really knows what went on among people 10,000 or 20,000 years ago. Maybe the earliest human religion was belief in a single supreme God, and animism was only a later corruption of this noble belief. This theory happened to fit better with what the Judaeo-Christian Scriptures seemed to say, that the first human beings knew that there was one supreme God, so this theory was more popular among people who adhered to traditional religious beliefs. The anthropologist Rev. Wilhelm Schmidt (1868-1954) promoted this idea in the early decades of this century.

The dust has settled somewhat since the days of the most turbulent arguments. Though there is always some room for revision, the best statement that can now be made is that what we call primitive religion is probably the earliest form of religion, and that primitive religion is animistic religion. But animism is also still part of life today, even in modern industrial nations, as is belief in mana. And animism is just an early form of religion, not necessarily the basic nature of religion. (A thesis of this book is that religion is basically a response to mystery, a response that can take primitive, archaic, historic, or modern forms.)

There are numerous forms of contemporary belief in mana. People still believe in good luck and bad luck. Some baseball players will not play without their lucky cap or socks. Actors refrain from wishing one another well because that is unlucky. They say "break a leg" instead. Hostesses will not seat thirteen people at a table and hotels have no thirteenth floor. Some people wear blessed medals or use holy water for protection.

Belief in mana is sometimes disguised in pseudo-scientific forms. Some people claim that the pyramid shape can focus cosmic rays to clear your mind, preserve raw hamburger, and sharpen razor blades. The magician who used to move objects by "magic" now advertises his exceptional ESP talent of telekinesis, which empowers him to bend forks with his mind and stop clocks at a distance.

Belief in spirits is less common today than it once was, yet we still buy books of stories of haunted houses. People fear ghosts, hold seances to talk with the dead, and claim to be reincarnations of ancient heroes. Many today ask the spirit of St. Anthony for help in locating lost articles. We hear stories at night of demonic possession and tremble a little, even in our skepticism.

Animism today also sometimes appears in the guise of science.

Researchers have discovered that people whose hearts have stopped beating for a time report similar "out-of-the-body" experiences. We are tempted to take this as scientific evidence that we are all embodied spirits. When strange lights are seen in the sky, it somehow seems possible to believe there are living beings within the unidentified flying objects. Unseen beings from outer space are replacing some of the invisible spirits that hovered around our ancestors.

The overall life, culture, and religion of the primitive tribes that exist today may be like surviving remnants of the common beginnings of all human culture. But the modern "tribes" that are the great industrialized and computerized nations contain other forms of the long-ago past in all the little ways we find mana-like powers and spirits all around us still.

The Culture of the Primitives

The numinous is ordinary. The numinous elements, living and nonliving, that are part of the primitive person's reality blend into the everyday and ordinary aspects of that reality. A child grows up memorizing the names and habits of invisible spirits and living cousins without thinking of one of them as being more "religious" than the others. They are different but all part of the same world. The child learns which snakes to avoid, which rocks have spirits, and which tree is full of mana, all as part of everyday practical knowledge. The spirits are part of the neighborhood; the numinous powers are all part of the family's homeland.

The world is a loose collection of powers and beings. There is no overall unified order to the spirits and mana-powers. Each spirit has its own story; each bit of magical power has its location or use. The world as it now exists is the result of a thousand different and mostly unconnected events. The porcupine has quills because once it was a person who burned someone's hut. The owners of the hut threw spears at the person, sticking him all over. The person crawled into a log and came out days later looking as he does now, with tiny spears all over his body. Clouds are wet and snakes are shiny and people die and no one should marry a brother or sister, each for a different reason. The world cannot be understood any more than that. Once upon a time, certain different things happened for different reasons, and that is why the world is the way it is today. Primitive people are as intelligent as people of any culture. They show great ingenuity in the countless ways they categorize and cross-categorize things. But their culture does not prompt them to use their intelligence in the same ways as other cultures, as we will see.

The collection of customs rules life. Collections of customs give form to the tribe and prevent it from breaking up into chaos. Many times fights erupt out of jealousy, anger, or pettiness. A small argument leads to great insults, and then to physical injury or even death. Suddenly whole families are caught up in tensions that could destroy the tribe. Customs may dictate who must pay reparation to whom, who is to be banished from the tribe, how to restore peace. Custom and chaos sway back and forth in uneasy balance. Words of wisdom from one person or an astute reading of omens by another may provide guidance. But those tribes with the stronger and more effective customs, we can presume, are the ones that endure in the face of the human impatience, irritability, passion, and pettiness that is part of life everywhere.

Tribespeople live day by day and generation by generation, juggling a thousand forces both numinous and ordinary, balancing between customs and impulses. There are rarely any plans for long-term developments. There is no well-structured social hierarchy, no kings, no full-time priests. There are just the people in families, bands, and tribes, digging up edible roots, planning a feast, preparing an initiation ritual, appeasing an irritated spirit, cooking a meal, making signs to ward off sorcery, nursing a child, stealing from an enemy, falling in love, growing old, and telling the stories about how things are in the world.

From Primitive to Archaic Culture

As far back as 10,000 years ago, some part of the human family transformed its existence by inventing agriculture. Primitive people lived by hunting and gathering, sometimes by simple herding. But a few people learned to plant some of the food they had been used to gathering in the wild. Various grains were developed over the centuries that could be planted, tended, and harvested in bulk. Soon larger numbers of people could live off of the produce of one area of land.

Villages turned into towns where there were distinctions between an upper and lower class of people, the rulers and the ruled. Cities appeared. Eventually, social and economic classes multiplied: landowners, the military, merchants, peasants. The role of chief or king took on clear identity. Even religion was put into the hands of full-time specialists, the priests, who offered sacrifices to gods, and prophets, whose job was to read omens. Religious beliefs changed with these changes in culture. The primitive beliefs in mana and spirits were retained (as they still are in weaker form even today), but were absorbed into a somewhat different pattern of belief known now as archaic religion.

The distinction between primitive and archaic culture is artificially neat. Some primitive tribes use slash-and-burn horticultural (garden) methods (cutting, burning the vegetation on a jungle plot and planting tubers for a season or two until that plot no longer yields well, then moving on). Some primitive or early archaic tribes are pastoral, herding animals. But even artificially neat distinctions offer some useful categories to work with. Large-scale agriculture is a sign and cause of a different kind of culture, the archaic.

ARCHAIC RELIGION

The Birth of the Gods

The archaic stage of religious development is a stage in which people begin to think of some of the spirits as numinous beings of very great power, more awesome than ordinary spirits. We usually call these great spirits "gods." Like all spirits, they are personal in that they have thoughts and feelings. The word "personal" here does not necessarily mean friendly or warm. Although the gods can be helpful and kind, they can also be petty, vengeful, and destructive.

The gods are not as neighborly as other spirits. If they live nearby in a shrine or sacred place, they are like a great chief or king, endowed with majesty and deserving of respect and fear. Many of them live far away in the skies, on a high mountain, or deep in the earth. In any case, near or far, they are usually more distant from daily human doings than the ordinary spirits are.

The gods and spirits form a numinous civilization that is mixed into the human civilization. There is a hierarchy of power among people, from peasants to landlords and military leaders to kings. Among the gods and spirits it is often the same. Many local spirits might live their own lives on the whole, but still be under the power of a god. The spirits that live in underwater caves and in various harbors might all have to bow to the greater power of the great god of the sea. Occasionally, there is an explicit line of authority, as in the case of Zeus, who ruled all the sky gods because he was their father, or of Marduk, god of ancient Babylon, who ruled the other gods of that area as his reward for having defeated monstrous enemies of the gods.

The anthropologists have sometimes used the name "high god" to label a god who is not merely greater than an ordinary spirit but who dominates even other gods in some sense. The category of high god is a fuzzy one. Sometimes it applies to any god like Zeus or Marduk who is the dominant one, albeit not all-powerful. Other times the title "high god" belongs to the god who created the universe as it now exists, perhaps forming it out of some primordial ooze or out of the bodies of defeated monsters. Or perhaps one god is just so appreciated by people that the other gods are overshadowed. (Wilhelm Schmidt, mentioned earlier, claimed that all cultures have or had some form of high god, but this does not seem to be true of genuinely primitive cultures.)

Awesome as they are, the gods are not always of particularly noble or gracious character. The very size of their power tends to spoil them. Little spirits can be as willful, vain, and petty as children. Unfortunately, the gods are too, but they have such power that their whims must be respected. Even kings can act childishly, so it is no surprise if gods do too. When the gods go on a rampage, bringing floods or epidemics, people can only cower in fear, offer the greatest gifts they can find, and hope that their offerings and praise will eventually soothe the divine anger. Archaic people do not always expect much of what we would call emotional maturity in their gods.

Religion and culture develop together. When chiefs and kings appear among the people, gods appear among the spirits. When a hierarchy of classes arises in society, a hierarchy of powers arises among the spirits. When cultures perceive a larger world of manifold and changing complexities, the lives of the gods then also inhabit larger spaces and become complex stories of various plans, struggles, victories, and defeats.

This is inevitable. On the one hand, people can really conceive of only what their own language, tradition, and experiences prepare them to be able to find words for. On the other hand, since they do have new experiences, they will eventually find the language to begin to describe them in new ways. Whether religion comes from the active presence of the numinous among people or from human imagination or from both, it will still be conceived of and portrayed in ways that the life experiences of the people incline them. Religiousness, like all aspects of life, finds its expression in the cultural forms available to people.

Great Mana

Just as the archaic cultures think some spirit-beings are great enough to be gods, they also think of some mana-power as very great. Most great power was usually personified; even time (Chronos) was portrayed as a god in ancient Greek thought, as were heaven and earth (Uranus and Geia), rather than nonpersonal or nonliving forces. Yet, occasionally there have been forms of belief in some great nonliving numinous forces.

The ancient Chinese, for example, perceived two complementary forces, the Yang and the Yin, at work in all aspects of the universe. Both the Aztecs and the ancient Hindu priests believed that in their rituals they generated a kind of cosmic power. (A later chapter will say more on all of these.)

A set of beliefs in a great mana-like power that is still relatively strong today is astrology, a belief in the influence of the stars and planets on our lives. There is no way of knowing how long human societies have taken clear notice of the effect of the moon on the tides, or the general correlation of the twenty-eight-day lunar month with menstruation (a word based on mensis, the Latin word for "month"). Nor do we know which societies of the Northern Hemisphere first noticed that when the constellation Cancer arose highest at night, the days were longest and the sun brightest. But out of these and similar observations ancient peoples like the Babylonians and the Chinese devised elaborate descriptions of various kinds of numinous forces that emanate from the heavens and influence human affairs.

Perhaps equally ancient is the belief that numbers represent great mana. Sums and proportions have a wondrous regularity. With measurements, angles, and designs, for example, the end of the sun's retreat into winter and its return for spring can be identified. (The structures of Stonehenge in England are just one example of this.) Among the Babylonians, numerology shared popularity with astrology. There were "lucky" numbers, numbers with positive power. The numbers of a person's name established how the person's life would intertwine with the number-value of other places and peoples and powers.

Dealing with Gods and Great Mana

The primitive person lives as a near-equal to the numinous powers, the spirits, and the local forms of mana; but the archaic person faces numinous powers that loom large over the landscapes of life. The gods are too strong to be controlled by magic or any other means. At best, it is persuasion, not control, that a person must bring to bear on the gods. Worship appears for the first time in history.

No one need worship spirits; they can be manipulated. But the gods are beyond human control. People must try to influence them with bribes and flattery, albeit with great respect. Bribery must be given as respectful offerings; flattery must appear as dutiful worship. Long rituals and celebrations are expected. Formal shrines and temples become common. A whole priesthood with its temple rituals develops eventually. Worship becomes the major business of religion.

Even with all this, it can still be difficult to please the gods and keep them helpful, or at least harmless. Subject to their own passions, pride, and pettiness, they might still send a plague, destroy crops, or flood a city. But anger against them in such cases will not help. The gods can be like abusive parents; the children can only submit helplessly. To blame the parent may only evoke more punishment.

To some extent, people can adapt to great mana. Parents can choose a name for their child that has lucky numbers, the sum of which is also lucky. They can even try to arrange when pregnancy will occur so as to give birth to a child whose sun-sign, for example, is that of Leo, a force producing strong and generous leaders.

The forms of great mana hover over a person's life with such unavoidable and unchangeable force that the only course open to people is to submit. The stars and sun will not change in their course; the Yang and Yin of nature flow unaffected by human decision. Much of life, therefore, can only be an acceptance of what is and will be, with perhaps some modest improvements in things through the occasional help of spirits and gods, the use of magic, and a wise coordination of activities with the patterns of the great numinous forces.

Polytheism: A Name for Archaic Religion

The name alone says most about what archaic religion is: a belief in many (*poly*) gods (*theoi*). There is not a clear line between animism and polytheism, because there is no way to fix a standard as to just how powerful or important a spirit-being must be to deserve the title "god." The ordinary sky spirits of the Australian aborigines have been called gods by some outsiders. On the other hand, the high god of the Delaware Indians, for example, was referred to by many colonial residents of America as a Great

Spirit. In general, though, it is useful to reserve the name "god" for a spirit of great power, superior to other spirits and people.

Polytheism developed after animism. Most primitive societies today do not exhibit beliefs in extremely powerful spirits. Some societies we loosely call "primitive" believe in a high god, but these often are not really primitive societies. They are mostly archaic cultures with a chief or king. The truly primitive societies, such as those of the Congo pygmies, the Kalahari bushpeople, or many of the Australian aborigines, have neither chief nor powerful gods. The best estimate is that primitive animism preceded archaic polytheism, and that the belief in local mana, which is part of animistic religion, preceded the belief in great mana found in archaic cultures.

Archaic Religion Today

Archaic beliefs are still fairly common. There are first of all explicit forms of polytheism alive today. Many cultures of Africa have been polytheistic to this day. The popular religion of India is strongly polytheistic, with gods almost beyond numbering filling up the spaces of the universe.

There are also less obvious ways in which the old gods have been replaced by their equivalents. In some major branches of Christianity, the saints in heaven are accorded great power. Strictly speaking, they are not to be worshipped as gods, because they are totally subordinate to the one God. Yet people appeal to them and have formal and elaborate ceremonies in their honor in order to benefit from their great influence. In his own sinister way, the Satan of popular Christian belief is also a spirit of godlike (though not God-like) power.

The old beliefs in great mana exist today also. Astrology is still strong enough to generate a multi-million dollar set of businesses of book publishing, chart reading, and newspaper columns. Those who believe in pyramid-power sometimes speak of this power as an awesome cosmic force. Those who use TM, transcendental meditation, often interpret it as a way to tap a numinous energy that flows through the whole universe.

As is the case with belief in small mana, belief in great mana today has also taken on quasi-scientific forms, disguising its sense of the numinous in technical jargon. Pyramid-power can be couched in the language physics uses to speak of cosmic rays. Biorhythms sound very scientific when explained by enthusiasts, yet belief in them is part of an ancient quest for harmony with the numinous patterns of nature. The mystery of the numinous is only half-tamed and half-hidden beneath all the technical language. Archaic beliefs live with primitive ones in our midst and within us. We never entirely lose our own primitive and archaic inclinations.

Archaic Culture

Archaic culture is one of greater complexity than the primitive. In archaic cultures the numinous powers range from the ordinary everyday spirits and magic inherited from primitive times, to the awesome and more distant gods and great mana. This greater range of the numinous is a clue to the greater world in which archaic people live. Life in the large village or in the city is a life with a more complex kind of knowledge about the world. There are more social roles and thus more complex relationships to be learned. There is often opportunity for more forms of trade with outside cultures. Local villages, each with their own customs, fall under the influence of a powerful city. Eventually, small empires arise, as in ancient China, India, Mesopotamia, and Egypt.

One result of this is that the universe appears to archaic cultures as no longer merely a collection of events and patterns to be learned and assimilated as the one single way reality is and life is. Instead, the universe looks complex enough to require more complex explanatory stories about it. There are more options about how to live, and so each culture needs some reasons why its ways are better than other ways. It is the great myths of archaic cultures that portray and explain the complexities of life to archaic people. There will be more on this when we speak of myths in the next chapter.

The complex facts of reality are not just scattered facts; they are organized into categories and put into a hierarchy of power or importance. In Egypt, the sun that gives light and life was above all life, so the sun was the most important god, called Amen or Ra. Lesser gods had to take a lesser position. Osiris and Horus had special presence, though, in the Pharaoh and the Pharaoh's power over the Egyptians. So these gods outranked most others.

In the ancient religion of the Indo-European people, whose language and thought is the parent of much of Western language, the sky is the dominant numinous realm. The power of sun and storm, of light and darkness, overwhelmed all else. So the sky god was high god. In ancient Greece his name was Zeus. Under the high god was often a hierarchy of other specific gods. Under Zeus, for example, were his children such as Aphrodite, Helios,

Hermes, Athena. Below the gods were the extraordinary beings such as the giants and the monsters. Below the extraordinary beings were the ordinary ones, the spirits and the humans.

This hierarchical ranking was rough and unsettled. Alliances of power were made and broken. Competing major gods might divide reality among them, as Zeus took the sky and open air, Poseidon the sea, and Hades the underground. Archaic cultures perceive a greater amount of unifying order in reality than do primitive cultures, but it is an incomplete order. There is no overall unity such as monotheism or other great historic forms of belief will expect to find, as we will see.

Summary

This chapter has presented some interpretations of the ways primitive and archaic societies perceive numinous mysteries, as mana and spirits and and great mana and gods. Primitive religion is a way of living with various numinous powers in a relatively small universe. Mana and spirits are plentiful, each to be dealt with to make life run smoothly. Archaic religion, an aspect of a more complexly structured society, still acknowledges magic and spirits at hand, but also worships the more distant powerful spirit-beings known as gods, whose influences can extend over many parts of the world.

Behind the fact of such beliefs is the question of why these beliefs exist. The various answers people offer are valuable because they give us clues about our own human character, needs, and hopes. That is the topic of the next chapter.

FOR FURTHER REFLECTION

1. List all the kinds of mana-like powers, spirits, and numinous realities in general that people today believe in. (Look at the magazines sold at your supermarket checkout counter to get some ideas.)

2. To what extent do you find it reasonable to believe in numinous powers like spirits, magic, or gods? Explain why you do or do not.

3. Explain how coherent or integrated the many forces of the universe seem to you. What sort of single underlying unifying order is there to all things, if any?

4. Are you comfortable with the claim that religious ideas and practices change as the culture changes? Is this true of the religious traditions you are most familiar with, including your own? Explain.

SUGGESTED READINGS

Sam Gill, *Beyond the Primitive: The Religion of Nonliterate Peoples,* *1982;* an interpretation of primitive religion.

Ronald M. and Catherine H. Berndt, *Man, Land, and Myth in North Australia, 1970;* a detailed study of a primitive people.

Christopher Hallpike, *The Foundations of Primitive Thought, 1979;* a closely argued case that primitive culture is indeed primitive.

Daisie and Michael Radner, *Science and Unreason,* 1982; describes many contemporary pseudo-scientific forms of primitive and archaic style beliefs.

Eric Hansen, *Stranger in the Forest: On Foot Across Borneo,* 1988; an account of primitive cultures now touched by the outside world.

John Middleton, *The Lugbara of Uganda, 1964;* especially ch. 6; in general on an early archaic society.

Dennis Werner, *Amazon Journey;* an account of an anthropologist's two years with a primitive people of Brazil.

The Human Quest

The Origin and Function of Belief in the Numinous

THE FACT OF BELIEF

Every culture in the history of humankind has included belief in the numinous as a major part of its understanding of reality. In fact, most people in history have considered it self-evident that the gods are real, or that the ancestors guide them, or that demons cause sickness. Does the sun rise and water run downhill and the eagle soar in the sky? Of course. Do spirits roam and magic exist? Of course. The numinous and the non-numinous are equally obvious, especially to people of primitive and archaic cultures.

Later developments in human history, though, included some degree of disbelief. In the historic cultures, people began to doubt some primitive and archaic beliefs. In contemporary times, there are those who doubt all beliefs in the numinous. In theory such doubts would have been possible all along; the numinous beings are usually invisible, after all. Why believe in something you cannot see? The evidence that magic truly works is shaky, it now seems to us. How is it that most people preceding us have believed in it or in some equivalent mana-power?

The possibility of doubt makes it all the more striking that so few doubts have existed. If disbelief could have existed at any time, the fact that it has been quite rare indicates something about human beings in general.

Individual religious traditions have proposed that the reason for belief lies in the actions of the divine power. Western religions, for example, have claimed that they believe in God because this God revealed himself to them. But these same believers do not think that Zeus really appeared to the Greeks, or nature spirits to primitives. Have all the gods and spirits and mana-powers that people have believed in really given reliable and obvious evidence of their existence? If some of these do not really exist, why is it that almost every culture in history has believed in them nonetheless? Closely allied with this is the question of why people have not only believed, but have found their beliefs to be very important to them.

The answers to these questions can tell us much about us humans, about our character and needs. An investigation into the fact of nearly universal human belief in the numinous is an investigation into ourselves.

There are four kinds of answers offered here. They are not the whole story of human existence, but they say a great deal about us. The four kinds of answers concern the search for intelligibility, the need for psychological security, the problem of social stability, and the human sense of the sacred. All four are answers to why humans perceive a numinous dimension in the endless mysteries of life.

THE SEARCH FOR INTELLIGIBILITY

Ancient and modern beliefs in magic, spirits, and gods often appear to us to be a sign of ignorance. There is some truth in that. At least we presume that we now have a better understanding of various things that were once thought to be numinous powers. But there is another side to animism and polytheism worth noting. Belief in spirits and gods, as well as in magic and great mana, represents acts of intelligence such as no other animal on this planet ever approaches. Even in our ignorance and superstition we are engaged in rather important mental processes: conscious attention, categorizing and naming, intellectual reflection. We can see this human power of consciousness and understanding at work in the various forms of belief in the numinous.

Belief in Mana

Every animal lives in an environment of wonders and never knows it. A woodchuck meandering through the woods is following its genetic programming: when hungry, start moving. Its eyes register the sight of a large brown thing in motion. It freezes for a moment, then darts away to pause in the nearest shelter, then to ramble on again. As best as anyone has ever been able to tell, the woodchuck has not had a conscious thought about any of this. It simply has senses that feed impressions into the central nervous system which computes the next response partly by its genetic programming and partly as the result of a non-thinking kind of learning or conditioning.

Many animals employ some sort of signals. Chimpanzees have even been taught some sign language. But not even the most well-trained chimpanzee has yet shown much talent for what a three-year-old human child can do rather easily, that is to stop and take deliberate, conscious note of events that seem significant or interesting, to consciously wonder about the cause of those events, and then to invent or discover ways of accounting for those events and language for categorizing them.

With this talent humankind has spent centuries taking note of events, labeling them, and devising explanations for them. People expect events to have causes. Any time we can name or describe the cause of an event we feel we have explained it. Many causes are clear and ordinary. A neighbor has a black eye because she ran into a tree. The bread is burnt because the fire was too hot. But there are other causes that are not so clear. Why does a sore on your leg not heal up? Why is the rain so abundant this year? If there is no visible cause, then it is obvious that there is an invisible cause. Evidently, the world is full of invisible powers because so many things happen without any visible cause.

The human race has been strangely insistent on finding or devising explicit and specific explanations for the events of life. We humans have been very reluctant ever to say merely that some things just happen for no particular reason or because of no particular cause. Primitive people (and others) ignore the possibility that events might be just random and accidental. When primitives take conscious note of things and categorize them, there is no category labeled "pure chance." There are always causes for things, visible and invisible.

The more valuable or troublesome events in life are the ones most important to explain. Health and sickness, food and hunger, peace and war are issues that stir up people. Whatever causes them is more deserving of concern. The invisible causes of any of these things evoke an extra sense of awe, because as invisible they are a little more mysterious. These are the causes more likely to be treated as numinous. They are the ones that go by such names as mana, magic, omens, spirits, and gods.

A major reason, it seems then, why people believe in mana-like powers is just the human tendency to insist that things be explained. However foolish or superstitious some beliefs might appear to us now, every belief represents human confidence that we can make sense out of things by discovering their causes. This confidence is based on our basic faith in the intelligibility of reality and in our power as thinking beings to understand it.

This often leads to superstitious belief, a mistaken belief in a cause-and-effect relationship. The psychologist B. F. Skinner has provided a good model for showing how this can happen. Skinner had a large box with a lever and a food tray. Every time a pigeon in the box pushed the lever, a food pellet dropped into the tray. Pigeons put in the box soon learned to push the lever in order to get food (although this "learning" is probably not conscious learning). One of the pigeons was not merely fat from eating well; it was also a little dizzy. It would turn in a complete circle, then push the lever and go to the tray for its food pellet. Apparently, the pigeon had once turned in a circle and then pushed the lever, thereby learning that a combination of turning and pushing produced food. Skinner called this superstitious behavior.

Today, a baseball player who wears a new cap and then hits a home run feels that wearing that cap helps his batting. In primitive society the person who hears a crow cry just before bad news arrives thinks of crows as bad omens. Pigeons, ballplayers, primitives, and all of us have an inclination to believe that when one thing precedes a second, it caused the second to happen. By definition, that is superstitious if it produces a mistaken belief in a cause that does not exist, or in a cause-and-effect relationship that does not exist.

It is worth noting, though, that not all belief in invisible causes is superstitious. Natives of Peru knew that the bark of the cinchona tree had the magic power to cure the fever that came from walking too near to the swamp where demons of illness lived. Today we agree. The quinine in the bark does in fact have the power to cure malarial fever. We simply no longer call this a numinous power. To us it has become too ordinary and easy to understand. There is genuine power there; there is genuine cause-and-effect relationship. The primitive person may well be right to believe that there are explanations for what happens, even if the particular explanation the person uses does not now appear to be a very good one.

Belief in Spirits

Belief in spirits is also a sign of the human impulse to make sense out of things. In fact, belief in spirits adds an implicit extra explanatory note about the numinous powers beyond what mere belief in mana provides. Magic, mana, luck, and other nonliving powers are just indescribable power. What it is like or why it should have an effect on things is unknown; it is simply mysterious. Spirits are somewhat mysterious also. No one can be sure of their habits, desires, activities, presence, or absence. They too are invisible. Yet, to think of numinous powers as living beings says something more about them. It explains their activities as motivated by the same kinds of desires and impulses that affect us. The spirits may be whimsical and arbitrary and unpredictable. Nonetheless, they do have motivations that we can understand to help us make some sense out of their behavior: they hurt us because they are angry or mean; they help us because they are friendly or because they like our gifts.

The tendency to believe in spirits sometimes goes by the name "projection," a process of explaining various events by projecting our own very familiar inner thoughts and feelings out into the world around us, believing that other people or even other things act for the same reasons we act. It appears that we project our inner states not just onto other people but also onto objects and animals and even invisible beings. We begin our lives projecting our inner life out into the world. Why does the sun set? Because it feels tired after being up all day. In fact, as children we often create invisible friends to talk to and play with. We start our lives projecting personality into many things. Perhaps it is just easy to continue to think this way, at least a little bit, when we grow up. It provides a handy explanation why some strange things happen. "The spirit led me." "The god saved me from drowning." "The devil made me do it."

There are some kinds of human experience that could seem like good evidence for the existence of spirits. Edward Tylor (who invented the word "animism"), made two different guesses, in fact, about ways in which people could feel that they had concrete evidence of how real spirits are.

First of all, there are many states of consciousness in which people find themselves face to face with talking animals or dead ancestors or numinous beings with magical powers. The most common state is dreams. Everyone dreams, and sooner or later in our dreams we find ourselves talking with great-uncle Louis who died seven years ago, or perhaps with a wise elephant who understands human language. Primitive and archaic people, inclined to animism anyway, are likely to interpret these dreams as real experiences of real people, real animals, and real spirits. Since spirits are mysterious beings, it makes sense that they should show themselves only in those rather strange kinds of experiences we call dreams, when it seems that our own inner spirit has entered a world where the usual rules do not apply.

Dreams are not the only altered state of consciousness. Native Americans of the northern plains had the practice of going alone to a hill or woods to fast, meditate, and wait. After days with no food the soul would be prepared. A spirit, often that of an animal, would appear and be a sign of what character and style in life the person should possess. Native Americans of Mexico have long used the mana-filled mushrooms to open their souls to special visions, some of them visions of the spirit-world. Many cultures have known that alcohol contains spirit power that can change people's perception and personality, and allow them to be strange beings. (Or maybe this is mana-power.) Altered states of consciousness, Tylor noted, are common to people everywhere. No wonder so many people have seen spirits.

Add to this a clue that language gives us and we can discover another kind of evidence for the reality of spirits. Many languages use the same word for both "breath" and "spirit." "Spirit" in the Christian New Testament is *pneuma* in Greek. This is the same word used in the English word "pneumonia," "breath illness." This breath is the power of life. When it leaves a person's body, the person dies, though it may go on living invisibly. At least that is how primitive people may have reasoned, Tylor surmised.

Primitive Folk Tales and Archaic Myths

So far, we have talked about belief in mana and spirits as a way primitive people explain their world. But the word "explain" is not quite enough. Belief in spirits and mana does not merely explain the world; it also portrays it in story form so that the primitive person can feel at home in it and identify intimately with its ways.

Primitives have many folk tales about reality, sometimes called myths but simpler in form than most myths. An Australian aborigine story, for example, tells how their land was created before the beginning in "dreamtime." This was before the first sunrise, when there was no light and the earth was flat and naked. Then the old blind woman, Mudungkala, rose out of the ground with three infants, a boy and two girls. She crawled around on her hands and knees, leaving hills and paths for water behind her. Then she decreed that vegetation should grow and animals appear so that her children and the generations to come would have food. That is why the world looks as it does now.

Stories such as this tend to remain popular as explanations for things, even in archaic and later cultures. But among primitives, a story like that about Mudungkala also provides a chance for people to relive the events at the beginning of things in a dreamtime, one that merges with that of the original time. In rituals the tribe can re-enact the first events that made the world as it is. In this way, the people portray the world to themselves as it is. They name it and its aspects once again in a vivid way, as though to repeat to themselves who they are and what their world is like.

In general, the most primitive tribal groups have the least overall interconnected order to their simple stories. Australian aborigines, Kalahari bushpeople, the Yanomamo of Brazil-Venezuela, New Guinea mountain people, to cite a few, are all people who have many separate stories to explain things. They take it for granted that there are explanations for things, but their explanations are disconnected. The stories often bear little or no relation to each other, may even contradict each other. On festive occasions when bands of the tribe get together, they may each tell their tales, one after the other, sometimes in a kind of historical sequence, but with no single uniting theme, plot, or conclusions. The stories are often like a child's who has just returned from a big amusement park. She will tell of her adventures and the strange creatures and powers she has seen, one after the other, rambling on until memory or energy fails. The primitive folk tales are told with an adult sense of humor and care for details, but they nonetheless have the flavor of smaller stories unconnected with each other, except that they are about the same single world.

Among even somewhat primitive tribes, however, there is sometimes the beginning of a larger ordering of things, some initial sense of a unity to the explanations of things. In the Pacific Northwest one group of Native Americans tell a simple but well-rounded story of the beginning of human life (a story that may have been influenced by contact with outside civilization). The Old One descended on a cloud from the sky to the surface of the only thing that existed, the formless waters. From five hairs of his head he created five young women. He gave to each of them the choice of what to be. One chose to be a bad woman and to bear children who, like her, would fight, steal, and commit adultery. Another chose to be good and to bear children who, like her, would be wise, just, honest, and peaceful. The third woman chose to become the earth; the fourth, fire; the fifth, sweet water. From these five came the world in which people live. From them come all people, both good and bad. The Old One promised that eventually the good people would outnumber the evil and then all things would be made good.

This is a very direct story explaining how the world and its inhabitants came to be. It treats fire and water not just as accidental aspects of life, but rather as important natural forces established at the beginning of things. It explains the source of human evil, making a kind of sense of why it should exist at all; and it even promises an ideal future, when conflict will end. The beginning of life, its present condition, and its future fulfillment are all brought together in one story.

This group of tales includes stories of other sky beings. The sun, moon, and stars are in the sky now, but they were not always there. Father Sun mated with Mother Earth, but Earth nagged him, saying he was nasty, ugly, and too hot. So Sun abandoned her, taking moon and stars with him. The Old One had to step in to put things back in order, the same order that exists now. At the same time the Old One taught people who did not yet know how to think or speak, how to make fire and to fish, to dig roots and build lodges, to sing and dance, or to do anything. All of life, therefore, is not just a set of random practices. The order of the universe and of human life alike come from the work and wisdom of the Old One. Behind the evident confusion and disorder of events in life, there is a set of reasons for things.

As human societies began to grow larger and more complex, so did the stories about the gods and the origins of things. As one city conquered others and united them into a kingdom, all the gods of the various cities had somehow to be put in order of importance in relation to each other. By 3000 B. C., the ancient Egyptian kingdom had an official state religion that emphasized the importance of some gods over others. By the second millennium B.C., the same thing was occurring in China, India, and Mesopotamia.

The various complex stories about the gods are called myths. What you and I first think of when we hear the word "myth" is "false story," for we no longer believe in most of them. But there is another side, one that should not be overlooked: these myths arise from the human belief that reality is intelligible. Myths are invented or accepted by people because they do not just settle for experiencing things but want to discover the sense of things. Around the world, people tell stories of how the world came to be as it is, where people come from, why there is evil and death, why there are laws and customs, why there is winter, even why turtles are slow and snakes have no legs. Some stories are so simple as to be brief folk tales. Others are grand myths tying together many aspects of life. All of them are the result of human intelligence beginning to make sense of things in the face of mystery, in however stumbling a way.

They have their impact on people, though not the way textbooks or formal education does. The myths are like motion pictures we might see today that speak directly to our own concerns and feelings by drawing us into the story to the point where we begin to interpret our own lives in terms of the story. We accept the values by which the heroine or hero lives; we imagine ourselves facing the same dangers or challenges and overcoming them with the same virtues or skills. The world of the story of the myth becomes part of the life of the person, helping to establish the person's identity and values and place in the scheme of things. Though their historical facts may not be correct, folk tales and myths are often quite accurate at expressing the inner feelings and character of human life.

PSYCHOLOGICAL COMFORT

When the tales, myths, and beliefs about the numinous provide a way to name and explain mysterious aspects of life, it is not just intellectual satisfaction that is achieved; there is also great psychological comfort in these stories. Without such stories to make sense of it, the world often appears chaotic, full of random forces that intrude upon the more reliable patterns of life. If the unexpected is truly random and accidental, then there is no sense to it. Perhaps what orderliness there is in life can even be destroyed by mindless and senseless powers. Perhaps, as the Aztecs came to fear, the universe can come crashing down. (See Chapter Three.)

Merely to assert that every event has an explanation, a story behind it, is to express an implicit trust that life makes sense, that the dimension of mysterious powers is not a dimension of raw chaos threatening life, but one of some coherence and intelligibility. However threatening various numinous spirits, gods, and powers may be, they are less threatening to human security than the alternative possibility that behind the strange events of life there is just random senselessness.

Primitive and archaic cultures do not say such things explicitly. They do not write philosophical or psychological analyses about how their stories function. But the outside observer can say it for them: they bring coherence to their lives when they tell their "creation" stories. Over and over again in folk tales and great myths the world is brought into its present order out of a chaotic condition. A kind of sense is imposed by the ancestors, the Old One, the gods, on the formless waters, on the dark and lifeless earth, or on the monsters of chaos and disorder that live in the depths. The ability to believe that the numinous conquers chaos provides psychological comfort.

An added feeling of security comes from the fact that if you can name and describe the numinous powers that affect your life, you can expect to be able to exert some influence on them at times. From knowledge comes power. Mana can be manipulated by magical procedures to cure your children and your goats. The spirits who have dried up all the berries can be bribed or flattered into making new sweet berries grow. A child can be sacrificed to appease the great god who has sent a killing sickness in punishment for committing incest. There are many terrifying events in life. It would be very discouraging to feel helpless to deal with them. Techniques of magic, and worship all provide a feeling of competence to do something about problems.

An influential but rather antireligious interpretation of the psychological function of religion is that of Sigmund Freud (1856-1939). As children, Freud claimed, we obviously experience a great deal of helplessness. Our parents provide us with guidance and protection, thereby taking some of the anxiety out of our helplessness. But we grow up and discover we still are somewhat helpless in the face of disease, injustice, natural disaster, betrayals, and death. Our parents are not as strong as they once were. It is now evident they too are limited humans, helpless as we are.

Our childhood experiences have prepared us to seek a solution to our helplessness by relying on a superior being, a parent, to guide and protect us. Thus we readily devote ourselves to a god, especially a high god with great power, who can continue to care for us as our parents did. We can appeal to this divine protector for aid; we can rely on the god for guidance. In addition, we can feel that a strong parental figure cares for us once again, one who might even love and cherish us (though gods are often not all that loving; Freud was talking about belief in God also).

Freud was an atheist. He thought religion was a neurotic illusion that we cling to out of psychological need. Yet, even one who believes in and values a given religious tradition can agree with Freud's claim that religion is a source of psychological comfort. It is safe to expect that anything in human history so widespread and powerful as religion must be fulfulling some important human needs. Otherwise, even if it were completely true, people would have no need for it. (We will see more about the psychological function of religion in later chapters.)

THE SOCIOLOGICAL VALUE OF RELIGION

Belief in the existence of numinous powers is reinforced by the social dimension of human existence. As social animals, our lives are bound up with one another. Even the simplest tribe has a set of techniques for caring for children, distributing food, preventing fights, assigning mates and marital responsibilities, and so forth. There have to be some specifically stated rules: it is all right to steal from an enemy but not from kinfolk. There are various roles to be defined: men hunt and plant yams; women tend the gardens and cook the food. There are institutional patterns: the mother and mother's brother carry the basic responsibility for raising the mother's children. Every group, tribe, or culture has rules, roles, and institutions that make their lives together coherent instead of chaotic and deadly.

Belief in numinous powers makes some of these social arrangements intelligible by attributing them to the ancestors or gods. Why must the young girl about to be married avoid everyone's sight for three days of fasting? Why can we eat pigs but not foxes? The answer to such questions is often simply that things have always been this way. But many times part of the answer is that this is how things were established at the beginning by sacred ancestor-beings, or how they have been decreed by the gods. By their actions and choices the numinous beings have made our lives to be what they are.

This explanation does not just satisfy the mind's curiosity; it also helps to maintain the customs. Human beings live close to social chaos in many ways. Disputes over pigs, huts, insults, marriage, or a hundred other things bring people into conflicts that can seriously impair the group's ability to get on with the activities that sustain their lives. There could be endless disagreements on how they should live with one another. The demands of the moment could lead to confusing changes in rules and roles. To primitive people, however, it appears that the tribe must adhere to its traditional patterns because there is no real alternative. The patterns were set up at the beginning by the ancestors, so that is the way it is. Reality is a "one-possibility-thing," as someone once expressed it. No one can go back and redo the origins. As it was in the beginning, so it must always be. Individual people can rebel, if they choose, but that puts them outside the one correct order of the tribe. It is even possible that the spirits, perhaps those of the ancestors, may punish them for that. By such beliefs primitive people not only explain but also uphold their social patterns.

Archaic people do the same. They are a little more sophisticated on the average, especially the great archaic civilizations. They trade with outsiders more extensively, or interact with them in war. Through this they gain greater knowledge about different possible rules, roles, and institutions in the world. If these are only human inventions, then a person might feel more free to break them. But archaic people typically claim that their social order was dictated by the gods, or at least is upheld by them.

A person can still choose to break the rules, but the gods will send punishment for this. The gods, in fact, expect society to actively defend the laws the gods have set up. If society does not punish the person caught in incest, the gods may punish the whole society.

A striking aspect of how religious beliefs help to maintain cultural patterns is that the people involved often do not realize that their beliefs are functioning that way. There are various examples of this.

Incest is forbidden in some form or another in every society. There is a good reason for this. A group that freely allows incest can weaken itself by increasing the prevalence of various genetic diseases. It may be that banning incest also decreases family tensions and promotes useful marriage alliances with other groups. Often, however, the only reason that a people explicitly gives for avoiding incest is that it is contrary to the original and sacred order of things. The dreamtime stories of the primal days tell of terrible things that happened to one of the original ancestral people who had sexual relations with someone too closely related. That is how things started; that is how they still are.

These stories usually do not sound explicitly religious to us now. But in primitive societies the religious and the everyday blend together. The punishment that comes from incest arrives like magic. It is taboo, bad mana, to commit incest.

The anthropologist Marvin Harris offers a different kind of example from an archaic-style belief system, that of the religious respect in India for the cow. Many non-Indians mock this respect, saying it is foolish and even harmful, that the cows get in people's way, that the cows consume good food but cannot be eaten for food. This criticism is partly mistaken. Cows give milk and provide cow chips for cooking. When the cows die naturally, the outcasts of society can eat them for badly needed protein. Their hides can then be used for leather goods.

More significantly, reverence for the cow has a special benefit that is ordinarily not recognized at all. In times of drought people go hungry, Harris notes, and become tempted to slaughter the cattle for food. But those who do so condemn themselves to long-term starvation because the cows and oxen are needed for plowing the fields. Without oxen, people could not feed themselves when the drought ended and the rains returned. So it is important that people have a strong motive not to kill and eat the cattle, even when that would keep some of them alive in the short run. In the villages where the strongest religious respect for the cow is maintained, the continuing existence of that village and its custom of veneration is most assured. Harris points out, though, that the villagers do not give this survival benefit as the reason for respecting the cow. They say it is because the cow is holy as an earthly form of the great mother goddess, Kali.

Today it is difficult to realize how thoroughly most societies in history have based their cultural patterns on religious beliefs. There are a few remnants of this today in modern industrialized society. Many people, for example, still say that the rules of marriage are not human inventions but have been decreed by God: one man and one woman entering into a life-long partnership wherein sexual relations are legitimate and in which the husband is the boss. Like other traditional beliefs, this one is undergoing some revision today. Less and less of our culture is explicitly based on religious beliefs.

In most of history until today, just the opposite has been true. The rules, roles, and institutions of a culture have been consistently portrayed by people as having originated in the choices and actions of numinous beings, whether the ancestors, gods, or God, and as still supported by those numinous beings. This belief has been the major force in cultures throughout history to sustain their rules and patterns, and to help maintain stability and order.

Once again, folk tales and myths are important. These stories tell of the days when the social order was established and how it came to be that men of the fox clan cannot marry women of the frog clan, or that a chief of the villages had power to be the judge over land disputes, or that the king was given power by the high god of the city to make laws. As the story tells it, so it is and must be.

EXPERIENCE OF THE SACRED

The three types of reasons for belief described here so far can all be used in such a way as to cast doubt on the truth of religious beliefs. By describing the motivations people might have to believe, they show that people might believe in numinous realities even if none existed. Mystery exists: unanswered questions, unexplained events, uncertainty about the future, confusion about how to live. To deal with mystery, perhaps human beings would feel compelled to invent numinous powers out of their dream experiences, their imaginations, their tendency to "projection," their wishful thinking, their needs for psychological comfort and social stability.

This sort of suspicion has gone by the name of reductionism. This name is used to suggest the idea that all religious beliefs can be reduced to the status of fictions or illusions, by claiming that they are nothing more than ideas we humans invent to achieve security in the face of our intellectual, psychological, and sociological insecurities.

Reductionism began as a by-product of rational inquiry, as in philosophy or science. Science explains events by showing their natural causes. Anthropologists, psychologists, and sociologists have all tried to be scientific by showing the natural causes of religious behavior. Having found all sorts of possible natural causes for religious belief, the science-minded have sometimes declared that these are the only causes, that people have no genuine experiences of true numinous powers or beings, not even of God, as causes of their religious beliefs. So belief in the numinous is entirely a mistake, the reductionists claim.

Everyone tends to be reductionist about other people's beliefs. We take it for granted that we are being objective and scientific when we explain belief in magic and gods as false beliefs. The thoroughgoing reductionist just extends this attitude toward all religion. Be objective, this person says, and admit that all religion is false.

This is not quite as objective or scientific as it might sound, though. It would be difficult to show that all religious belief is false, to establish that there is no numinous reality of any sort. It is always possible that our intellectual, psychological, and sociological needs only heighten our sensitivity to the numinous dimension rather than lead us to invent it.

Mircea Eliade (1907-1984), the historian of religion, has made a special point of this. The experience of the sacred (the numinous) has been so overwhelmingly prevalent in human history, Eliade argues, that it is not very objective or scientific to casually dismiss it as though none of it could be legitimate.

In *The Sacred and the Profane* (1961) and many other books, Eliade indicates how thoroughly a sense of the sacred permeates the atmosphere of human existence. Awareness of the sacred dimension resolves many of the tensions of life and also keeps people open to further values and realities that transcend our present limits. The sacred is, therefore, too important to be dismissed, Eliade insists.

What Eliade suggests is that many specific beliefs about magic and gods and such may well be false or inadequate, but it may also be that these are just the limited attempts we have so far made to express the mysterious dimension that surrounds us. However inadequate various specific beliefs have been, there may nonetheless be a sacred or numinous reality, one perceived only in various cloudy ways, but one that is still too important to ignore.

As the next chapter will explain, classic historic religions—Judaism, Christianity, Islam, Hinduism, Buddhism, Taoism—have all given some indirect support to the idea that we can be correct in believing in the reality of the numinous or sacred, even while we are incorrect in our way of describing it. These religious traditions all say that there is an Ultimate Reality that is the final answer to life, but one which human language and concepts can never adequately capture. Perhaps belief in spirits and magic and gods is also just an inadequate way to express the reality of the numinous, the sacred.

It is certainly true that the dimension of mystery is always present in life; it is also true that this mystery eventually must be addressed by the human spirit seeking to discover the truth and value of being human. No one can adequately explore the human condition without taking the story of religion seriously, because that has been the heart of the human effort to address mystery.

Summary

This has been a brief look at three kinds of theories about why we humans have so readily and so often believed in mana powers, in spirits, and in gods. Theories claim that we have intellectual, psychological, and sociological motivations that might lead us to appreciate or even invent belief in numinous powers and beings. But Eliade adds a fourth possible explanation: belief in the numinous or sacred arises because there really is such a dimension to reality, one which people have experienced and expressed in limited ways but which is there nonetheless. Even if some specific beliefs are only human inventions, they may still be legitimate attempts to come to terms with a genuinely numinous aspect of reality.

The style of belief found in primitive and archaic cultures is not restricted to those cultures. People today still find that style of belief comfortable in many ways. But there is yet another style with another set of beliefs that has embraced archaic and primitive thoughts in a much larger and well-integrated framework. That is the style of historic culture and religion, the topic of the next chapter.

FOR FURTHER REFLECTION

1. Are there really any compelling reasons not to believe in magic, spirits, and gods? Describe the ones that make most sense to you.

2. Do you think that there are adequate non-religious answers available about why all events happen as they do, and why all of reality is the way it is?

3. To appreciate the power of myth, describe some story, motion picture, television drama, or play that seemed so real and vivid to you that you imaged yourself as part of the story.

4. Do you think it is true that people think of gods or God as a super parent? Why? If so, is this good, bad, or just a fact?

5. Do you know people who now claim that there is one correct social order that is commanded or supported by God?

6. If almost everyone in history has believed in the existence of the numinous, does that make it more reasonable for you also to believe in it? Explain.

7. Can we human beings get along all right without belief in the numinous? Intellectually? Psychologically? Socially? Explain.

SUGGESTED READINGS

W. Richard Comstock, *The Study of Religion and Primitive Religion*, 1971; ch. 1 on various theories of the origin and function of religion.

Joseph Campbell, *Myths to Live By*, 1972; ch. 2 on the emergence of human culture through myths.

Marvin Harris, *Cannibals and Kings*, 1977; a theory of what turned primitive societies into archaic ones.

Sigmund Freud, *The Future of an Illusion*, 1964; a brief critique of religious belief.

Peter Berger, *The Sacred Canopy*, 1969; chs. 1-4 in particular (difficult to read), on the sociological function of religion.

Mircea Eliade, *The Sacred and the Profane*, 1961; ch. 4 in particular.

Barbara Sproul, *Primitive Myths*, 1979; a collection of folk tales and myths on the origins of things from many primitive and archaic cultures.

Len Biallas, *Myths: Gods, Heroes, and Saviors*, 1986; the basic types of myths as stories of life's main challenges.

CHAPTER THREE

A Supreme
and Awesome Unity

God and Other Ultimates
in Historic Religions

HISTORIC RELIGION

The Axial Age: One Order to Reality
Around the 6th century B.C., many major cultures began to use a broadly systematic, logical mode of thought. Many individuals may have thought this way on their own in previous times, but it was not until sometime around 600 B.C. or later that this thought style became publicly influential and valued. The philosopher Karl Jaspers thought this was a breakthrough so important that he labeled this era the axial age, as though all history revolved around it as on its axis. It was the time when major civilizations learned to stand back mentally from the universe and from them-

selves in order to look beyond individual events and patterns toward a single final explanation for everything.

In various cultural centers, East and West, this more thoroughly logical systematic style of thinking gained enough influence to transform those cultures. That may sound a bit vague at this point, but this chapter will explain it more concretely as we go along. We will start with an initial comparison of beliefs about order in the universe.

If a person looks superficially at the world without any mental categories to sort things out, reality is just a collection of things and happenings with no particular order. Even primitive cultures, however, are able to look at reality and see order. They see cause-and-effect relationships. They sometimes perceive general categories like the numinous and the ordinary, the personal and the nonpersonal, the important and the irrelevant, the rewarding and the threatening. They usually have vastly detailed categories for foods, plants, terrain, weather, and spirits.

Archaic polytheistic cultures recognize larger, partially systematic order, represented by their great myths that connect many events into a single narrative, and by their belief in gods whose power unites many parts of reality. The world does in fact look the way a polytheist pictures it. Reality is a mixture of many specific things and various large patterns. Trees, rocks, lakes, and clouds are all individually influenced by or are a part of large valleys or major weather patterns. The many activities of the city, the shops and the gate-guards, the streets and the temples, the neighborhoods, the festivals, are all influenced by the king. Thus there is some large-scale order to reality, order that archaic cultures attribute to gods of the land or the weather or the city and so on.

There is, though, no total order. The land needs water but the skies withhold it this season. The god of the underworld erupts through the mountain, pouring down ash and fire. The great god of the city is defeated by the god of a neighboring city in a battle where the king is killed. Life goes on, both ordered and disordered, always a little dangerous and confusing.

Once there were only archaic and primitive cultures, in which people accepted reality as it appeared, partly stable and ordered, partly disordered and unreliable. This was reality. What else is there to do with reality except to acknowledge it and accept it? Neighborly spirits lived close at hand; the gods were more distant and awesome, requiring worship. Society dealt with them individually or grouped a few of them together, hoping to keep the numinous beings happy and helpful as much as possible. Life was as it appeared. All that people could do was to scratch out as much safety and happiness from it as they could.

Then came the axial age, when human consciousness dared to go beyond how things appeared in order to discover a universal order that rose above, "transcended," all the separate parts of reality, an order that included all those parts in its all-encompassing unity. Philosophy appeared. This included attempts to describe the ultimate principles and patterns and stuff of the entire universe at once and to show how it all logically fits together in one coherent system. Science appeared also, as part of philosophy, trying to do what philosophy in general did, to provide an all-embracing set of explanations of how all things work and why. This new consciousness also included a vision of how human life fit within the logically coherent system of the universe, and how life therefore might be made whole and ideal rather than torn between the conflicting forces of earthly life. This new consciousness produced a new way of being religious, one built upon the achievements of primitive and archaic forms, but one that absorbed them into a more unitary and idealizing religiousness. This is now called historic religion.

Historic religion took many forms in the East and West, each arising out of its own cultural context. But beneath all the varieties of forms and ideas are four characteristics common to historic stages of religiousness. These are beliefs 1) that there is an ultimate unity to all things, 2) that the source of the unity lies beyond or beneath the complexities, changes, and limits of this world, 3) that this source of ultimate unity is a reality of total perfection, and 4) that such perfection must be an incomprehensible Absolute (a word that will be explained later). In briefer terms, historic religion focuses on a numinous reality that is a universally unifying and perfect Absolute. The rest of this chapter will explain what that means.

HISTORIC RELIGION IN THE WEST

A Personal Supreme Being

According to the major Western religions, there is a universal and unifying order to reality because there is a supreme and transcendent personal Being that created and rules the entire universe from end to end. Belief in such a Being is called monotheism.

Most people in the West today would probably call themselves monotheists because they believe in an all-powerful Creator-Being called God or Yahweh or Allah. The era of polytheism is over, it would seem. Yet monotheism is a more austere and difficult kind of belief than we are usually aware of. It is hard to think the way a thoroughgoing monotheist does. A look at some history will make this more clear.

Near-Monotheism: Two Cases From History

One of the oddities of history is what appears to be a kind of monotheism that appeared in Egypt for a brief period of about twenty years, long before such an idea existed in other cultures. Whether it was a true monotheism or not is still disputed.

As far back as 3000 B.C., Egypt was a united kingdom with a vigorous archaic culture. In these early times the pharaoh was an earthly presence of the highest of the gods, the sun-god Ra. Through the rise and fall of many dynasties, the sun god remained supreme, though he came to be called Amen or Amen-Ra. By the beginning of the 14th century B.C., Egypt was attaining its greatest power, extending its rule to Mesopotamia. It was as though the sun god Amen-Ra, whose divine power was present in the pharaoh, was extending his control over the whole known earth.

But this was not yet a monotheism. Other important gods existed such as Osiris, descendant of Ra in some accounts, the god of life especially of life after death, as well as Osiris's son Horus, also identified with the pharaoh in those times. (Yes, it is very complicated. Archaic cultures do not make all their stories neatly logical and coherent the way historic cultures do.) All these polytheistic complexities suddenly gave way to an apparent monotheism, in the reign of Amenhotep IV (or Amenophis IV in some spellings) in the 14th century B.C.

This new pharaoh changed his name to Ikhnaton (or Akhenaton) in honor of a new sun god, Aton. Ikhnaton's name means "one who is devoted to Aton," and devoted he was. The pharaoh declared the old gods banished, and outlawed public worship of them. Some scholars have claimed that Ikhnaton was promoting a true monotheism, with Aton as the sole god over all the universe. As long as Ikhnaton lived, Aton had to be worshipped in the public temples as the sole and supreme god. But when Ikhnaton died, so did worship of Aton. The next pharaoh to ascend the throne was Ikhnaton's son-in-law, Tutankhamen, the famous "king Tut," whose name signals the return to worship of Amen as sun god, as well as of all the other traditional gods.

If the worship of Aton was true monotheism, it was not accepted enthusiastically by the people of Egypt. The old priestly caste that worshipped Amen may have resented their loss of power under the new god Aton. The people of Egypt, like all people, probably thought that the traditional gods were better for them. They were used to the stability and security represented by the old ways. On a local level, people also may have felt that Aton was too distant to be of use to them. The gods of the river, of life after death, of fertility—each had a special function. Each of these gods was closer to hand, although still somewhat awesome, in comparison with a god so big that he ruled the universe. While Aton was running the whole world, who would answer their prayers concerning their individual needs? Egypt, like the rest of the world, was not prepared for monotheism at that time.

Six or seven hundred years later, another near-monotheism appeared in Persia (modern Iran). The people of this part of the world had long lived by animistic and polytheistic beliefs. They saw the world as full of the spirits of their ancestors as well as other spirits and gods. An unusual aspect of their belief was that the spirits were either good or evil but not both. Most of the spirits and gods people have believed in throughout history have been an ordinary humanlike mixture of good and evil. These ancient Persians, however, perceived the human world as a battleground between the forces of good and the forces of evil. The evil in the world exists not as most people have thought, just because people and spirits alike all have their unpleasant side, their moments of anger or spite. Evil is a stronger and more unremitting force. It is a power that is simply evil. It is the power of the evil spirits, called daevas. Good people are fortunate, though, because they can expect help against the daevas from good spirits known as ahuras.

About 600 B.C., a man named Zarathustra began to interpret these older Persian beliefs in a new way, founding a religion that is known to us after the ancient Greek form of his name, Zoroaster. There are very few Zoroastrians in the world today. The last sizable group are the Parsees (Persians) of Bombay, India. But Zoroastrianism left its mark on the other major western religions. According to one early version of Zarathustra's thought there is one supreme god named Ahura Mazda ("wise Lord") or Ormuzd. This wisest of good spirits was perfectly good, hating evil. He was the creator of the entire universe, originally a beautiful place of joy and happiness. But Ahura Mazda had an opposite, the evil one named Ahriman. The goodness of the world was offensive to Ahriman so he began to curse it, bringing war, disease, suffering, and death. It was Ahriman who created the daevas, and together with them tried to seduce the minds and hearts of humans to follow evil ways.

Ahura Mazda immediately set about fighting to bring goodness out of all this evil. For 3000 years there would be a battle between all the forces of good and of evil. People would have to take sides, choosing to follow Ahura Mazda or Ahriman. In the end, this whole world would be destroyed in the conflict, and all people would meet in judgment. Those who had pursued goodness would cross a wide bridge into Paradise, a lovely garden. Those who had followed the ways of Ahriman, father of lies, would find the same bridge thin as a knife's edge and would fall from it into the burning pit as they deserved.

In one version of these beliefs, after 3000 more years, the former sinners, purged by fire of their evil, would be released from the pit and rejoin the good people in a perfect world prepared by Ahura Mazda. Then all evil and all its effects would have been totally destroyed. Ahura Mazda's power and goodness would have unquestioned supremacy over everything.

Extant historical documents are not fully clear about Zarathustra's actual teachings, but it looks as though he was struggling toward a true monotheism. Ahura Mazda was creator of the entire universe and in the end would exercise complete power over everything. Yet he had to engage in actual battle with Ahriman, just as the gods of polytheism sometimes fought one another. If monotheism is a belief in a God whose power is total, then a being like Ahura Mazda is not quite God-like because his power is limited by another such as Ahriman, even if for just a time.

The problem that Zarathustra and later Zoroastrians faced was how to reconcile belief in a supreme and perfectly good Creator with the all too evident fact of evil in the world. If the Creator is all good, then it seemed he could not be willing to tolerate evil. He would not merely eliminate it all at the end of time; he would not allow it to exist in the first place. But evil does exist. Rather than accept the idea that Ahura Mazda was uncaring or imperfectly good or incompetent, Zoroastrian thought chose an alternative: Ahura Mazda is not all-powerful. He is the most powerful, finally able to conquer even Ahriman and all the forces of evil Ahriman created to help him. But Ahura Mazda does not have all power. He is not unqualifiedly supreme.

Many people who are supposedly pure monotheists may actually be closer to the Zoroastrian type of belief. As long as the god they worshipped is most powerful, one who will win out in the long run, that is enough. It is sufficient, perhaps, to picture the god as not too distant from the troubles of human life, not so absolutely supreme as to seem as distant from people as Aton once seemed to the ordinary Egyptian. A god that has to battle against forces of evil, as people themselves must do, is one that may be easier to identify with. But this is a limited god, not quite an all-powerful God.

The God of Western Religion

The formal belief of Judaism, Christianity, and Islam define Yahweh/God/Allah not merely as the most powerful god but as the absolutely, totally supreme Reality from all eternity, Creator and ruler of everything, limited in no way at all. By custom the name for this Creator is spelled with a capital letter: God. There is a history behind this belief in God, a history that can make clearer what an unqualified monotheism is.

The major formative influence in Western monotheism is the early history of Jewish monotheism, which developed out of the religious beliefs of the ancient Hebrews. These people were Semitic nomads who settled in the land of Canaan (present-day Palestine/Israel) sometime in the second millennium B.C. Some of them ended up as slaves in Egypt. A pivotal event in the history of Western civilization was the escape of some of these slaves from Egypt under the leadership of Moses about 1250 B.C., an event known as the Exodus. Moses came to the slaves from the Sinai peninsula where he had been living, and brought them a new god called Yahweh, who would be able to protect them from the Egyptian gods in their attempt to escape.

Moses might have been a monotheist of some sort, believing that no God existed except Yahweh, though many scholars now doubt this. It is clear that Moses' Hebrew followers were not monotheists. Like all people of their time, they showed great willingness to worship any god they thought might help them. When these Hebrews eventually settled in Canaan (Palestine), they happily worshipped the local high gods, Baal and his consort Astarte, gods of fertility and the skies. For that matter, the Hebrews also believed in spirits, sorcerers, and omens. They and their descendants were polytheists and animists at heart. It probably would not have occurred to them to take seriously the idea that no god existed except one absolutely supreme God.

Yahweh was nonetheless a very important god to them. He was clearly a good war god because he had led the Hebrews to victory in many battles. In general, Yahweh was a good god for historical events like wars, escape from Egypt, the invasion of and settling in Canaan. But their Canaanite neighbors and, eventually, kinfolk taught them that Baal was the god to worship for fertility in the family, flocks, and fields. And Hebrews and Canaanites alike would presume that when visiting in foreign countries such as Egypt or Babylon, it would be prudent to pay homage to Amen-Ra or Marduk.

A step closer toward monotheism was the belief that grew among the Hebrews, perhaps from as early as the time of Moses, that Yahweh was a jealous god, not one to share worship with other gods. Although the Hebrews believed that many gods existed, they sometimes nonetheless insisted that they should ignore all gods except for the one that was distinctively theirs, who specially guarded and guided them and gave them their identity through their laws and customs. The name "henotheism," invented in 1880 by German religion scholar F. Max Müller to identify a similar kind of exclusive worship of a local god in areas of India, has sometimes been stretched to include the Hebrew notion of a devotion to Yahweh alone.

There is a famous story in the history of Israel illustrating this form of henotheism. In the 9th century B.C., Ahab, king of the northern tribes of Israel, had a wife named Jezebel. She came from Phoenicia where her father, also a king, had followed the royal ways approved by Baal, the main god of many Phoenicians. The ways of Baal allowed the king great powers over his subjects. The ways of Yahweh, however, coming from a time before there were kings over Israel, demanded what today could be called civil and social rights. With Jezebel's support Ahab was acting like a tyrant, contrary to Yahweh's customs.

From out of the desert appeared a wild-looking man, Elijah. He challenged the ways of Baal by proclaiming that if Ahab did not follow Yahweh's customs, Yahweh would cause a drought. This was a striking challenge because rain was supposedly under Baal's power. Eventually, the contest between Yahweh and Baal was focused on Mount Carmel near the Mediterranean where altars were set up, one to each god. The priests and prophets of

Baal danced, sweated, sang, and cut themselves to get Baal to show a sign of his power. Nothing happened. Elijah suggested that Baal was hard of hearing or off resting. Then, at Elijah's prayer, Yahweh sent a mighty bolt from heaven to burn up the offering and show his power. Before long, there appeared on the horizon a small cloud, "no bigger than a man's fist." The cloud grew quickly until it let loose a downpour. Yahweh had shown that he was God of nature's fertile rain. For generations after this, Yahweh's followers would try to urge that other gods be ignored, that people abandon Baal and worship only Yahweh. Yahweh might not be the only god that existed, his followers said, but he was the only one his people should acknowledge as their god. He could take care of all their needs—war, fertility, and anything else.

This henotheism was only partially successful. For the next 200 years and more, people were still inclined to hedge their bets, catering to all gods who might have some power. Then came a catastrophe that established belief in Yahweh as a genuine monotheism. In 587 B.C., Babylon conquered Jerusalem, capital of Judea. All the leading Judeans (the word "Jew" derives from this) were taken into captivity so they could not instigate a new rebellion against Babylon. The city walls of Jerusalem were destroyed as was the glorious temple of Yahweh built by Solomon. The Judeans were in exile, living in a foreign land ruled by the great god Marduk. Many of the Judeans undoubtedly came to the most logical conclusion, that Marduk had defeated Yahweh. Other Judeans, however, a "faithful remnant," intensified their loyalty to Yahweh. Babylon was Yahweh's tool, they said, used by him to test them and purify them, to teach them that Yahweh alone is God, that all other gods are but lifeless clay and sticks. Yahweh is so great a God as to be God over all the nations of the earth. There is no God but Yahweh.

This Jewish monotheism has proclaimed itself in the famous prayer, "Hear, O Israel, the Lord our God, the Lord is one." Christianity inherited this belief, as did Islam: "There is no god but God (Allah)." Jews, Christians, and Muslims are sometimes highly conscious of the differences among them, but all three share Jewish monotheism.

The Jewish-Christian-Islamic God is a God we probably all think we can define rather easily. It is the Creator, Lord of the Universe. But it is not really easy to pin down what is meant by "God." Here is a list of five major characteristics that the three main Western monotheisms have traditionally agreed upon. You may want to test your conception of God against these.

First of all, God is all-powerful ("omnipotent"). This does not mean merely that God has more power than anything or anyone else, such as Ahura Mazda had. It means literally that *nothing* exists except that God has created it and sustains it in being. Nothing can happen except that God makes it happen that way or allows it to happen. God's control over the course of all events is known as Providence. Every lily that grows, sparrow that flies, volcano that erupts, does so under God's providential guidance. Human beings are said to have free will. But to exist at all depends on God's power; to continue to have freedom depends on God's decision to make people free; and God may influence free will very much (though different groups disagree on how much).

Secondly, the Western God is all-knowing ("omniscient"). There is absolutely nothing that happens that God does not know. God sees all, down to the most minute detail. The traditional belief, in fact, has claimed that God knows everything that will ever happen, that God has known perfectly from before the beginning of time every event that would ever take place.

Whatever any person freely decides to do, God already knew about that free choice and took it into account, along with every free choice ever to be made as part of the divine plan. Therefore, it would seem, everything is bound to turn out exactly as God has planned all along. The control that God exercises over the eventual destiny or outcome of each person's life is often called predestination, or sometimes predeterminism.

Western monotheism has not been consistently predeterministic. Islam has favored this view most strongly. All things happen "as Allah wills." In Christianity, a line of thought that runs from St. Augustine in the 4th century to John Calvin in the 16th says that individuals are predestined by God even before their birth to end up in heaven or in hell after death. Jewish thought has been the least predeterministic or predestinarian of all.

A third traditional concept about God in the West is that God is perfectly good. In the earlier parts of the Judaic Scriptures, God is pictured as sometimes angry and vengeful. But eventually the Jews began to conceive of God as utterly perfect and, therefore, utterly good. Human weaknesses such as emotional outbursts of jealousy or impatience seemed increasingly inappropriate for God. Some religious believers then and now, however, have not considered jealousy, anger, impatience, or vengeance to be imperfections. They manage to assert simultaneously that God does have something like these emotions but is also perfectly good. The idea of "good" can vary, evidently.

An equally serious problem with the concept of God as perfectly good is that there seems to be a great deal of evil in the world. One cause of evil is human free choice. People have freely decided to murder and torture one another, or to allow pain and hunger when it could be prevented. Why are people like this? The events of nature also cause evil. In the course of human existence, a billion people have been killed or crippled by disease, drought, earthquake, and flood. For the most part these have all been things that human beings were powerless to prevent. Why is nature like this? An all-good God cannot be callous or indifferent to such things. An all-powerful and all-knowing God presumably could have arranged things to operate less destructively (unless omnipotence and omniscience are somehow compatible with incompetence).

Western religions have faced the problems posed by the existence of evil and have produced various answers. Such answers are called "theodicies," a word coined by the philosopher Gottfried Leibniz (1646–1716) in the early 18th century. (Theodicy literally means "justifying [the ways] of God.") One theodicy is the story of the original sin of humankind committed in the garden of Eden, as told in the third chapter of the book of Genesis. It wasn't God but human sin that caused evil by throwing life and nature itself into disorder. Most recently, some theology has suggested, like Zoroastrian thought long ago, that God has limited power and so should not be blamed for everything that goes wrong. For centuries people have struggled with this problem of evil, producing various answers. The notion of a perfectly good God is not as simple a notion as it first seems.

The fourth major characteristic of the Western God is personness. This can be a tricky concept because it can have a variety of meanings. The Yahweh of early Hebrew thought was very much a person, as were Baal and Marduk and other gods. They were divine persons rather than human ones, but they thought and acted like humans and had emotional needs and feelings like humans. These gods were anthropomorphic ("human-form"), not necessarily in appearance but in their personalities.

Early monotheism retained much of the anthropomorphic language about God from earlier polytheistic (or henotheistic) times, but it reinterpreted this language. The all-powerful God was beyond all humanlike limitations and weaknesses. The personhood of God was what a person would be like if a person were not confined to bodily forms and were totally perfect in every way possible. Judaism came to conceive of God, for example, as utterly perfect wisdom. Christian texts spoke of God as pure love. Islam describes God as perfectly merciful and compassionate. These are all characteristics of a person, yet a perfect Person in this case and not a merely humanlike god such as Zeus.

As monotheism continued to develop in the West, the formal theologies moved even further away from any suggestion of anthropomorphic thought. While the average religious person spoke of God as attentive and caring, as wise and merciful, the theologies warned people not to take such language too literally. Theologians proposed that "God" is the name for the infinite, changeless, eternal Being that is the Cause of all else, a Being beyond the capacity of a finite mind to understand it or a language to describe it.

When people say that God is personal, therefore, what they should mean according to the theologies is that God is in some incomprehensible way what the total perfection of life, consciousness, goodness, and free choice are like when these are aspects of an infinite and eternal Reality (in a way not comprehensible to us).

This theological way of speaking avoids anthropomorphic talk about God, or at least asserts that anthropomorphic talk is useful poetic images but not literal truth. But there is a price to pay. A God that cannot be described literally as a caring and attentive person may be a God too incomprehensible to satisfy many people's needs. Most people might well prefer a very good, powerful, personally attentive but limited god, someone like Zeus turned into a benevolent helper, to an infinite and eternal but incomprehensible perfection of personness.

The fifth major characteristic of God in much of Western theology nevertheless calls for such nonanthropomorphic language. It is that God is Absolute, which means that God is unqualifiedly beyond every limitation of any kind whatsoever. God is not only totally perfect, God is beyond even perfections as we humans could conceive of them. God is the infinite, the incomprehensible fullness that is eternal Mystery. God is the Absolute.

This rather extreme and abstract way of thinking arose in a way that was perhaps inevitable. Once people begin to search behind the confusions and imperfections of the world for a supreme and unifying perfection, the found it hard to stop at any finite reality. "God" is the name given to the absolutely ultimate cause of everything, the final answer, the origin and goal of all else. God can be this only if God is truly ultimate, beyond which there is nothing else. If there is anything beyond God or independent of God in any way at all, then God is not the ultimate unifying cause of all that is, for there is at least some other and competing reality, such as Ahriman was to Ahura Mazda's supremacy.

A way to conceive of God as unqualifiedly ultimate is to do what a Christian theologian, Anselm, did in the 11th century. He defined God as "that than which nothing greater can be conceived." God, therefore, is not merely a being that happens to be greater than anything else. "God" is the name for that being which by its nature is necessarily greater than anything and everything else that even might exist. "God" is the name for a reality which cannot be "second" in any way to anything. The only way to be that great, it seems, is to exceed every possible limitation. And that is to be infinite. So the traditional argument went.

That conclusion eliminates all anthropomorphism. In fact, it makes it hard to say anything. A finite reality can be defined; its limits are what describe it. It is like this and not like that. But if God is totally unlimited, then God is actually beyond all categories and labels. God is called a Mystery, then, not merely because God's ways are sometimes puzzling but because the absoluteness of God is always beyond what any finite mind can conceive.

In spite of this, Jews, Christians, and Muslims do describe God—by a balancing of ideas. On the one hand, God is the supreme personal Creator from whom all else receives its existence, in some sense totally good, all-powerful, and all-knowing. On the other hand, God is Absolute, the infinite Mystery. God somehow is goodness, somehow personness, somehow power, but all in ways beyond human understanding.

If you find it difficult to deal with the notion of God as Absolute, you are far from alone. Nonetheless, it seems to be an idea that the human mind drives toward in its search to make sense of reality in the face of mystery. Most people do not feel any individual need to affirm the utter absoluteness of God. Yet in the major religious traditions some such idea occurs anyway. This is evident not just in Western monotheism but in Eastern thought also.

HISTORIC RELIGION IN THE EAST

Nonpersonal Ultimates

To speak of religion in the East is even more of an oversimplification than to speak of a single monotheism in the West. There is not one, but two major centers of ancient civilization in the East: India and China. Each of these two has a complex religious history. Neither gave birth to only one form of religiousness, but they both produced religious movements that portrayed an ultimate numinous reality as nonpersonal rather than personal. The infinite and universal power in some Eastern religious traditions is not so much a Being as a Force, not a personal reality but simply a Cause. It may be easier to understand this way of thinking by beginning with a description of some less than infinite nonpersonal forces that have appeared in cultures other than Eastern ones.

Non-Eastern Numinous Forces of Great Power

The Aztecs of Central Mexico believed that the earth and heavens had been brought out of chaos three different times, each time ending in horrible destruction. Now, they believed, we live in the fourth and last age. The universe must be held together, for there will be no other chance beyond this. If the universe collapses again, the gods themselves would fall into destruction. And so, day after day, year after year, the Aztecs offered up human sacrifices on the altars. Originally such sacrifices seem to have been conceived of only as offerings to the gods, but eventually they were treated also as rituals that generated the cosmic energy necessary to keep the universe together, gods and all. This great ritual force was capable of powering the entire universe and maintaining its coherence. (Whether this belief represents archaic or an incipient historic consciousness is difficult to say.)

In ancient Greek mythology before the axial age, three numinous beings, the Fates, controlled the destinies of all people. By the axial age or during it, some Greeks came to think of the Fates as a single, nonpersonal Force that assigned humans and gods alike their situation and status in life. One of the most useless and dangerous things a person could do, therefore, was to aspire to rise above the station in life Fate had assigned. Such desire was called *hubris*, pride. It was the arrogance of daring to believe that you could accomplish more or be more than Fate had decreed.

Out of this belief in Fate, perhaps, came a similar notion, that of a group of philosophers known as Stoics (because their founder

Zeno [c. 490–c. 430 B.C.] had lectured on a porch [*stoa* in Greek]). The Stoic movement took place after the axial age had begun and was explicit in believing that there was a universal power that ruled even the gods. Every event in history is predetermined by a cosmic *Logos*, or principle of rational order, they said. (Out of respect for tradition the Stoics called this Zeus, thereby transforming the god Zeus from a personlike being into a cosmic Force.) So it is useless to fight against the course that events take. Our only freedom as humans is to choose to acquiesce calmly or to rebel in vain against the Logic of the universe.

Just slightly earlier another Greek philosopher had developed a theory about a supreme force that is hard to classify as personal or nonpersonal. That is the Unmoved Mover, described by the great Aristotle (384–322) around 330 B.C. He decided that there must be some continuing and primal force or being unceasingly producing motion or change in the universe, otherwise everything in the world would naturally grind to a halt. Oddly enough, Aristotle reasoned, the prime force that made everything else must itself be unmoving, because if *it* moved it would then not be the prime or first mover Aristotle wanted to talk about. This would result in an infinite regression, i.e., an infinite series of movers moved by another mover, which in turn was moved by another, and so on. Aristotle claimed that there had to be a *First* Mover, itself unmoved and unmoving, for us to make sense of the continuing fact of motion in the world. (He never doubted that we could make sense of reality.)

The only kind of reality Aristotle knew about that could remain motionless yet move other beings was something desirable. An ice cold drink on a hot day can move us into action without its having to do anything except be there in front of us. So the unmoved mover must be the supremely desirable reality. This in turn meant to Aristotle that it must be perfect in every way. An imperfect reality would not be supremely desirable. The most perfect kind of thing Aristotle knew of was thought, for it is thinking that reveals to us what is perfect and eternal. So the unmoved mover must be pure thought. But there is nothing higher than the unmoved mover. If it is thought, it must be self-thinking thought, not a thought dependent on someone else's mind. Aristotle concluded then that the ongoing cause of all activity in the whole universe is a self-thinking thought, perfectly desirable, the Unmoved Mover.

A self-thinking thought, a *Logos* that controls our lives and keeps us each in our places, a ritual-power, generated from human sacrifices to keep the universe moving—this is a strange collection of beliefs. Yet each of these represents an attempt by some people to make sense of reality as best they could. Each group or person became aware of some puzzle or mystery: Why does the universe act as it does? What makes it go? How does it influence our lives? Is there anything a person can do in response? The desire to make sense out of life in the face of mystery is one that no culture seems able to resist. Each tries to respond to mystery as best it can, given its history, culture, and experiences. China and India gave their own responses also.

The Taoism of China

Long before recorded history began, the peoples of China were animists and polytheists. By historical times many Chinese worshipped a high god. In the Shang dynasty of the 18th to 11th centuries B.C., the great Ti, ruler of heavens, watched over the Shang kings. A neighboring kingdom ruled by the Chou dynasty also had a high god, one called T'ien, "heaven." In the 11th century B.C. the Chou conquered the Shang and combined the two gods into one. Shang-Ti and T'ien became just two different names for one high god of the skies (as Amen and Ra in Egypt had become one sun god instead of two).

T'ien or Shang-Ti was a personlike god. Ancient Chinese literature speaks of T'ien as one who sees all and hears all, who blesses and protects people and punishes the wicked, who in fact created the Chinese people with their particular character. The Chou dynasty encouraged people to think of T'ien as the one who upheld the power of the king as long as he ruled wisely and benevolently, and who would overthrow a corrupt dynasty like the Shang in order to provide a new and good government for the people.

But from ancient times in China there was another belief, this one in a regular, natural order of things. The day and the night follow one another and the seasons progress year after year. All things follow a pattern of growth and decline, everything is balanced by its opposite. The Chinese summed all of this up into one fundamental pattern—Yang/Yin.

There is a Yang aspect to nature that is warm, dry, male, of heaven; and a Yin aspect to balance it, which is cool, moist, female, of earth. The list of opposites can be extended indefinitely: active and passive, loud and quiet, hard and soft, and so on. In discovering the Yang/Yin, the Chinese had found a way to organize all the categories of nature into one grand scheme. Human intelligence was at work again, refusing to accept the world as a variety of disconnected happenings, forms, or things. The Chinese mind sought a higher unifying order running throughout all reality.

The Yang/Yin are opposites, but not antagonists. They blend into one another. They are the alternating aspects of nature. There are moments when one or the other dominates. The hot and dry longest day of summer and the cold and wet shortest day of winter are such times. But these extreme days are also the moment of a return back to the mingled moderation of spring or fall when Yang/Yin are more even balanced. The moon that wanes also waxes; the seed that flowers withers and drops new seed to the ground. Yang/Yin are not good/evil; both are valuable and necessary aspects of the unity of nature. They are not gods or spirits, but the fundamental forces of nature.

From about the 8th century B.C., the Chou dynasty itself fell into corruption. The rule of law broke down and no one could be sure of receiving justice in the courts, protection from bandits or from greedy landowners. It was the time known as "the warring states." Most of the Chinese continued to pray to T'ien (Shang-Ti) or the ancestors. Some Chinese, however became skeptical about T'ien. As the centuries went by, conflict continued. It seemed that T'ien was either powerless or callous. Hope in help from the high god diminished.

Out of all this came a particular school of thought known as Taoism. Sometime between 600 and 300 B.C., two writings appeared, one by a legendary Lao-Tzu, another by Chuang-Tzu. These two works are in agreement that there is one supreme force, a truly ultimate one. It includes everything that exists within the scope of its influence. It has universal power and presence. This ultimate reality is called Tao (pronounced "dow").

The word "tao" is a rather ordinary one. It means way, or pattern, or order. The Chinese had long sought the right way (tao) to live and to organize society. For most Chinese the ancestors and the high god T'ien/Shang-Ti had been of major importance in establishing the correct way. The writings ascribed to Lao-Tzu and Chuang-Tzu proposed something different. We all know that there is a way to nature, they said. This is the Yang/Yin pattern, the eternal process of the world. These are the two forces at work in the three parts of the universe: heaven, earth, and living beings. These three parts move through the four seasons, which in turn are a blending of the five elements: earth, water, fire, wood, and metal. But ultimately, behind the five, four, three, and two, is One. That is the Tao that is the way of all the universe. ("Tao bore one, one bore two, two bore three; three bore ten thousand things," says The Book of the Tao, in its usual obscure way.)

This ultimate Tao is beyond all categories of five or four or three or two. It cannot fit within any definition at all. Therefore it is ineffable, unable to be spoken. Whatever can be expressed, thought, felt, or imagined, is not Tao. "That which imparts form to forms is itself formless," says Chuang-Tzu. Tao is self-existent; there is nothing that accounts for its existence. It just is. Eternal and unchangeable, it is not outside the universe but is in and through all. It is the nameless principle behind all the happenings in the world.

Western scholars have sometimes translated the word Tao as "God." It is easy to see why. The ultimate Tao, like God in the West, is the universal ultimate power at work in all that happens. This view is close to pantheism, a notion that all of nature is divine and worthy of worship. It would be more accurate to call Taoist belief a near-pantheism in that it considers all of the events of nature to be manifestations of the supreme power called Tao, which lies within nature, but is not identical with it.

On the other hand, the ultimate Tao is not what Westerners usually expect when they think of God. The Tao is not a supreme Person who knows what is going on in the world and who guides the path of history. The Tao does not and cannot hear or respond to prayer. The Tao is not caring toward people, but neither is it uncaring. It is beyond such categories. It simply is, eternally and unchangeably incomprehensible. It is the nonpersonal way from which there somehow emanates the Yang/Yin way of nature.

In actual practice most of those who call themselves Taoists today acknowledge the reality of Tao but do not devote much time or attention to it. This is partly because the Tao is nonpersonal and cannot care for people or listen to them. Most Taoists are involved on a daily basis with the spirits and the ancestral beings that are personal. They are also happy to be concerned with the smaller nonpersonal power in omens, mana-filled rituals, and various smaller forms of Yang/Yin. If ordinary people pay scant attention to the supreme Tao, it is probably because this ultimate Tao, like all ultimate realities, is a little too hard to grasp, too general or abstract or philosophical to evoke ongoing interest. Yet belief in it shows again how far the human mind can reach.

The Ultimate Reality in the Religions of India

It is impossible to represent the range of religious thought that has developed in India. Hindu, Buddhist, Sikh, and Jain religious traditions had their origins there. Hindu thought alone can count many different theological schools as well as hundreds of local traditions. But we can describe a few particularly significant Indian themes about the ultimate.

There is, for example, the extremely austere theme of earliest Buddhism. The Buddha (c. 563–c. 483 B.C.), prince Siddhartha Gautama, was a very practical person in his own way. He proposed that human salvation consisted in achieving nirvana, a sort of self-extinguishing (more about this later). The condition of nirvana was the ultimate reality, according to the Buddha. What was nirvana like? Do not ask, the Buddha replied. No one can know. There is no use wasting time on empty speculations. This answer did not satisfy the Buddhists for long, however. Shortly after his time and down to today, a majority of Buddhists began to describe the ultimate as a kind of supreme divinity, once manifested in the prince Siddhartha as well as in other earthly and godly beings.

Buddhism came out of an older and still enduring Hindu tradition, one that in India reabsorbed Buddhism into itself. In this there are two lines of thought about the ultimate that have converged at least partially and have had major influence. One originally concerned the power of ritual; the other was about a search into a person's innermost self.

The best starting point in discussing any Hindu traditions is the Vedas. From about 1500 to 500 B.C., a set of sacred writings was assembled, focusing on the ritual prayers of ancient Hindu practice but containing all sorts of information, instruction, and, in the later works, even philosophical interpretations. In the 6th century B.C., the axial age, a late segment of the Veda literature appeared, known as the Upanishads, a set of commentaries on ritual, the universe, and the gods. Until this time Hindu belief and ritual had been polytheistic, but the Upanishads added something important.

From very ancient times the priestly caste, those whose right and duty it was to perform the ritual, had emphasized the importance of ritual power. A word for ritual-power (sometimes translated as "prayer") begins with the letters *brhm*. The priests therefore were called brahmins and the mana-like power generated by the ritual was called something like "brahman." By the 6th century B.C., the Upanishads proclaimed that Brahman was not just a power, but was the ultimate power in the universe.

As time went on, various schools of thought developed this notion further. Taking the Upanishads and other Vedic literature as their inspiration, a number of Hindu thinkers asserted that there is one supreme and ultimate reality, infinite and incomprehensible, that lies behind the entire universe, a reality to be called Brahman. It is the ocean of Being, the fullness of Power, the Really Real.

This idea eventually intersected with another ancient tradition, belief in the Atman, a belief in a kind of "Self" (a word to be used cautiously). As early as the time of the Upanishads, some Hindu thought had begun to turn inward, away from the outer world. The world we live in is one of confusion and pain, of unreliable things that come and go. To find some peace, a person may try to close off the world and retreat into the inner self. One of the ways this was described in Hindu thought was to compare it metaphorically to falling asleep to the outer world in order to find something else inside the person.

In dreams or special states of consciousness a person perceives a reality that is not subject to the usual limitations imposed by time and space. Dreams are partial freedom from the world. In deep, dreamless sleep a person goes a step further, beyond even the dream-reality into a kind of no-self, a state of non-consciousness as though the self had disappeared for a time. But this is a temporary no-self. The inner self of a person actually lasts through this dreamless sleep, as is evident when the person wakes up. The dreamless state was just a temporary freedom from involvement in the passing jumble of events in life. To attain a fuller freedom a person must go even deeper, beyond even dreamlessness, to get totally beyond individual self. It is not easy to take this metaphorical journey beyond waking and dreams and dreamless sleep into full no-self. The path to it is not through actual sleep (Chapter Five will describe the path). Few ever achieve it. But what the path leads to is the ultimate Self. It is called Atman, a word that originally meant just inner self or spirit (or breath or air, as in "*atm*osphere). It is the infinite and universal Self, the truly ultimate reality. At times it is called pure consciousness as befits a Self, or pure bliss as a kind of state of consciousness. Yet because it is truly the Ultimate, it is also eternal, unchanging, and unbounded. It is a consciousness and bliss utterly beyond what we can comprehend.

Different Hindu thinkers responded to ideas about Brahman and Atman in different ways. Many decided that since each was

said to be ultimate reality and there could be only one truly ultimate reality, it must therefore be that Brahman was Atman and
vice versa. To some this meant that Brahman-Atman was and is
pure Consciousness, as though Brahman-atman were the ultimate
Self or Personness. Another school of thought pushed the ideal of
ultimateness all the way. The truly ultimate is that beyond which
there can be nothing else. As ultimate, it must therefore be the infinite. As infinite, it must therefore be beyond all categories, even
the categories of consciousness and bliss. Brahman-Atman then
must be Nirguna Brahman: Brahman without attributes. This is
all certainly confusing. But it is difficult to think clearly about a reality that lies beyond the ability of thought to grasp it.

A fairly extreme but widely held position is that of the Hindu
thinker, Shankara. He lived and wrote in the 9th century A.D., relatively recently, and he claimed to be bringing to completion what
was already in the Vedic writings. He argued that Brahman is indeed the incomprehensible, infinite, ultimate Reality. It has the
fullness of realness and infinitely so. That means that in some
sense nothing is really real, except Brahman's eternal and changeless "realness." At this point, other thinkers concluded that because the world is real it is therefore part of Brahman. Not Shankara. He concluded that the world we live in and perceive and take
to be real is just the opposite. It is a shadowy, unsubstantial thing.
It is "maya," a word sometimes translated as "illusion." Like those
concerned with the inner self and Atman, but in his own way,
Shankara turned away from the world. Brahman-Atman alone is
real, he declared, in its infinite incomprehensibility.

This is the extreme of a belief in a nonpersonal Ultimate. The
Tao is nonpersonal and ultimate, but the Taoist values this world
and its Yang/Yin order as manifesting the universal influence of
the Tao. The Brahmanist who accepts Shankara's ideas claims that
nothing is truly real except the infinite and incomprehensible Nirguna Brahman. The world has no true existence. Nor do you and I
have any true existence, except that we have within us beneath
our individual selfhood the Self (Atman), which is actually even
beyond Self, for it is ultimately identical with Nirguna Brahman.

TALKING ABOUT THE INCOMPREHENSIBLE

It is difficult to try to make sense out of a position that says that
we are not real the way we think we are, and that the best way to

think about the Ultimate is to recognize that it is unthinkable. But within the complexly woven threads of Hindu tradition there is a basic thought common to East and West. It is that beyond or beneath the various events and things of life as we experience it and comprehend it, there is a single and infinite incomprehensible reality: God as Absolute, the formless Tao, Nirguna Brahman. In the West, in China, and in India, three major historical centers of world civilization, religious thought passed beyond animism and polytheism, beyond even everyday monotheism, in search of the ultimate unity to everything. The search has led to a great mystery, the incomprehensible and absolute Ultimate.

The different civilizations followed different clues toward the Ultimate. Western religion pursued the idea of a personal Creator-God. By asking who created everything, it arrived at the notion of the Absolute from whom somehow reality comes. Chinese Taoism looked to the Yang/Yin order of nature as its best clue to the ultimate, and discovered a nonpersonal Cause of the patterns of nature. Hindu Brahmanist thought speculated both on the Atman-Self within a person and on the nonpersonal sacred power in rituals in order eventually to find the ultimate Brahman-without-attributes.

The differences among these three approaches deserve books of their own, but what is the same is this: all three discovered an Ultimate, a reality that transcends or exceeds all boundaries and all comprehension. All three concluded that to understand that we cannot really understand is the most valid understanding. All three concluded that the Ultimate is Mystery.

If the religious traditions had stopped at that and insisted firmly on nothing but that, these traditions might quickly have lost strength among most people. Ordinary religiousness includes more than an awed acknowledgment that the Ultimate is Mystery. Mystics may relish contemplating the infinite Mystery. Most people, however, seek something else in their religion.

These traditions remained alive for two reasons. The first is that most religious believers have not worried much about these rather abstract conclusions. In India, for example, most people worship one or more gods rather than focus on the absolute Being of Brahman-Atman. Each of the gods is said to be a lesser symbol of the supreme divine Self (Atman), which in turn is somehow a mode of presence of Brahman. But the people do not worry too much about that. It is enough to worship the gods. Similarly, in China Taoism takes a less abstract and popular form, attending to the ancestors, manipulating magic powers, and dealing with spirits. They do not break their heads over the formless Tao.

In the West, people are usually happy to speak in somewhat anthropomorphic ways about God. Jews, Christians, and Muslims will say that God is a Mystery and certainly not an anthropomorphic being like Zeus. Yet they will also speak of God's love or mercy or God's plans and activities the way we all speak of human persons, without worrying much about how precisely correct this is. Religious traditions do not usually insist that all believers hold to the most austerely proper and rigorously logical forms of speaking about the supreme numinous reality, be it God, Tao, or Brahman.

The second reason why religious traditions have been able both to claim that the supreme reality is an incomprehensible Ultimate and to have it still remain important to them is that they have found workable ways of talking about the incomprehensible. They do this by focusing on the clues to the Ultimate. The existence of persons, the order of the world, reflections on ritual-power and on the inner layers of one's self—these point in the direction of the Ultimate. In the Western historic religions, for example, God is said to be personal. This is taken to mean that when we understand what a person is, life and consciousness, freedom and love, we are then orienting ourselves in the direction of what God is, rather than away from God. It is legitimate, therefore, to call God personal, although it must always be added that the ultimate nature of divine personhood is utterly beyond all limitations and therefore exists in a way that cannot be comprehended. (If you find such a philosophical qualification too technical and intellectualist to want to include it as part of your daily religious thoughts, the religious traditions will not insist upon it.)

Summary

This chapter has provided a survey of various ways different religious traditions have agreed that behind the diversity and conflicts of life there is a single unifying Ultimate Reality. Because it is ultimate, it is also beyond any human ability to describe it adequately. As a result, each culture has its own perspectives about the Ultimate. Each perspective provides a different view of the value and reality of human personness, of nature, of the universe.

It is striking that we humans should find it possible to believe in and care about an ultimate unity to all things. It is doubly striking that we should maintain this belief even if it leads us into ultimate incomprehensibility—into Mystery. The next chapter will explore the human condition to see what it is about us that perpetuates such belief as the core of historic religion.

FOR FURTHER REFLECTION

1. How disorderly does this world appear to you? Do you find it plausible that there is an ultimate unity to all things? Does the religion you know best claim that there is such a unity? Explain.

2. If you had to describe the main characteristics of God, would you agree with the image presented here of the Judaeo-Christian-Islamic God? Why? Why not?

3. Would you call the nonliving Tao by the name "God?" What about Atman-Brahman? Explain.

4. Where do you look for the best clue as to what is truly ultimate? What clue or clues are most meaningful to you?

5. What value can you see, if any, in saying that God is an ultimate Mystery? Are you comfortable with this idea? Explain.

SUGGESTED READINGS

Karl Jaspers, *The Origin and Goal of History*, 1953; ch. 1 on the axial age.

Ninian Smart, *The World's Religions*, 1989; clear, thorough, and up-to-date.

Walter Kaufman, *Religion in Four Dimensions*, 1976; a more provocative interpretation of the major religions of the world.

Bernhard W. Anderson, *Understanding the Old Testament*, 3rd ed., 1975; a thorough interpretation based on modern critical methods.

Saravasti Chennakesavan, *A Critical Study of Hinduism*, 1974.

Kenneth K. S. Ch'en, *Buddhism, The Light of Asia*, 1968.

Herrlee G. Creed, *What Is Taoism?*, 1970.

The Endless Quest

The Human Basis
of Belief in an Ultimate

Chapter Two described many reasons that outside observers can find why people believe in magic, spirits, and gods. Animism and polytheism offer ways of making sense out of the events of life. These beliefs provide psychological comfort and social stability. Most of us usually assume that belief in a single, universal Ultimate such as God also offers equivalent mental, emotional, and social benefits. But it should be clear now from Chapter Three that monotheism and its equivalents can be somewhat discomforting. Belief in a single Ultimate sounds quite simple: It is belief in one God instead of many. But this belief is actually rather sophisticated; it claims that contrary to appearances there is a universal unity to everything. It passes beyond familiar anthropomorphisms into austere statements about infinity and incomprehensibility. In spite of this, it is a belief that has been maintained firmly and widely for many centuries. That is what needs to be explained.

GOD AS A MERELY PERFECT PERSON

It is odd to speak of God as "merely" perfect person, but the Supreme Being in the belief of most monotheists is probably pictured in a mildly anthropomorphic way. Awesome as such a being may be, this is not the kind of unqualified monotheism or its equivalent that belief in an Absolute is. A "merely" perfect Being is one that exceeds by far the gods of polytheism, but is described in words that can suggest something less than the truly infinite and ultimate reality.

As a perfect person, God is totally good. No person need fear that God will be fickle, unreliable, unfair, petty, greedy, or vain. The gods suffer from all these liabilities that we ordinary humans also experience, because the gods are not perfectly good as God is. Sometimes supposedly monotheistic religious leaders or writings will still refer to God as though God were only a god, saying that God is impatient or angry or needs attention. But monotheism intends to establish at least this minimum about God, that God's goodness is totally unflawed. This could mean, for example, that when God is poetically portrayed as a parent, the image that would be best is that of a perfect parent who recognizes that the way to respond to a child's faults and failings is by loving and supportive effort, by compassion and understanding, by using corrective measures when necessary but never out of anger or impatience or to fulfill selfish needs.

A perfect God is also all-knowing and thus will never harm anyone through mistake, inattention, or ignorance, as mere gods might do. There is no real need ever to call God's attention to problems as must be done with the gods. Nothing that God does is aimless or useless, even if people fail to understand the purpose behind it. Of equal importance is that an all-knowing God is one who truly understands a person. Other people fail to see us as we are or appreciate what we have to offer. Others ignore us at those times we most need to be accepted. Others pressure us into play-acting our lives to earn their approval. But God sees within, knows a person fully and accurately. As all-good, God does not merely know us in our inner selves, feelings, and needs, but cherishes us deeply.

A perfect God is all-powerful. While God's knowledge and goodness lead God to know and choose exactly what is best for every person, "All-powerful" means that God can also accomplish what is best; no power in the universe can stand against God's choice. If anything seems evil or chaotic, we can nonetheless be assured that it happens only as the all-powerful, all-knowing, and all-good God has chosen to make it happen or at least has allowed it to happen as part of a larger divine plan. If human beings have any special needs for miraculous help, divine care, special guidance, or even life after death, there is no doubt that God can provide such things.

The gods also can provide some divine guidance and care. They can even give life after death, if that is needed. Miracles, divine commandments, special attention, and eternal life are not things that only God can do. What belief in God adds is the confidence that because God is perfect as the gods are not, people can place unqualified and unhesitating trust in God. God will never fail us because of limitations such as inattentiveness, carelessness, ignorance, weakness, confusion, or emotional immaturity.

This portrayal of God as Perfect Person makes it obvious why many people have adhered to at least some limited form of monotheism throughout centuries. Belief in a perfect God can offer much more psychological comfort than belief in lesser numinous powers and beings. Whatever can be done with mana or magic or luck, God can do better and is guaranteed to do what is best. Whatever it is the spirits or even the gods can provide, God can do more and will do it with unfailing love. This same God is also a more certain reference point for social stability than the gods can be. When God delivers laws to be obeyed or provides wisdom for guidance or establishes patterns of human life, every person can be sure that they are the best possible laws, wisdom, and patterns. Conformity to them will never be wasted effort, for God knows all and controls all.

With all this, God is pictured in somewhat anthropomorphic terms as like a parent or friend. God is a friendly and helpful Being rather than just an incomprehensible Absolute. God is Lord, Leader, or Lawgiver, not just an Ultimate. Yet the great religious traditions have claimed that although the portrait of God as a Perfect Person is a legitimate use of human images to point in the direction of the truth, it is not the literal truth; it is only a set of metaphors we use to express the inexpressible. The religious traditions have continued to insist that the true nature of the Ultimate, whether God or Brahman or the Tao, is incomprehensible.

So there is a further question here about why anyone would want to maintain belief in that aspect of the Supreme reality.

As we have seen, most people do not care about the Ultimate as such. Hindus pay more attention to gods, Taoists to spirits, Christians to somewhat anthropomorphic images. In general, most people of history ordinarily might even be quite content with a near-God such as Ahura Mazda, all-good and all-knowing but finite in power, struggling with us against the forces of evil.

In spite of this, the historical religions have maintained that we all should push beyond our anthropomorphisms, beyond the comfort and security of an image of God as a merely perfect person, on to belief that the ultimate truth is that God is infinite and incomprehensible, that there is a Nirguna Brahman beyond perfect Self, that the Tao is formless. There are philosophical reasons why the traditions have described the Ultimate this way. We will see these reasons in a later chapter about proving the existence of God (or equivalent). Some religious thinkers say that we have semimystical experiences of infinite mystery upon which the universe and our lives depend. That too will be discussed in another chapter. This chapter has a more ordinary question to answer.

The search in the next few pages is for the way our lives end up presenting to us a dimension of ultimacy that we cannot easily avoid. We will understand a great deal about ourselves as human beings when we understand why the rather austere and difficult notion of the Ultimate as incomprehensible Mystery has been maintained at the core of major religious traditions. What we will be looking for are the kinds of feelings and ideas that everyone might have sooner or later in life that would make a person aware of questions so big and disturbing that only belief in some truly Ultimate or Absolute reality could provide a positive answer to them. Thousands of years ago, our ancestors set out to find answers to the many mysteries of life. They did not know it, but they were setting out on an endless quest. The human mind has such an unlimited capacity to wonder and question that it is in the very nature of humanness to live in the presence of infinite mystery. The next section will try to explain that.

THE ULTIMATE QUESTIONS

There are certain questions that we are capable of asking because we have human minds, but that are odd because they can only be answered (if at all) in the way historic religion does, by talking about an ultimate reality that is relevant to the entire universe at once. These questions are not universally asked. It may be that most people would just as soon avoid being bothered by them. Still, the questions are universal in a different sense: they ask about the whole of all things at once. These are ultimate questions, seeking the final or ultimate explanation for everything at once. The ultimate explanation for everything in a pure monotheism or its equivalent is a single reality (rather than multiple realities, as in polytheism), and a single reality that is the Cause or Power or Being behind the whole of things.

There is really just one ultimate question, though it has many aspects: "Why is everything?" It will be easier here to sneak up on the one single ultimate question by looking at three different forms the question might take:

1. What is the origin of everything (if any)?
2. What is the order or nature of everything (if any)?
3. What is the purpose of everything (if any)?

These three questions ask about the entire universe at once, where it all comes from, what it is like, and where it is going. Because we are part of this universe, these questions appear also as: Where did we come from? Who are we? Where are we going?

It required many thousands of years of human development before whole civilizations became aware of these universal questions. It is as though human cultural development preceding the axial age had not yet reached the stage in which such questions made sense. This is also true of each individual. Not until adolescence do human beings begin to achieve the capacity to recognize the significance and range of the ultimate questions. Even then we do not find it easy to exercise that capacity. It takes practice before we get used to thinking in such broad, all-inclusive, and abstract ways. Only since the axial age has it been easy to find a number of cultures that encourage the use of this ability.

Asking the Questions in a Contemporary Context

From primitive times people have been asking about the origin, nature, and goal of things. As we have already seen, primitive peoples explain each bit and piece of reality by relating it to some folk tale. Archaic people tell their greater myths about how the god or gods brought order out of chaos and how the present division of authority among gods came to be. Historic religion looks further, for a single unifying all-inclusive explanation of all things.

It is difficult for us to try to appreciate how new ideas about reality have startled people in a different culture into asking ultimate questions. We may never be able to share the sensibilities of former generations and other societies. Rather than try to reproduce the complex analyses of the Chinese, Indian, or Jewish thinkers of ancient times, we can get a better idea of how ultimate questions can arise by considering information that is part of our own era, information from astronomy about the physical universe. It is seemingly harmless information, but if any of it begins to evoke some uneasiness and stir up some uncomfortable questions in your mind, then you will know a little better how previous generations as long ago as 500 or 600 B.C. felt when they stumbled across ultimate questions in their own cultural contexts.

Current astronomical theory says that the universe is about 15 billion years old. The estimates vary and new information could change them, but generally speaking this picture of the universe is a well-supported theory. About 15 billion years ago, it says, all the stuff/energy that is the universe today was condensed so compactly that less than a teaspoonful would have a mass equivalent to the entire universe. The density was so great that its own heat made this stuff/energy explode, scattering itself outward, spinning and crashing and expanding on and on until today. The universe we live in is that explosion still scattering outward. All the stars and galaxies of stars and the matter/energy in between are spinning particles and clusters of stuff blowing outward since the "big bang" that began 15 billion years ago.

Perhaps this exploding universe will expand endlessly, with everything becoming more and more scattered and with all stuff/energy spreading itself ever thinner until the universe that we know becomes dead, every bit of it lost from every other bit in the unending cold. Another possibility is that the mutual gravitational attraction of every bit for every other bit will slow down and stop the expansion of the universe and then drag it back together, faster and faster, all of it falling in toward everything else until it is so condensed again that there will be another big bang and the universe will start all over again, and then again, and so on. Such a cycle would recur about every 80 billion years or less, the theory has it. It seems there would be an endless series of cycles: explosion and collapse, explosion and collapse, one after the other.

Meanwhile, we live in this currently expanding universe. It is a very large one. To get an idea of the amount of matter and space involved, begin with a pea about one-third of an inch in diameter.

Let that stand for the earth (a little less than 8000 miles in diameter). Put the pea next to a very large beach ball, one full yard in diameter. That is the sun (864,000 miles in diameter). Now put the pea at one end of a football field and the ball at the far other end, about 110 yards apart. That approximates the distance between earth and sun (93 million miles). The earth is quite close to the sun compared to the outermost planets. Pluto is 40 times as far from the sun as earth is.

If the whole solar system out to Pluto were shrunk to one inch, on that scale the nearest star would be 90 yards away. Our solar system is three-fourths of the way out from the center of a cluster of stars known to us as the Milky Way, a galaxy with as many as four hundred billion stars. There are an estimated hundred billion galaxies in the known universe, each of them averaging another hundred billion stars or so. This speck of rock called earth is nowhere in particular in a universe where even our entire Milky Way galaxy is lost among a hundred billion others. In a few million years our sun will follow the normal course in the life of a small to medium-sized star, first bloating out into a "red giant" burning the earth raw and then collapsing and dying.

The astronomical theories have disturbing implications. They may imply that the whole universe is a rather chaotic collection of random events, that we tiny humans are the slightest specks of life on a rocky mote whirling in vast emptiness as a momentary phase in the unending aimlessness of time and space. Is that the whole story of the ultimate origin, order, and purpose of the entire universe?

How should we respond to a question like that? We can ignore it and get on with the practical things of life. That is a successful tactic most of the time. We can also fall back on traditional religious beliefs and just say that no matter what the universe looks like to astronomers we are sure it is all under God's purposeful guidance. That usually works well for many people. But to understand better the human significance of ultimate questions we will have to wade into them more deeply. We might even get in over our heads here and there, looking at problems we cannot answer. It will all help, though, in understanding why ultimacy, universality, infinity, and other such incomprehensibles keep intruding into human history in historic religions.

What Is the Origin of Everything?

This is the first form of the ultimate questions, the most intellectually abstract of the three. There is a dilemma inherent in any attempt to ask about the origin of everything. Neither of the two horns of the dilemma is a comfortable place to sit. One is the possibility that there is no origin, that the stuff of the universe always existed, everlastingly before every person's life and, seemingly, everlastingly after. Things keep on happening, one after another, every event passing away endlessly, all events and lives swallowed up eventually in an infinite series of changes.

There are mind-breaking aspects to this. Can the universe really go on endlessly? If it could cease to exist or if the energy that composes it could ever be extinguished, then an infinity of time already passed should have been time enough for this to happen. Inasmuch as the universe is still active, then perhaps it goes on endlessly. That would be the same, it seems, as going nowhere in particular, because wherever or however the universe ends up at some given point in time, it will never stop there but go on and on and on. Our minds can circle restlessly around on possibilities like these.

The other horn of the dilemma, that the universe did originate some infinite amount of time ago, is embodied in the scientific theory of the big bang 15 billion years ago. The next question, then, is why there existed any stuff/energy to go "bang" in the first place. Where did it come from? The monotheist answers this easily: God created it. But the answer is not as simple as it looks. Why is there a God? Did someone or something create God?

The traditional answer is that no one created God because God always existed. This is a troublesome response, as the philosopher David Hume (1711-1776) pointed out about two centuries ago. If we think the universe had to have a start, what is it about God that says God did not have a start but can start everything else? Or if God could have existed endlessly, why not the universe also? But then if the universe could have existed forever, what need is there for a God? If the universe has existed forever, in fact, then all the problems from the first horn of the dilemma are back with us.

Indian and Western historic religions found it necessary in the face of such puzzles to make a major shift in their idea of the ultimate reality. God or Brahman are not everlasting, they said. To last endlessly is to endure through time. The Ultimate is not everlasting, they proclaimed; rather, it is eternal, meaning that it stands outside of time; it is timeless. It causes time, or affects the events of time, or is the reality hidden behind the appearances of time. But in the eternal Ultimate there is only utter changelessness. There is no before or during or after. It is because the world experiences time that it gives rise to questions about its long-ago origins. That is why there must be an eternal (timeless) ultimate to account for the world's existence. That which is outside of time need have no origin, the argument goes.

We have seen another kind of logic that led to this conclusion. In the East and West the supreme Reality is thought to be totally perfect. Anything imperfect is a limited or flawed reality, like a god or great mana. The reality behind all the universe must be unlimited or unflawed. Whatever changes is good or perfect in its own way perhaps (if it really exists at all), but it is not totally perfect. Whatever changes is always passing away in some respect. The totally perfect, therefore, is beyond change. What is beyond change is timeless, for time is nothing but change. So the logic went, at least. It is perhaps not watertight logic, but it is the kind of thought that the West and East engaged in beginning in the axial age.

We may be a little intrigued by thoughts like this, or just tired and confused trying to sort it out, wondering whether it is really worth the effort. There is very little in our daily lives that makes such thoughts useful. But in the axial age about 2500 years ago, this kind of thinking became an explicit part of human history. Human minds then opened wide enough to wonder about everlasting duration and timeless eternity. Ever since then, we have been asking questions that are so broad that they point toward infinite, absolute and changeless perfection. This beginning leads to other ultimate questions, some more directly related to our ordinary life.

What Order and Purpose Is There to the Universe?

However you or your culture answers the question about the origin of everything, a further question remains unanswered: What order is there in reality as a whole?

In the extreme it is possible to ask whether there is any real order at all. The astronomers' portrait of the universe as the fragments of an explosion is a hint that perhaps any kind of orderliness or pattern is just a momentary accident. In general, our basic faith in the intelligibility of reality usually overcomes our doubts; we feel sure that somehow things do make sense. This basic faith, though, is always being challenged by reality.

Order does exist to some degree; that much seems obvious. We can make a certain amount of sense of things. The success of science seems to be evidence that reality is intelligible and predictable. But the order is incomplete. Science says that nature on the whole is a cosmic explosion still chaotically fragmenting. Likewise in every person's life there is some chaos, confusion, conflict, and destruction. The simple faith that reality makes sense may then be too sweeping a judgment. Perhaps the evidence should lead us to say that reality makes only partial and temporary and local sense, that everywhere there are conflicting forces at work, that there is no universal order such as historic religions claim but only partial areas of order, as polytheistic interpretations see it.

Even if we find some way to assert that there is a basic order to all things, this order may not be to our liking. Perhaps this order is just a mindless fate to which we can only submit. Perhaps it is a dead, mechanical, automatic process. The laws and patterns of nature are all rather orderly in that they follow certain basic physical laws. But the laws may just operate without purpose or meaning. Order without purpose can be as humanly empty as chaos. Everything then runs smoothly but uselessly.

A person may well reject the ideas that our existence is an accident, subject to uncontrolled forms of chaos, or is order but of a mindless and purposeless sort. But is it bothersome or unsettling to you to take these kinds of ideas seriously? If so, then the questions of ultimate order and purpose are important to you. We do not always notice their importance because we tend to live by the unconscious faith that reality is intelligible, that there is purposeful order to it. It is not until that faith is somehow challenged that we become aware of its place in our lives.

Primitive, archaic, and historic people have all felt the threat of chaos, but it is the historic religious traditions that have worried and reflected most deeply about it. They have found ways to express their faith that in the end chaos is not victorious. The Taoist is confident that all moments of disorder will be balanced out in the long run by the Tao. The Western monotheist claims that even seeming disorder is controlled by God, who maintains a true order to everything even if that is not apparent to us. In India the Shankara school neatly eliminates disorder by declaring that all the events of the universe are not truly real, but only "maya." In each case the supreme reality must be of such power or of such a nature to assure that every event in the universe is assimilated in some way into an ultimate order or perfection.

It is an awesomely massive and complex universe to bring under a single order. There is an enormous extent of time and of real events and possible events, of countless billions of happenings

even under a single jungle rock, much less in a whole forest, conti-
nent, planet, solar system, or galaxy. Is there a God or cosmic
force that can and does bring the events of a 100 billion galaxies
into a coherent and meaningful order on each of a billion billion
days? Questions like these have helped sustain the historic religions in their belief that the one God or Ultimate must be not merely a Perfect Person or Self but the infinite Absolute, able to encom-
pass the immensity of the universe within its eternal power.

What Order and Purpose Is There to Our Lives?

All the thoughts about the universe, about its origin, order, and
purpose, would be just interesting speculation were it not that the
order and purpose to our lives is bound up in such questions. We
do not often experience the connection. Our implicit faith in the
intelligibility and value of life usually remains strong. We believe
that to live and act and choose, to work and to plan and to love,
are all somehow deeply meaningful.

Once in a while, though, reality falls apart in front of us and
lays bare a frightening emptiness. Most of us only catch glimpses
of this emptiness and comfort ourselves with the thought that it is
not really there. Very few become convinced that emptiness is the
final truth; some may be fortunate enough never to perceive it at
all. Yet most people eventually get a brief look behind the seeming order and purpose of life into mysteries that can upset their
natural faith in life.

The Unfairness of Life

One major way that reality challenges our faith that life is
meaningful is by its "unfairness." By definition, life would be fair
if every person could expect to get out of life exactly what he or
she deserves. If life were fully fair, the innocent would never
starve to death or suffer a long and painful disease. If life were
fully fair, those who conscientiously work and sacrifice to help
those they love would never lose everything to flood or earthquake. The fact of reading this book probably means that by accident of birth you have received food, shelter, and education during your life, enjoyed the luxury of not worrying about intestinal
parasites, of not expecting to be killed in a revolution, of living a
reasonably long life. These are luxuries in the sense that most people in history would consider them true privileges. Have we done
something wonderfully meritorious to have deserved these privileges? Probably not. Life is not fair.

It is one of the peculiarities of our contemporary situation that life appears basically fair to us because we are protected against many of the deadly uncertainties of life. But even we can occasionally break through the comfort of our conditions into a sudden outrage at the unfairness of life. We too can be crippled by disease or made blind. Our children, our parents, our loved ones can suddenly die in a stupid accident.

The Fact of Death

There is a second major aspect of life that can stir up a deep uneasiness about the ultimate meaning of life. That is the fact of death. During our lives we build up a pattern of goals and accomplishments. We live toward the future, to enjoy, to do, to create. And then one day we discover that most of our future is behind us. There is a time limit. We all die. We will never enjoy all that we hope to enjoy. We will never find all the love, success, happiness, fulfillment we once had as goals worth living for. For a brief moment, the moving forces of the universe have produced the particular spark of life that is our identity, a brief candle glowing brightly and then sputtering out.

The fact of death easily becomes a symbol of our finiteness. Every person's life is a quick flash of hope, burning among a billion others, passing away like a billion others to be replaced by another countless billion. People leave behind families, monuments, great books and works of art, philosophies, nations, even religions. But everything is limited, partial, passing. In 10,000 years all but the very greatest or very worst will have been forgotten. A million years from now, a brief time on the cosmic scale, little will be left. "Eat, drink, and be merry, for tomorrow we die," said the Christian apostle Paul, mocking what he thought to be the Epicurean philosophy of life. If death brings an end to everything, then there is no lasting purpose to anything. In the infinite immensity of time, all things become dusty death.

Religious Answers to Death and Life's Unfairness

There are various ways to deal with the challenges to life's meaning. Some people manage to ignore the challenges. Others manage to maintain their basic faith in the worthwhileness of life out of some inner optimism. For most people, however, it is their religious beliefs that meet the challenges.

Historic religion has a special power to overcome the threats of death and unfairness. The belief that there is one ultimate Being or Power is already a belief in a final order, in spite of apparent conflicts and contradictions in life. Belief in a God is a belief that the disorder of unfairness is conquered finally in some way by the ordering power of divine Providence. Belief in Brahman is a belief that the disorder of unfairness and death is only part of "maya" (illusion). Belief in the Tao is a belief in a transcendent order that reconciles all temporary disorder in some way. Likewise, belief that death is not just a passing away but a meaningful incorporation into an eternal reality beyond this life, is a belief common to most historic religions.

When people face death and unfairness, belief in a God who is a merely perfect person turns out to be helpful, but isn't always enough. As long as each person thinks mainly of his or her own experiences of life's unfairness and of the approach of death, the person may be satisfied with a God who is guaranteed to be perfectly fair and loving and able to give everlasting life to that person. But larger questions can intrude. The death of millions through starvation and the unfairness of children dying hungry in the world can pull the mind into wonderment about what it all ultimately means. The questing consciousness of human thought can begin to nose around the edges of infinity by asking where it all comes from, whether it all hangs together in some way, whether there really is some ultimate purpose to all things that can never be swallowed up by billions of years of time or by an endless sequence of happenings.

It is in answer to such thoughts that the historic religions have proposed there is an Ultimate that is more than even a merely perfect person (though in Western thought the Ultimate is also somehow the infinite perfection of personness). As a result, there are whole theological libraries laboring over how to comprehend and speak about the incomprehensible Ultimate.

In all these libraries of thought about the Ultimate is another topic, half-hidden, one a little closer to our lives than abstract discussions of the Ultimate. This is our own human orientation to the Ultimate or the infinite. From the first pages we have talked about our orientation to mystery and even about our capacity for the infinite. Our bare ability to think about the kinds of ultimate questions we have been pondering is of very special importance and needs to be addressed more explicitly.

THE CAPACITY FOR THE INFINITE

Our Peculiar Kind of Consciousness

The ultimate questions represent something odd about human life: we are unsure where we fit in reality. Where do we come from? What are we part of? Where are we going? We do not always know for sure; at least, the human race has had a hard time trying to answer those questions. The most significant thing is that we are aware that we are unsure. We are aware that these questions exist and can be asked, and that we do not have the answers. We are the consciously uncertain animal.

Once again, compare a human being to any other animal. Those animals are simply a part of nature. Each is aware of its environment, the air and smells and moisture in it, the earth and mud and rocks, trees and shrubs and stumps, rivers and rain, birds and insects and mammals. None of the animals, however, consciously names these things and wonders where they came from or what their purpose is. The animals are born, develop, live and die, in accordance with the patterns evolution has produced so far, and they do this without thinking about it. They do not ponder the meaning of their lives or ever worry about their future success. They simply live, from moment to moment, meal to meal.

We humans have some things in common with those animals. We also are born, live for a while, and die. We also have moments of pleasure and pain. But we can also think about these things in layer upon layer of conscious awareness. On any given day we may be consciously aware of feelings of excitement about someone we are going to meet, or of feelings of frustration over failing to achieve something we hoped for. To be aware of having these feelings is a special consciousness. It is not just having the feelings, but also being consciously able to say, "I am excited," or "I am feeling frustrated." We simultaneously remember times when we were less excited or frustrated. We can make conscious comparisons in our minds and feel better or worse through these comparisons. We can also consciously picture to ourselves others we know or have read about and use this mental picture as a basis of comparison. We can even consciously imagine possible future conditions for ourselves in which our excitement is spoiled or our frustration is overcome. We can make ourselves happy or sad by our memories, imaginings, and comparisons. We can create worlds of possibilities by which we measure what we actually have or lack.

This is an extraordinary ability; it is self-awareness. We can consciously possess our own selfhood by being able to say, "I am." It is also called self-transcendence. When we look at ourselves, at our lives, actions, and options, we are rising above (transcending) our ongoing existence, as it were, in order to look it over and reflect on it. In this lies our power of self-determination. Because we can rise above our ongoing life and look it over, we are in a position to direct that life, to choose in various ways what it will be like. This capacity for self-transcendence is therefore our freedom. It distinguishes us from all other beings. It is what makes us distinctively human.

The Condition of Estrangement

Because we can consciously remember, imagine, reflect, compare, and see ourselves in a thousand ways, we can also stand in front of a mirror and say, "I wish that I could be. . . ." We all have the kind of consciousness that allows us to dream of being as strong, good looking, intelligent, free, courageous, wealthy, famous, healthy, loved and loving as someone else, real or imagined.

We all know that wishful thinking is not very profitable, except when it's about things that we could accomplish by hard work and training. We know that much of life must simply be accepted and endured. We know that the right attitude about what is can bring us happiness, instead of misery about what is not. We learn to deal with our consciousness of what might be, with our imagination and dreams. The significant thing about humans is that we must *learn* to deal with these. Life is not automatic; we are not born into a programmed pattern of behavior to fit into a special niche in nature. We are adrift in reality, struggling perhaps to find a place, a home, a center of security and identity; or working to establish a direction, a set of goals that we can trust to guide us in our decisions.

Nothing is a greater blessing or advantage than our power to imagine what does not yet exist, to work with our minds, comparing options and reflecting on possibilities. Out of this has come our language, civilization, art, and humor. The uncertainty and desires that arise because of our kind of consciousness gives us our openness to change and the motivation to grow. But there is a price we pay. While our consciousness makes us the animal that is most fully alive, that same consciousness also makes us the only animal that foresees its own death. The consciousness that makes us desire wholeness and happiness also makes us estranged.

Estrangement is an unusual word with a simple meaning: to be separate. In romantic contexts the word "estrangement" is used to describe a change from a feeling of affection to one of indifference or hatred. Philosophers and theologians employ the word at times to reflect something of the romantic meaning in a new way. Human existence is like the tragic condition of two lovers who sought happiness with each other but somehow find themselves lonely and frustrated. The unity they once thought they had has turned out to be an illusion and mockery. Where they hoped to find meaning there is now nothing. It would be too painful to think about this often, so they do their best to forget or ignore the bright wholeness they once had. But there is now a feeling of restlessness within, a deep-down, unnamed sense of wrongness to life, a state of separation or estrangement.

The historic religions often declare that our whole lives are basically ones of estrangement from some ideal reality or some perfect Ultimate. The human ability to look at the conditions of existence and discover basic problems in life reached its greatest strength precisely when the human mind became able to dream of perfection. The same consciousness that allows us to dream of an ideal unity to things, of perfect goodness, knowledge, and love, also thereby allows us to recognize that in this ordinary life things fall far short of such perfection.

In the historic religions that arose in India and the West there is a sense of estrangement from the conditions of human life. These historic religions have described life as fallen, corrupt, sinful, or an illusion. They see it as flawed beyond repair. (It will not be until the rise of the modern stage of religion that an appreciation of life in this world will regain strength.)

Forms of Estrangement

A modern theologian, Paul Tillich (1886–1965), described estrangement by separating it into three aspects. A review of these kinds of estrangement can help a person today see the sort of thing historic religions have said about life all along.

First of all, we can feel estranged from nature and the universe. We are cosmic orphans, as one person expressed it; we have no clear and settled place in nature. Physically we are natural beings, yet our minds allow us to step back from nature and look at it and decide whether to accept it or reject it, enjoy it or avoid it. We often like to see ourselves as part of a grand natural order. Yet that natural order includes our death. We like to admire the grandeur of nature, yet nature is so immensely grand that perhaps it is only a cosmic collection of accidents with no particular place for human consciousness. In the midst of nature's beauty there is also nature's destructiveness through disease and drought and earthquake.

Secondly, we can be estranged from one another. Every human being has a strong need to belong, to be accepted, to be loved. Each of us can look at the person next to us and recognize a common humanness in a common need to be close to someone. Yet there is probably no person who has ever lived that achieved so full and lasting a relationship that all loneliness disappeared. Communication between any two people is always a little bit off. Misunderstandings arise. Lack of trust and openness is part of life. Jealousy, hatred, insecurity, boredom, irritation, possessiveness, bigotry—all cut little scars into the skin of life, making us tough enough to survive but also tough enough to be separate from one another in self-defense. Every one of us needs acceptance and support. Every one receives some rejection and abandonment. We dull our minds and harden our feelings a bit so that we are not too painfully aware of it. We learn the courage to live with it, but we are still estranged from one another.

Thirdly, we are even estranged from ourselves. Each of us as a child was taught what we must not be. We found ways of talking, dressing, laughing, and playing that earned approval from family, teachers, or friends. We did not always feel comfortable with some of these roles; we often faked it. We still do. When we were children, people occasionally told us that we were selfish or jealous and we felt like saying, "No, I'm not," because we had been taught that good little girls or boys were not like that. Without really being conscious of it, we have all learned to lie to ourselves about some of our true feelings in order to preserve our own self-esteem. A young boy walks to the seashore with his father and is frightened by the big waves. The father says, "You are not afraid, are you?" The child learns from this to pretend, even to himself, that he is not afraid. A teenage girl has sexual feelings but denies them to herself because someone has taught her that those feelings make her dirty-minded. These kinds of examples are endless because they are so ordinary. There may be someone who lives comfortably without pretense of any kind; there may be someone who does not lie to himself or herself in hidden ways, but such a person would be very rare.

We do not have a ready-made identity. We must search for one as the years pass, creating it as we go. It is never ideal. We dream of who we might be. We look for unity with others, and sometimes try to please them so they will like us. We hope always for an "at-home-ness" with the universe, others, and self, but it never works quite right. Most importantly, we are conscious of that. Because we can imagine what life might be like, we are conscious that life as it exists is flawed.

Overcoming Estrangement

Sometimes we hope to overcome these flaws by human effort. Perhaps someday we will learn to understand ourselves, each other, and the universe, and from that understanding develop techniques for eliminating the sources of estrangement. Perhaps medicine can eventually prolong life so that no one need die until death finally looks appealing as a permanent rest (or a transition to a new condition). Perhaps psychology, sociology, and other fields of study will enable us to grow up happy and self-accepting, loving and open and supportive toward one another.

If we achieve such a marvelous state, however, perhaps we will become restless again by wondering what the point of it all might be, what the ultimate purpose or value is in living, however pleasant it might be. Now we can become restless because our minds enable us to look past present conditions to something better. Even in some supposedly ideal state our minds will still have the power to imagine, wonder, and dream. Even the smallest flaw, the humblest question about purpose, the slightest bit of unfairness, could make us wonder again and worry. Our minds have been dreaming of perfection at least since the beginning of the axial age. Perhaps such dreams and the estrangement they can can bring will never be eliminated unless we eliminate our ability to think.

It is the historic religions that have often decided that earthly life is fundamentally flawed beyond correction. The world we live in, historic religions say, must therefore be transformed, destroyed, or abandoned completely in favor of a different kind of existence. The new world or other realm cannot be one that only improves on current life. (Primitive and archaic religions, as we will see, have settled for dreams of improvements on life.) Historic religion is the religious consciousness of those who ask universal questions, who can dream of absolute unqualified perfection. Our human power of conscious awareness gives us an inner ability to seek that which transcends all limitations and overcomes all estrangement totally. In the following chapters we will see this more concretely.

Summary

This chapter has reviewed aspects of our existence that lead us beyond local spirits, magic, powerful gods, and great mana forces, behind the finite and comprehensible, to wonderment about what is ultimate and beyond all limitation. There are many specific issues that do this: the general ultimate questions, the problem of life's fairness and of death, the forms of estrangement. The power of these issues to take us beyond the finite is a sign of our own human capacity for the infinite. In the last analysis, it is this capacity that leaves us always open to the infinite Mystery that goes by all the names described in Chapter Three.

END OF PART I

We are not yet at an end in talking about the stages in the development of religion. There is still the modern stage. But that stage is so recent that it is as yet only a small part of the overall story of religion. The following chapters, therefore, will explore more of the ways in which primitive, archaic, and historic religions have dealt with the mysteries of life. That will provide the background to understand better what is happening to religion today.

Very likely in the course of this study you will eventually discover that you are a modern person in some ways but, like most people, also partly historic and archaic and even primitive to a degree, with all of it mixed together in the flow of your life, thoughts, and feelings. The kinds of salvation from estrangement that appeal to you or make sense to you will provide some clues on this. That is the topic of Part II.

FOR FURTHER REFLECTION

1. Express as clearly as you can the difference between a merely perfect Person and an Absolute.
2. How do you feel about making the idea of a merely Perfect Person only a way of imaging or symbolizing an Absolute Reality? Explain.

3. Is it possible that in 500 years or more we humans will have learned to overcome the three major forms of estrangement? Explain.
4. Describe any ways you think of earthly life as fundamentally flawed or even hopelessly corrupt.
5. In what ways do you see yourself as a being with a capacity for the infinite? Explain.
6. In your own words describe fully some example of a way in which our minds can ask questions so big that not even belief in God as a Perfect Person is adequate to answer them.

SUGGESTED READINGS

John Haught, *What Is God?*, 1986; an analysis of different ideas about God.

James Drane, *The Possibility of God*, 1976; on the human condition and ultimate restlessness.

Paul Tillich, *Systematic Theology*, Vol. ll, 1957; pp. 66-72 on estrangement.

John Passmore, *The Perfectibility of Man*, 1970; a scholarly survey of Western theories of the ultimate nature and destiny of humankind, of the sources of evil, and of how to overcome it.

James W. Sire, *The Universe Next Door: A Basic World View Catalogue*, 1976; a description of how several religious and non-religious world views interpret the basic human situation.

Victor Frankl, *Man's Search for Meaning*, 1967; told by a survivor of a Nazi concentration camp.

PART II

SALVATIONS

Estrangement appears in many forms. The historic and modern religions are the most conscious of life's flaws, but primitive and archaic religions also can be restless with life. Human beings, whatever their culture, feel some need to overcome life's limitations and failings.

There are nonreligious means people can use to eliminate sources of estrangement. Human techniques for handling nature and social relations and self-development might produce the technology, sociology, and psychology to solve human problems. Medical progress, for example, has eliminated smallpox, one of nature's great killers. Perhaps developments in the social sciences may eventually eliminate war. In general, the various sciences approach the threatening mysteries of life as problems to be solved. Compared to many of the religious techniques of the past, such as the use of magic and invocations of the gods, science is doing much better in dealing with many of the former mysteries. Science is saving people from many sources of estrangement that primitive and archaic religions could not deal with particularly well.

Not all mysteries, though, can be turned into mere practical problems to be solved. At each stage of cultural development, there have been mysteries that were both threatening and unavoidable, for which there was no technology or science available. The previous chapter on universal or ultimate questions should make clear that the mysteries of life, including the estranging presence of death, unfairness, and other basic evils, are not easily dissolved into technical problems to be solved. The human mind can always chew on the wretched possibility that ultimately nothing makes any sense. There always remains the human ability to wonder and compare and question and to become restless with the limitations of life.

A mystery is threatening. When it cannot be solved as a problem is solved, its threat is unrelenting. Life in the presence of an unrelenting threat would be hellish. Religions save people from this hellishness by seeing another side to mystery, not just as threat but as promise. Religion saves people from feelings of estrangement by perceiving in the mysteries of life a numinous presence and power that offers hope. Earlier, religion was defined as a response to mystery. A fuller definition is this: religion is a response to mystery as a numinous reality that has the power to provide salvation from estrangement.

The following three chapters are about forms of religious salvation. There will be many examples of various religious beliefs in salvation, because there have been a great many notions about how best to be saved from the estranging threats that life poses. To bring some order out of the wealth of traditions, the chapters have been divided in terms of the kinds of threatening estrangements. Chapter Five will be about ideas of an ideal life or universe as answers to estrangement from nature or the universe. Chapter Six will be about ideal communities or forms of social existence as answers to estrangement from others. And Chapter Seven will be about ways of achieving an ideal selfhood as answers to estrangement from self. Each of these chapters will in turn describe primitive, archaic, and historic forms of beliefs and practices.

Beneath all these divisions and examples there is still a common human story. All the many beliefs and behaviors described here are signs of the human condition as beings with the conscious ability to ask endless questions and thereby discover mystery, and to have faith that the mystery is a numinous power that upholds— rather than destroys—the ultimate meaningfulness of life.

CHAPTER FIVE

Peace, Paradise, and Perfection

Reality as It Should Be

This universe is not always kind to us. We live lives of troubles and uncertainties, and dream of an ideal situation where nothing threatens our safety and meaningfulness. Every religious tradition has some way of acknowledging that life is not what we would like it to be, and of portraying ideal conditions that can be achieved through proper relations to the numinous powers. The traditions usually describe simultaneously how to achieve the ideal world and to establish or maintain ideal relations with others as well as an ideal self, so these three elements will appear somewhat intermingled here. But the emphasis in this chapter is on ideas about beliefs in an ideal world, a place or condition or universe that does not cause a sense of wrongness.

PRIMITIVE SALVATION: AN UNBOTHERED LIFE

The primitive person accepts the world as it is. The tribesperson knows that it is not perfect; there is disorder within it; there are powers that cause disease and hunger. Nonetheless, the tribesperson has an unthinking faith in the universe as it appears, accepting it as reality and trusting that it can provide for a comfortable and safe life. For the primitive person, salvation consists mainly of a defense of the stable order of the world against disruptive forces.

There are three ways the comforting pattern of life can be disrupted. The first source of disruption is a breakdown in proper tribal order. This order was established at the beginning of time, the original time of the world just a few generations prior to what living memory can reach, by ancestral figures and various spirit-beings. This is the one real way to behave, the right way, the safe way. This order is composed of all the customs, laws, roles, and other behavioral patterns that make the tribespeople who they are. Violation of these patterns causes chaos and confusion, fights and family disputes, bad luck and punishment from the numinous. Maintaining the one correct order produces peace and happiness.

To preserve the order given in the primal time is to stay in contact with those times. Thus the Australian aborigines use the ritual retelling of these stories of the beginning as "dreamtime," when they identify themselves with their origin and become one with it again. In the modern world we value the changes that time brings, but for the primitive person time is an enemy because it contains the risk of change; it brings confusion and danger. It is better to maintain a kind of timeless identity between the "now" and the "then" of the beginning, and to avoid any future not identical with then and now. That is one form of salvation for the primitive person.

Even if the proper tribal order were faithfully maintained, there is still a second source of disruption: the activities or influences of mana-like forces and spirits. It is not enough, then, just to try to maintain correct roles, customs, and so forth; it is also important to learn about and to use the many techniques that can control the numinous powers. The spirits must be kept happy or at a distance. Mana-like power must be controlled magically or avoided. All these things contribute to saving the tribesperson from powers that can upset daily living.

The breakdown of proper order and the intrusion of dangerous numinous powers into life are the two main threats in this life that a tribesperson seeks to be saved from. Salvation from them means that day by day there would be good food, physical health, familial and tribal peace, individual happiness. But almost every tribe acknowledges the presence of a third disruptive force, one of great importance: death.

Some primitive tribes believe that only the death of very old and weak people is natural. All other deaths are caused by sorcerers using magic or by angry spirits. A number of New Guinea tribes believe that death is caused by enemy tribes using sorcery, and that the death of a tribesperson by sickness requires vengeance. The oracles are checked to discover which enemy caused the disease; then the tribe goes to war against that enemy. Very old people sometimes believe that even their deaths can be put off indefinitely by the proper magic. After all, no one has to die just today or even tomorrow. At least one more day of life is possible, and then one more. So the old men and women who feel their strength failing may try to hold on to life with the help of various charms, potions, and spells.

No amount of magic or vengeance, however, prevents death from finally coming. Many tribes hold farewell rites to put the dead person's spirit to rest or send it away so that it will not return to cause trouble. It is fairly common for primitive people to assume that it is better to be alive than dead, and that spirits of the dead are apt to cause trouble out of envy for the living.

A common alternative belief is that those who have died live in a different place, but one more or less like the one they have just left. The Apatani hill people of Burma and Tibet believe that those who die pass on to a land of the dead which is very much like the usual Apatani village. The guardian spirits there ask the new spirit how much land he owned, how many wives and chickens and pigs he had (in a usual male chauvinistic way), and how many cattle he sacrificed to the spirits. These spirits then assign the new spirit to the same possessions he had before, including the cattle he sacrificed. The new spirit lives another normal life this way until he grows old and dies once more. Then he passes on to yet another Apatani village of the dead, and so on. By such beliefs, the sting is taken from death, even though the new life hoped for is very ordinary. Primitives like their lives, accepting them as the way things are. It does not usually occur to them to imagine a new life after death that is radically different from the life they know, except that it is often pictured as more boring and dreary.

ARCHAIC SALVATION: AN IDEALIZED LIFE

Archaic people live in a bigger and more complicated universe than primitive people do. They know more about the world, about other cultures, about complexities in their own society. They have a greater sense that there are other ways of life than their own. One way they show this is by picturing the gods as somehow different from themselves, living apart from people in their own reality. Another way is by dreaming sometimes of an ideal life that they themselves would like to lead, one quite different from the normal human situation in the world, which would save them from many of life's limitations and miseries.

Primitives seek to stabilize and maintain life as they know it, but one that is freed from irregularities and sorcery. Archaic people look beyond the conditions of life as they experience it to a vision of a better life, one they can imagine even if they do not expect to attain it. Different cultures have different beliefs, some quite simple and others more complex. They often contain elements retained from a more primitive past. That means it is often difficult to classify some of the beliefs as primitive or archaic, but we can follow a rule of thumb that has some validity: archaic religion is more conscious that this ordinary life is flawed, and is more desirous of a different and utopian mode of existence. Primitive people seek a good life. Archaic people dream of a better life.

The Golden Age and the Fall

One way archaic people show their awareness that life is seriously flawed is by their stories or myths about a time back in the beginning when life was not flawed. These stories also make some sense out of the disconcerting fact that life is now flawed, by describing an original mistake or evil deed that caused the present miseries. A good number of cultures have some story of an ideal primordial state without sickness or death, without anger or war, without drought or flood, without vermin or poisonous animals. This past and ideal state is called a "golden age."

The story in the Hebrew Scriptures about the garden of Eden is an example of belief in a golden age. In this early Hebrew story Yahweh is pictured a little like a god of polytheistic beliefs (he walks in the garden in the afternoon to be cooled by the breeze). This Yahweh created a man and a woman and a garden of plenty where they lived. In the garden was the tree of life from which they could eat and therefore live forever, it seems. But there was another tree also, of the knowledge of good and evil, from which they were forbidden to eat. A serpent persuaded the woman to eat from this tree (women are frequently blamed for humankind's troubles—by men, of course). She persuaded the man to eat from it also. As punishment, the couple was expelled from the garden. They were cursed so that ever since then people have had to earn their bread with sweat and weariness, women bear children with pain, and all people die and return to dust. Once there was a golden age, but because of the primordial act of disobedience rust, rot, and sadness now afflict everything.

Similarly, the Nuer tribe of north central Africa tells of a time when heaven and earth were joined. The heaven in this story is not some invisible realm but simply the sky above where a great sky god named Kwoth lives. People once lived in heaven too. They were happy and healthy; they did not die. Heaven and earth were joined by a rope. One day a mischievous hyena cut the rope. Those people who had been temporarily down on earth gathering some food were trapped here. Unable to return to heaven, people now grow old and weak and eventually die. Today their descendents are born, live for some years, and then also die. In another African story, that of the Tutsi, the ancestor of humankind, Nyina-kigwa, lived in heaven. She broke her word to Imana, the high god of the sky. As a consequence, she and her children had to leave the heavenly realm and fell to earth, where there was—and is to this day—hunger, suffering, and death.

People today, in our supposedly forward-looking age, still look backwards to the beginnings, to the original ideal society. Atlantis, Mu, Lemuria are all names of mythical or legendary empires of great power and accomplishments. Various books speculate that earth was once visited by space people. There are many tales of the wisdom of the Ancients, of the secrets of lost civilizations. Other longings for a golden age dream not of a once-great civilization but a life in touch with nature, uncorrupted by civilization. The pollution in our skies, earth, and seas today make the vision of nature pure once again all the more appealing. Each of these ideas represents a belief that once things were better than they are now, that our present limits and liabilities are not natural or inevitable, but the result of some fall from truth, wisdom, and power. If all of us felt truly at home in our present world, such stories would be less popular than they have been.

Sometimes the story about the original error or fall offers no particular hope that the error can ever be rectified. There is a kind of numb acceptance of the sad conditions of life. The Nuer tribe story that tells of the hyena and the rope does not hope for a day when heaven and earth will be reconnected, although they do believe that the high god Kwoth will continue to care for them on earth. The Tutsi, however, who tell of Nyinakigwa's fall, believe that one day Imana will no longer be angry and will allow all of Nyinakigwa's children to return to the sky, to happiness and unlimited life. Such a hope for the future, when the present sadness will be eliminated, is a hope common to much of humankind.

The Millennium

"Millennium" has come to be the label for any future utopia or ideal society. The best known milleniarist beliefs in Western culture are those based on Jewish apocalypticism, which in turn may be based on Zoroastrian ideas described in Chapter Three. The word "apocalypse" is an ancient Greek word meaning "revelation." During the period of approximately 150 B.C. to A.D. 100, many supposed revelations were circulating in Jerusalem and other places. A few of these writings are now part of Judaic and Christian Scriptures, in the books of Daniel and Revelation, for example. They were said to be revelations about future events from God or an angel or some ancient hero. Generally speaking, they promised that foreign domination over Jerusalem would be overthrown by God's power. He would send his anointed one ("messiah" in Hebrew) who would then rule over a perfect world. As the prophet Isaiah had once promised, Israel would be a light to all nations, bringing peace and prosperity. In the Christian version, Jesus the Christ would return to rule.

Some of these writings predicted a catastrophic end to this world-order. Fire would fall from the skies, the earth would tremble, the armies of good would clash with the armies of evil. Finally, all evil forces would be defeated. Then a new earth and a new sky above would be built out of the rubble. All those who had remained on the side of good would live on in the new earth, the heavenly kingdom of God on earth. In some of these revelations it was said that good people who had died would be raised up from the dead and live on also in the new kingdom.

The word "apocalyptic" has come to be used to label all visions that predict a violent and sudden destruction of this world-order in order to usher in a new ideal one. Even today, anyone who predicts a catastrophic end of the world is said to be preaching apocalyptic ideas. In the Christian New Testament the last book is the book of Revelation (Apocalypse). It too predicts the end of the world. There will be worldwide upheavals and natural catastrophes. The forces of good and evil, people, angels, and demons, will face off. On the plains of Meggido in Israel (Armageddon) the climactic battle between the Christ (Greek for "anointed," i.e., "messiah") and the Anti-Christ will take place. There the power of God will overcome the power of Satan. Then God will send the Christ to rule over a perfect kingdom centered on Jerusalem for a thousand years. (Later Satan will briefly be released only to be defeated again permanently.) The word for one thousand years is "millennium." Those who wait for the thousand-year reign of Christ are said to be waiting for the millennium to arrive.

Various Christians have used the book of Revelation as a guide to interpret the signs of their own times. Many early Christians awaited the end of this world-order in their own times. Centuries later some believed that the book of Revelation meant that Christ's reign would be made perfect at the end of a millennium in the year 1000 A.D. In Europe at that time many people left their farms and their families, devoted themselves to prayers and fasting, or went on pilgrimages to prepare themselves for the coming of the end. Today, major religious groups such as Seventh Day Adventists and Jehovah's Witnesses still expect the end of the world before too long, and many individual Christian ministers and believers see all around them the signs predicted in the book of Revelation coming true now, omens of the end of this world-order.

There are many beliefs outside of the Christian tradition that anthropologists have called millenniarist beliefs, regardless of whether there is any one-thousand-year period involved. Any expectation that this current world-order will soon be ended and a new utopian life created is now labeled "millenniarist." In North America at the end of the 19th century, the Native Americans of the Western plains began to preach a set of ideas associated with a ghost dance (or spirit dance). Dispossessed of their lands and the buffalo, dislocated and discouraged, they began to spread the belief that if they would return to the old tribal ways established by their ancestors, then the ancestors' spirits (ghosts) would set things right, defeating the foreign intruders, bringing back the buffalo, and creating a happy society. This was to happen soon, not in a thousand years. Nor was the happiness to last for just a thousand-year period. Nonetheless, anthropologists have called this a millenniarist movement.

Other movements today can also be called millenniarist, even in forms that do not appear to be religious. The hope of many communists, for example, had been that in a few generations the principles of Marxism would dominate the earth, bringing peace, prosperity, and happiness to the human race. Each of us at some times in our lives may have become attached to a utopian vision of a society to come, when everyone on earth would finally have learned to live in love and peace. Whether this utopia is ushered in by an apocalyptic catastrophe or by a gentle evolution, it would in either case now be called a millennium.

As you may be able to tell from the examples given, millenniarist thought is also sometimes part of historic religion. The line between archaic and historic thought is blurred, because historic modes of thought arise out of and borrow heavily from archaic culture, and continue to mingle with it. Like archaic thought, such beliefs are expressed in myth-like stories rather than in the systematic analyses found in historic theologies. They are also archaic in that the ideal life they seek is in an idealized world rather than an escape from the world entirely as is common in historic religion. Finally, such stories are archaic to the extent that they disregard the question of the Ultimate in a full sense. They settle for a god-like being powerful enough to win out eventually over all enemies, as Ahura Mazda wins out eventually over Ahriman.

HISTORIC RELIGION: PERFECTION

Humankind long ago lurched toward monotheism, stumbling into beliefs like those about Akhenaton and Zoroaster, approaching a clearer belief in a universal and unifying numinous Power. At the same time it began to despair of this world as a place for human happiness or fulfillment. The human mind became more and more accustomed to thinking about unqualified perfection, as it did when thinking of the Ultimate. Human imagination began also to look beyond this incorrigibly flawed earthly existence to a fully perfect reality beyond. A golden age or a millennium began to seem merely ideal, a great improvement, but not unqualifiedly perfect. Only an utterly other-worldly realm might suffice.

Salvation Through Cosmic Order
Before talking about the perfect reality beyond, however, we should give some attention to the idea of a perfect worldly order. This idea first arose in primitive times in the unspoken assump-

tion that there was an order established at the beginning of things that is the way things are and now must be. It is an idea that can be found in archaic thought such as the ancient Egyptian belief in ma'at, a word sometimes translated as "truth," which is the basic order of the universe. In both archaic and historic stages of religion in India there was belief in a cosmic pattern of justice known as karma, and in the basic natural set of duties—dharma—people should obey.

China has been a civilization thoroughly dominated by the belief that there is a proper order to all things and that adherence to this order provides salvation. The two main forms of this are found in the two religions native to China, Taoism and Confucianism. In each the historic interest in perfection eventually appeared, although these religions were more worldly than historic religion usually is. (In general, the history of China is harder to fit into Bellah's categories of religious evolution than are other traditions.)

Confucianism is as much a social philosophy as a religion. It arose about the same time as Taoist thought and shared Taoism's indifference toward the high god or gods. The movement stems from the wisdom writings ("Analects") of Kung Fu-Tzu ("Confucius" in Latinized form). Confucius preached social order based on a harmony among human beings. This in turn came from adherence to "li," proper behavior and observance of customs. Conformity to li would bring about salvation from family discord, from social injustice, from political unrest, and from war. By A.D. 1200, a neo-Confucian called Chu Hsi had elaborated on the concept of li and described it as the a cosmic right order to which all people ought to adhere.

Taoism also offered certain kinds of salvation through an understanding and acceptance of the eternal Tao and its major manifestation, the Ying/Yin pattern to all things. Some Taoists have always been more archaic than historic in their attitudes. In facing the problem of death, for example, many Taoists have sought to use their knowledge of Yang/Yin in a kind of magical way. They have analyzed the kinds of food people can eat to determine which has more Yang and less Yin. The ordinary person may want to mix beans and rice rather equally for lunch, because this would provide a nice balance of Yang and Yin aspects. Older people, however, are apparently losing Yang, the more active and energetic principle, and need more of it. For vigor in old age, then, go heavy on the beans. Some Taoists spent years devising strange mixtures of gold and other elements into various kinds of food, in order to create a potion that could extend life indefinitely.

The more philosophical Taoists, however, found their salvation from the threat of death through a correct attitude. Meditation on the patterns of nature would produce an inner sense of the fundamental rightness of the natural. Death is as natural as life. So the Taoist would learn to accept it without fear or concern. Chuang-Tzu, the ancient Taoist, was found humming and making pottery in his yard the day after his beloved wife of many years had died. His friends were shocked that he should act so cheerfully rather than be in mourning. Chuang-Tzu replied by asking what wisdom there was in mourning over what was as natural as eating or sleeping.

Belief in a perfect order in this world, whether of nature or of society, has not been the usual path taken by the historic religions of the West or of India, including the Buddhism that eventually became very strong in China and Japan. The historic Western and Indian religions looked away from this world to another world. Bellah characterizes them as world-rejecting religions.

Paradise: A Perfect World Beyond the World

Belief in an utterly perfect other-worldly realm did not appear suddenly in fully finished form. It began in early historic times with a belief in an otherworldly but earthlike paradise, and its counterpart, hell.

The archaic beliefs in a golden age or millennium portray an idealized life on earth, past or to come. Archaic societies have also believed in some existence after death, though they do not always expect much from it for most people. It is pictured at times as a shadowy life of boredom, as in the Hades of Greek thought, or as a lifeless place of unending sleep, as in the Sheol of ancient Hebrew beliefs. A few heroes or favorites of the gods might have a very pleasant time of it, but not most people. As the axial age arrived, however, belief in life after death took a new turn.

Discouraged thoroughly by the newly-perceived finitude of earthly life, estranged from life as it exists in this world, religious thinkers around the time of the axial age began to envision a perfect existence beyond this world. An early version of this is belief in a paradise. The word, which comes to us through a Greek form based on an old Persian word, meant a beautiful park with deer and fruit trees and flowing water. This is the sort of afterlife promised by Zoroaster to followers of Ahura Mazda. Islamic belief offers paradise after death to those Allah has chosen. Christians are promised eternal life in a heaven that is often portrayed as a paradise, although the trees and streams are sometimes replaced with clouds and harp-playing angels.

In the East, Hindus and Buddhists look forward to at least a temporary stay in a paradise, though this is not full and final salvation. Pure Land Buddhism, for example, popular in Japan and formerly also in China, made hope for paradise a focal idea in a way that includes other older ideas. According to this form of Buddhism, there was once a golden age on earth when people followed the ways of the Buddha and achieved enlightenment as Siddhartha Gautama did. But as time passed, people slowly became less and less enlightened and finally even lost their ability to follow the teachings of the Buddha at all. But the Buddha-power that existed in Siddhartha Gautama exists also in many beings, including the divine Amida-Buddha, a kind of god. Fortunately for people in this present fallen age, Amida has the power to transport those who trust him straight to a Pure Land after their deaths, to a paradise. In this Pure Land everyone can finally learn enlightenment as the Buddha did and then achieve the salvation that lies beyond all paradises (which we will talk about soon).

Hell: The Opposite of Paradise

In its earliest stages, historic religion has tended to believe not only in a perfect paradise rather than in just another life after death; it has also believed in various hells. Primitive and archaic religions believe that a person who is not buried properly, or whose death is not avenged, or who is not offered enough food through sacrifices, may end up troubled and unhappy. They have also pictured life after death as a shadowy and dreary state, not exactly hellish, but simply boring. Early historic religion, however, has a tendency to create full-scale hells, some temporary and some everlasting.

From Zoroaster to contemporary times, people in the West have often believed that there is a hell that is a place of everlasting fire and torment. Many have claimed that such beliefs should not be taken too literally, but the words traditionally used make of hell a truly terrible existence, a place of utter and unrelenting torment.

Some forms of Buddhism also have traditions about a hell or many hells. An educated Buddhist will say these descriptions are only poetic metaphors and not literally true, but popular beliefs portray hell very graphically. One such description portrays hell as a place of excrement, of bitter-tasting dung mixed with molten copper in which there are worms with diamond-sharp beaks. The sinner who dies awakens in hell being eaten by the worms. They start with his lips, tongue, and throat, until finally the sinner is eaten from inside out, only to find himself alive again and due for more punishment. (This particular hell is for anyone who kills a bird or animal for supper without feeling regret.)

Zoroastrian, Hindu, and Buddhist thought, each in its own way, offer some assurance that hell will not be everlasting. Terrible as it is, someday it will come to an end. All evil, even the evil of being in hell, can pass away.

Christianity has traditionally been less sparing. Those who have deserved hell will have to suffer there forever and ever. Some Christians in modern times have had doubts about how literally this should be taken. Perhaps, they have suggested, belief in an unending hell is just a dramatic way to express thorough antagonism to evil. An all-good God might also be all-forgiving. An all-powerful God might be able to conquer evil totally by leaving no pain or agony anywhere in existence.

The Realm of Pure Spirits and Unqualified Perfection

Western religions to this day have balanced the early historic belief in a paradise with a parallel belief in a fully spiritualized heaven, wherein even the limitations of paradise are surpassed. (As we will soon see, the religions of India did the same in their own way.) For most of us, the idea of a merely perfect God is more appealing than that of an Absolute. Likewise, a merely perfect paradise can be more attractive than a totally spiritualized heaven. Yet the same restless human mind that can conceive of the ultimate, infinite, and incomprehensible Reality, can also question the adequacy even of paradise.

The movement away from belief in a mere paradise began with a change in the idea of spirit. For primitive and archaic people, spirit is physical stuff like air or breath, thin and usually invisible but solid enough to feel. When primitive and archaic cultures speak of a life after death for human spirits, they imagine it as a kind of earthly life, a physical place suited for spirits. Usually, in fact, the belief in a life after death assumed that it was somehow a bodily life also. If life is to be really human life after death, it would have to include the whole human person, body and spirit as one. Primitive and archaic religions are often not clear on how this works, but they are nonetheless confident that the spirit that lives on after death does so in a village with huts and cattle, or in a utopia with wonderful bodily comforts, or in a physical Hades located somewhere underground.

When historic religion developed in the West, it at first retained a somewhat archaic belief in a this-worldly salvation for the whole person, body and spirit as one. The apocalyptic tradition in Judaism had looked for a kingdom of heaven on earth. The living would enjoy it and the religiously faithful who had already died would be resurrected into a new whole life in this millennial kingdom. Christianity inherited this belief and preached a bodily resurrection of the dead into the kingdom of God in the new earth following the apocalyptic end of the old one. The Koran, Islam's sacred book, describes paradise in ways that make it a heavenly garden full of physical comfort, though like later Judaism and Christianity it placed this paradise outside of this earth.

These Western religions, though, eventually minimized or ignored the physical aspect of life after death and described it in a purely spiritual way. They came to accept a more radically distinctive meaning to the word "spirit" as something utterly unphysical and unearthly. This was due to the influence of Greek philosophy.

In 399 B.C., the Greek philosopher Socrates (469-399 B.C.) died by drinking a cup of hemlock. He had been accused and found guilty by the citizens of Athens of denying the reality of the gods and of corrupting the youth of Athens by leading them away from traditional beliefs. He accepted the punishment as a way of showing his dedication to the ideas he stood for. But when it was time for him to die, his friends began to cry. To console them he gave them a few reasons to believe that it would only be his body that died, not his soul.

The story of Socrates's death is contained in a short work called the *Phaedo* written by Socrates's disciple, the great philosopher Plato (427?-347 B.C.). This story became one of the main sources in all of European civilization for the belief in the immortality of the soul. Plato begins his version of the argument with the idea that there are two major elements in each person, body and soul; and that these two elements are entirely different from each other.

Matter is limitation, Plato argued, using the figure of Socrates to say these things; whatever is material is imperfect, flawed, changeable, and therefore apt to decay. Spirit, on the other hand, belongs to the realm of what is perfect and changeless. The basic evidence for this is our own knowledge. The inner spirit-power we call mind is able to conceive of things as perfect and unflawed. For example, it can conceptualize the abstract idea of perfect oneness, a simple unity without parts, complexity, or division, even thought in the actual physical world no such perfect oneness exists. Similarly, the mind can conceive of perfect justice, a state wherein all things exist in perfect order, even though in the actual physical world justice is always partial and imperfect.

Plato concluded that there are two levels of reality: one is the flawed and limited space-time realm of matter; the other is the invisible and timeless realm of pure essences (also called Ideas or Forms). These essences are the basic, unchanging, and perfect natures reflected in mixed and confused form in the material world. Behind the material reality that we perceive lies the eternal realm of perfect and pure goodness, truth, beauty, oneness, justice, and so forth. If you cannot form any image of goodness as such, not this good thing and that good deed but just pure goodness, you are on the right track. Pure goodness, pure beauty, pure justice, apart from all concrete instances, belong to the perfect realm of essences, which no images are adequate to express. Only abstract concepts can categorize them. The fact that our minds can conceive of them abstractly is evidence that our mind is spirit, belonging not to material reality but to the eternal and perfect realm of essences.

It is very strange, in fact, Plato thought, that we live a bodily existence at all. Plato believed that the spirit is like a prisoner in the body. Some primordial flaw, some unknown ancient mistake has trapped us for a time in material existence, in time and space. But bodies die. The spirit cannot die, for it belongs to what is eternal and changeless. Our spirits, or souls, are immortal by their very nature.

We should use our time on earth to train our minds to be open to what is perfect and eternal in preparation for the death of the body. At that time our souls will pass back into the perfect realm of essences. Then we will spend a timeless forever in blissful contemplation of the perfection of the essences. This will be our salvation from all estrangement, for then we will have found our true home and perfect happiness without end.

To exist forever in mental contemplation of perfect essences is not the average person's idea of a joyous life after death. Nevertheless, from Plato's time until today the idea of the soul as a purely spiritual being, destined for a purely spiritual immortality, has had great influence. One effect of Plato's thought was to modify Christian ideas about life after death (as well as those of Islam and Judaism, in different ways).

The first Christians, as was mentioned, looked forward to an apocalyptic end of this world-order and the establishment of a millennial kingdom of God on a new earth. Those who had already died would experience a resurrection, body and soul, into new life in this kingdom. As it developed further, Christian tradition has usually continued to maintain that resurrection is bodily resurrection and not just a purely spiritual rebirth. But this tradition has often been overshadowed by an emphasis on the life of the soul that describes a state of heavenly existence for the soul after death, for example, as a "beatific vision." The happiness of the soul in heaven will thus consist in an eternal contemplation of God. The mental vision of God's absolute and infinite perfection will overwhelm the soul and produce in it unspeakable and unending bliss. There is little mention of any bodily existence in the usual language about this beatific vision.

Another aspect of Platonic thought that has had a more concrete effect in the West has been Plato's idea that materiality is a trap or prison and only the soul has eternal life and value. About the same time that apocalyptic ideas were gaining popularity among many Jews, a form of thought known as gnosticism was spreading among educated Greek-speaking people who were scattered all around the countries of the eastern Mediterranean. *Gnosis* is the Greek word for "knowledge." Gnostics were people who agreed with Plato that our inner self was an immortal soul belonging to the realm of perfect ideas. Most people, the gnostics argued, had lost sight of their true nature as minds that belong to the nonmaterial realm of spirit. In order to achieve a lasting freedom from being born into a physical body, people must come to know who they really are, and they must know this clearly and fully. They must devote their lives to the minds and not allow their bodies to distract them.

These gnostic attitudes were accepted by many people. They may have influenced Mani, a Persian who lived in the 3rd century A.D. and borrowed ideas from Zoroastrian, Buddhist, and Christian thought. Mani's movement, named Manicheism, preached that caring for the body would perpetuate the power of the body to hold the inner spirit captive. The way to liberation was the way of asceticism, the practice of denying oneself any pleasures. In particular, Mani declared that sex was the pleasure most to be avoided because it had great power to keep people interested in physical existence. Manicheism and many forms of gnosticism together influenced early Christianity. In spite of biblical statements that God intended there to be sex and that God made this physical world and called it good, a variety of Christian groups in history have declared that sex is either always sinful or at least mildly degrading, something to be avoided by anyone who is interested in spiritual values.

Platonic ideas also live on today, occasionally mixed with beliefs derived from Eastern thought, in a number of fairly significant religious movements. Christian Science, for example, the belief of the Church of Christ Scientist founded in Boston in the 19th century by Mary Baker Eddy, says that people are basically souls. A soul should have power over the lesser forces of matter. True spiritual understanding and faith should make medical help unnecessary; mind should be able to cure body. There are also a number of theosophical schools of belief that proclaim that we are souls, perhaps ones who have been assigned to these particular bodies and earthly lives in order to test and train us for greater spiritual and mental advances in a spirit realm or astral plane, as it is sometimes called.

The Western historic religions today have a mixture of belief in an ideal life after death that range from the somewhat archaic-style belief in a millennial kingdom on earth, to the early historic paradise-like heaven, to an utterly spiritual heaven. It is generally safe to characterize Western historic religions as religions that look for salvation in a life to be achieved when this current world has been utterly transformed or rejected. This otherworldly emphasis has lasted until today. (We will eventually see that modern religiousness includes a return to a fuller appreciation of this world.)

Salvation in Religions of India as Dissolution of the Self

To reject this world completely is a fairly drastic way to seek salvation from the estranging conditions of life. Major religious traditions in India have gone a step further. Hindus and Buddhists say that to escape fully from pain and frustration, to achieve final and lasting salvation, a person must escape not only from the world but even from individual selfhood. Only when there is no longer an individual "you" at all is there salvation.

While people of the West hope for life after death, the Hindu and Buddhists are afraid that we are all condemned to have to live again after death. Hindus say that each of us is a soul or self that is born into the world and dies, and then is reincarnated (re-embodied or re-enfleshed) again tens of thousands of times. In each one of these thousands of lives there will be suffering. If one or more life should be joyous or healthy it will end, and eventually it will be replaced by more suffering.

We earn happiness by our good deeds and by our acceptance of our duties. The law of justice called karma, which is built into the structure of the universe, guarantees that we are eventually repaid exactly for all our good and our evil in one or more of our reincarnations. But no person is perfect. We make mistakes, grow weak, and sin, and so we earn more suffering. Popular Hindu and Buddhist beliefs say also that we spend time between our incarnations on earth in a paradise or hell, as we have deserved. But even these pass away and we are each threatened again by rebirth into this world.

The Buddha, Prince Siddhartha Gautama, lived in Nepal in the 6th century B.C. As he was growing up, his father had protected him from the sight of human misery. One day he wandered from the palace and was shocked by the sight of a hungry and ragged old beggar. He abandoned his home and family to try to discover how such misery could exist and what could be done about it. After years of searching and learning, he finally reduced all his insights to a few sparse ideas: all life is suffering; we suffer because we have desires; the only salvation from suffering consists of letting go utterly of all desires, all attachments and cares. Those who let go completely will pass into the condition called nirvana when they die, instead of having to be reborn again. Nirvana is an extinction of individual self, a kind of not-being. It is also beyond comprehension, the Buddha said, so there is not much use in speculating on what it is like.

Since the time of the Buddha, many reinterpretations of his ideas have grown up and spread throughout the world. Many of these reinterpretations speak more positively of nirvana as a kind of spiritual heaven rather than as a not-being, but the original impulse of Buddhism was to simply let go completely of the world, of life, of self. This alone is salvation.

The Hindu tradition has similar ideas about final salvation. Being born again and again is the basic problem. The only way to escape it is to cease to be a self at all, to bring a complete end to one's individual identity. That leaves, then, only what alone was real in a person, the presence of the eternal Atman-Brahman. It is as though when the individual self lets go, it is dissolved back into the cosmic ocean of Brahman.

The Hindu tradition says it can take many thousands of lifetimes to reach this letting-go. When we are born for the first time (why this happens is not quite clear), we have many desires. We find value in pleasure. It is perfectly natural, says Hindu belief, for a person to take great joy in good food and comfortable sleep and intimately loving sex, in majestic scenery and the excitement of adventure, in the beauty of great art and in the smile of a child. But when a person has devoted a thousand or ten thousand life-times to pleasure, it will all become dull. Then a person may find life's values in success, in fame and power and wealth. But even-tually, through thousands of lives, a person will have achieved so many things so often that all success will be empty. Then a person will find life meaningful through devotion to the needs of others. A lifetime or ten thousand lifetimes can be spent in unselfish ser-vice: clothing the naked, feeding the hungry, consoling the wretched, loving the orphan, the bereaved, the lonely. But this too will prove to be an endless task, raising eventually in a person's mind a doubt about all life. Life itself will continuously produce more people to serve and be served. Generation after generation, the trail of human joy and misery goes on and endlessly on. Even-tually each person comes to face the ultimate question of the pur-pose of things: What is any of it truly worth?

Even an endless life in paradise is not enough to answer this question. To endure forever is not sufficient as a purpose. For what purpose does one endure? The Hindu sees that the human mind can ask the ultimate questions, and because it can a restless-ness will inevitably set in, even in paradise, and finally a sense of estrangement about all existence.

These are the kinds of thoughts that have led Hindus and Bud-dhists to proclaim that the only full and lasting salvation is to pass beyond all individual existence and to fade into the cosmic ultimate, Brahman to the Hindu and nirvana to the Buddhist. In both cases salvation consists of eternal and unchanging identity with the ultimate reality. This condition is beyond our imagina-tion because it is a union with the incomprehensible Mystery. Western religion usually denies that the individual self ceases to exist after death, but they too often proclaim that salvation is an incomprehensible and blissful union with the Ultimate mystery called God.

All of these ideas about salvation as an incomprehensible un-ion with the Ultimate may sound vague or abstract, as well as un-appealing. When we worry about life's limitations and experience a sense of estrangement, hope for a millennial utopia or a para-dise is usually satisfying enough. If paradise turned out to be boring in an eon or two, that would be time enough to start worrying about a subsequent form of salvation that was even more fulfilling. Yet the fact that Hindus, Buddhists, Christians, and others have looked beyond paradise to an incomprehensible and eternal union with limitless mystery indicates a continuing potential built into our humanness, a potential for the infinite. To be human is to be able to reach out endlessly more.

Summary

This chapter has been a survey of the various ways religious traditions have dreamed of an ideal context for human existence as a kind of salvation. A good life in primitive thought, a wonderfully ideal-worldly existence in archaic thought, an other-worldly paradise in early historic thought, and an utterly perfect existence in later historic thought is the general pattern of these dreams. (Later we will see that the modern style of religion has come to appreciate this world again.)

Any ideal context, though, is ideal only if it somehow provides also for our need for acceptance and our need for a sense of worthy selfhood. We need to be saved not merely from a flawed nature or world but also from our estrangement from others and from self. These are the topics of the next two chapters.

FOR FURTHER REFLECTION

1. Do you take it for granted that some aspect of ourselves survives physical death, or is this an implausible idea to you? Explain.

2. When you have thought about a life after death, how have you imagined it? Is it like earth in any way at all? Explain.

3. If there were no life beyond death, would this earthly existence be meaningful and sufficient in itself? Explain.

4. Can the world be improved enough to provide adequate earthly happiness for all people? Explain. Do you think that will ever happen?

5. How much sense does it make to you to hope for some kind of purely spiritial vision? How about a dissolution of self in relation to an infinite Ultimate? Explain.

SUGGESTED READINGS

Eric J. Sharpe and John R. Hinnels, eds., *Man and His Salvation*, 1974.

Bernard McGinn, *Visions of the End*, 1979; apocalyptic thought in the Middle Ages, with earlier background in ch. 1.

James B. Wiggens, "Death and Eschatology," in *Introduction to the Study of Religion*, T. William Hall, ed., 1978.

Peter Worseley, *The Trumpet Shall Sound*, 1968; on the millenniarist cargo cults of the southwest Pacific.

Byron Earhardt, *Japanese Religion*, 1974; p. 60 on a Golden Age and a Fall.

Daigan and Alicia Matsunaga, *The Buddist Concept of Hell*, 1972.

Karl Rahner, "Thomas Aquinas on the Incomprehensibility of God," in David Tracy, ed., *Celebrating the Medieval Heritage*, 1978; a rather philosophical interpretation of the beatific vision.

CHAPTER SIX

Neither Lost nor Alone

Belonging
as a Form of Salvation

When we hear the word "salvation," we usually think of a life after death where we are saved both from the trials of this life and from death itself. Most of the beliefs about salvation presented in Chapter Five involved some sort of life after death, but not all of them. The main theme was that of an ideal reality or world. Although many cultures expect such a world to be an alternative to this one, achieved after death or in the future, others think of that ideal reality as a here-and-now affair. Primitives seek a here-and-now proper order. Confucian and Taoist ideas emphasize a this-worldly utopia to be attained and maintained in our daily lives. These beliefs are clues to the fact that not all ideas about salvation involve life after death. Some of them are more concerned with a

112

person's daily sense of fulfillment or worth. This chapter and the next will both be concerned with that sort of salvation, a present and ongoing salvation from threats of estrangement, achieved through a sense of personal worth and at-home-ness in daily life by relation to some numinous reality.

This chapter will describe various ways religiousness provides a comforting and supportive sense of belonging. In the course of the descriptions, three complexities will come up that can be mentioned here. One is that belonging is a fairly broad word, which can include a feeling of being accepted by another person, as well as a conviction that one belongs to a whole community of persons. A person can also belong to a historical movement, a belief system, or a cosmic order—something more impersonal.

A second complexity is that the notion of belonging overlaps with the topics of both the previous chapter and the one following. There is no way to be perfectly clear when salvation is a matter of finding an ideal reality and when it is a matter of belonging. These two blend together, as the concrete illustrations here will show, and also blend with a person's identity, the topic of the next chapter. The categories of estrangement from universe and others and self are a little artificial. Our life is one; our problems are one; our salvations are also one. All is one because underneath all the categoried compartments of our lives is one basic reality, the human person conscious of self and therefore needing to have a sense that life is meaningful in the face of the mysteries that our consciousness allows us to perceive.

The third complexity is one created by the outsider's perspective on the study of religion, which we are taking here. The outsider can see a believer being saved from estrangement in ways the believer might not even recognize. Religious traditions sometimes tell the believer that just belonging to the tradition instead of being lost and alone is already a kind of salvation. We will see examples of this. But the outsider can see many instances when the feeling of belonging is not explicitly recognized by a tradition as a kind of salvation, even though this belonging does in fact free the believer from a painfully estranged state. To belong somewhere meaningful is immensely important to a person. To belong is a kind of salvation, even if it is not called that.

As usual, there is some advantage in dividing up the topic into smaller and more manageable categories. The categories are only approximations. How many ways can a person feel lost and alone? How many ways can a person find a sense of belonging?

In each case too many to count. But here are two main categories, each with subdivisions. The first involves a special one-on-one relation to a numinous being, power, or order. The second involves being part of a larger social context.

INDIVIDUAL DEVOTION
TO A NUMINOUS REALITY

Throughout time, people have devoted themselves to offering attention, praise, gifts, affection, and obedience to various numinous powers. Often these offerings are simply means of persuasion carefully calculated to bribe, flatter, or seduce a spirit or god into granting some favor. As was mentioned briefly in Chapter Two, the attention paid to the gods is at times a way of achieving a kind of psychological salvation through a sense of belonging. This world can be a dreary and disappointing place to many individuals. Hope for an afterlife, paradise, or heaven can sustain a weary and lonely person for a long time. Years of nothing but aloneness, however, of being only marginally significant to others, of being powerless in a world where others accomplish great things, is a very heavy burden to bear. Hope for eventual joy after death might not be enough to sustain a person. During life's long years there is a need for additional consolation and support. Devotion to a numinous reality can provide this.

Devotion to a Personal Numinous Being

Spirits, ancestors, saints, angels, gods, and God in many descriptions have in common the fact that they are not only numinous but are also personable. They are beings you can address as friendly, thoughtful, helpful, and even loving persons. Followers of the Hindu gods Shiva or Krishna or the goddess Sri carry their statues in processions, build beautiful temples to them, and surround their statues with lights, flowers, and burning incense. In every Chinese village there used to be a shrine or two to the local gods or spirits. A small food offering, a bunch of flowers, a carved bit of wood would be placed there to honor the spirit. The many local spirits in Japan each have had their own shrines, ceremonies, and days of celebration. Orthodox and Catholic Christians celebrate feast days of various saints and angels, with processions and other ceremonies. All these numinous personal beings are treated with respect, affection, and praise. This is partly to win their favor, but it is also simply to rejoice in having them as bene-factors and even friends.

The full value of having a numinous personal being as friend is manifest in the private side of devotion. Whether during a great public ceremony or in the quiet of a nearly empty shrine, each person can cherish the thought of the spirit, saint, or god whose attentiveness makes up for all the thoughtless people in life. The saint in heaven knows the innermost feelings of a person who is misunderstood by everyone else. The love given by Vishnu is not the critical and selfish love of a human partner, but a forgiving and generous love. To know that Jesus loves you with enormous and divine love washes away your insignificance or failure and makes you equal in worth to the greatest person who ever lived. In fact, the gods, spirits, and God are often said to have a special love and concern for the weak, the forgotten, those who suffer in life. The same burdens of powerlessness and pain that threaten to crush people actually make them more significant, more worthy of divine care and affection. This belief is a form of salvation from feelings of insignificance and aloneness.

Whether the devotion is public or private, it can vary in de-grees of intensity. For most religious people, to have devotion to a god or saint is important, but not all-important. In every relig-ious tradition, however, there are those who give their entire lives in service to a divine or numinous person. There are monks and nuns in East and West; priests, hermits, and gurus and prophets, who devote their entire lives to prayer, attention, and devotion to a form of the Buddha, to Shiva or his consort Kali, to Jesus, to Allah. We will see more about such people later. These find the entire worth of their lives in devotion to a numi-nous being.

As we have noted, there is a tendency around the world to be-lieve that suffering somehow merits special attention from the gods or God. As though the pains in life that come to a person by themselves were not enough, out of religious devotion people will inflict additional suffering upon themselves. People have beat themselves with whips, starved themselves, lived in cold and darkness, all to show their devotion to a god or God. Some pain in life is unavoidable; at other times pain is deliberately accepted as part of a training program; but religious movements have includ-ed people who believe that suffering is somehow pleasing to the numinous being whose attention, forgiveness, or love they seek. Religious people are sometimes masochistic in their devotion, though they would probably deny that the god or God is a sadist who enjoys seeing suffering.

There are various attempts to explain why this masochism appears in religion. To some extent it may be because religion is often a way of making sense of life's sufferings. First, we suffer, some of us much more than others. This can make life seem unfair or senseless. Second, we find a way of making sense of this mystery of suffering by a religious explanation: the spirits are punishing us for violating the customs; the gods are angry at our meager offerings; the balance of Tao's nature has been upset by our excesses; God is putting us to the test. Third, we then come to think of suffering as a good thing because it helps to maintain the customs, improve the offerings, balance nature, and prove our worth. Fourth, we go overboard and conclude that because suffering is good we should seek it.

There are other possible explanations for religious masochism. Perhaps childhood memories are unconsciously at work. When a child is hurt, parents grow very attentive and loving. Parents are sometimes angry at children until the children are punished; then the anger is gone. Perhaps suffering is a proof of devotion. We are touched by someone who makes sacrifices for us; we are sure then that someone truly cares for us. So we make sacrifices for our gods so they will know we truly love them. In any case, the greater our fears that the spirits or gods might not care for us, the greater the motivation to suffer in order to evoke their concern and merit their love. The greater a person's sense of guilt, the more a person might believe that only suffering can restore the person to favor in the god's eyes. If nothing else, religious masochism is a sign of the immense human need to be forgiven, accepted, and cherished. To achieve this is a form of salvation.

Devotion to the Right Order of Things

A person can live a life of devotion not only to personal beings such as spirits, gods, or God, but also to impersonal numinous order. We have seen how the primitive person devotes energy to maintaining the order established at the beginning times. And we have talked about the beliefs of Confucianists, Taoists, and Hindus who believe in a sacred cosmic order. It is possible to achieve a sense of belonging by harmonizing one's life with such order.

For some who believe in a cosmic right order, adherence to this order is only a *means* to a further state of salvation. By conforming to the cosmic law of karma, a person earns a better chance at eventually achieving the enlightenment that is the gateway to eternal not-being, nirvana. Yet in all cases where people believe in a cosmic order, there is also a here-and-now sense of belonging that is worth treating as a kind of salvation all by itself.

Each of us would like to be able to feel that our lives are lived well and wisely rather than poorly and stupidly. We have to make serious decisions about patterns of our life, and we worry at times that we have made the wrong decisions. Whatever we have accomplished, whatever our work or our social success or our accomplishments, we can all have some doubts about the worth and rightness of who we are. If we are sure that there is one correct way to exist, one natural pattern to things, then we can achieve a sense of rightness to our lives by conforming to that pattern. Thus the ancient Egyptians strove after ma'at, the Stoic deliberately accepted fate, the Taoists still seek to flow smoothly in life with the eternal currents of Yang/Yin, living in simple huts, raising a few chickens and radishes, at one with nature.

In each instance some degree of salvation from problems is achieved just for the practical reason that the one order of nature is the fact of things. People who struggle against the currents of nature and time are liable to wear themselves out and still lose in the long run. It is good practical wisdom to learn to cooperate with the laws of reality.

In addition to this practical common sense, there is also a psychological satisfaction that comes from feeling that we belong to the truth, to what is naturally correct, to what is the everlastingly right order of things. It does not matter as much, then, if on the surface our lives look unimportant, because the deeper truth is that our lives are at one with what alone is finally important, the cosmic order. It does not matter as much, then, if our lives appear to be unsuccessful, because underneath they are actually in harmony with the greatest and noblest reality, the universal and unifying supreme order of all things.

Devotion to the right order of things is often found as part of devotion to a personal numinous being. If the ancestors or gods established the rules of living, then adherence to the rules is a form of devotion to these sacred beings. A person belongs to the god by accepting the god's decrees. If it is a universal power such as God that has created the natural order, then the person who tries to do what is natural thereby belongs to God. The person who perceives a divine plan and follows it shows devotion to God. For many people, devotion to God is accompanied by a general belief that God has a hidden plan for all things. Whatever happens is God's will; so to accept all things, however confusing or threatening they may be, is a way of accepting and belonging to God and takes the terror out of the universe.

Mystical Devotion to an Absolute

Mystical experience is sometimes defined rather loosely as any overwhelming religious feeling. Those whom historic religions have called true mystics define mysticism a little more precisely than that. A mystic is one who has an intimate experience of the Absolute, the numinous reality that is infinite, eternal, and incomprehensible, the universal reality that embraces all things at once. It is the One beyond all limits. It is God the Absolute, Brahman the incomprehensible, Allah the infinite, or the formless and eternal Tao that the mystic encounters in mystical experience.

According to the mystics, this mystical encounter is not really describable, because it is not experienced in any usual sense of the word. It is not thinking or knowing because it is beyond them. It may produce certain feelings or emotional states, but it is beyond mere emotions. It is not a seeing or hearing or touching, although metaphors based on sensation or sensory images can provide some poetic ways of speaking about it. The mystics attempt to describe it by saying it is a being-at-one with the One that is All. It is a momentary eternity, a few minutes or hours of identity with the Everything in comparison with which the person is nothing. It is bliss; it is nothingness. It is ecstasy; it is emptiness. It is a rapture or utter peace. Then, when they have said all these things in an attempt to describe it, the mystics finally reaffirm that it is....It is ineffable. Words might help point a person toward mystical union with the Absolute, but only the experience of it can let a person "know" what it is.

Such experience sounds far removed from the life of a normal person; it is rare, indescribable, strange. But each of the great historic religions has had its mystics. In each major civilization there have been those who have sought and found union with the One as the highest and fullest mode of religious devotion. This devotion is a kind of salvation. Like all people, mystics are aware of the limitations of life. They too have suffered from a sense of estrangement, yet the union with the absolute One overrides estrangement by giving the mystic a sense of total belonging. Ordinary feelings of loneliness or dislocation are wiped out by the experience of belonging to the One in perfect union.

The mystics claim that after the mystical experience, the limitations of life no longer have much power to give rise to feelings of estrangement because in a moment of total union, peace, bliss, love, and belonging, all earthly limitations have by comparison been made trivial and unimportant. The mystics say that this rewarding feeling is not the real purpose of mystical union. Because the One they seek is alone truly and ultimately of lasting value, it is deserving of unqualified dedication and devotion for its own sake. That, they say, is the real reason they give themselves over to this One. But the sense of belonging to this One is still a form of fulfillment. It is a kind of salvation.

BELONGING TO A SACRED COMMUNITY

In many nations today, religion is a relatively private matter. People have the option of adhering—or not adhering—to any religious tradition. But this is a highly unusual situation. Down through history religion has been a shared social matter in a degree only suggested by what was said earlier in Chapter Two on the sociological function of religion. In spite of the option today of religious privacy and even solitude, most people still are religious in at least a semi-public way, in a community of believers. From this communal aspect of religion comes a sense of belonging.

Primitive Religious Community
Religion, community, and individual identity are inseparable in primitive society. Each person learns his or her identity by learning what the tribe sees as proper behavior, thoughts, and feelings. A given individual will, of course, have a unique personality, a special name, perhaps a singular role such as elder or warrior, but these will be within the bounds defined by tribal tradition. Moreover, the traditions are right because they were established at the beginning of things by the ancestors or the other original beings. Tribal customs are expressed and reinforced in religious ceremonies. Political, social, and economic decisions are made with the help of the spirits who communicate by signs and through dreams.

Primitive religious communities are straightforward and clear examples of what sociologists claim when they say that religion functions to support the social order. Religion does this by being an inseparable aspect of the social order, by being the sacred threads that tie all the pieces of social custom together, by being the inner supporting framework of every social structure. Through this the individual tribesperson gains a sense of belonging not only to the present pattern of tribal life but also to an unchanging, reliable, sacred order.

One of the great problems for tribal societies in today's world of quick travel and easy communication is that they must contend not only with occasional new ideas but also with the presence of constant newness. Primitive tribal societies are likely to have a defense against outside influences in a belief common to many tribes, that what happens to outsiders is of no significance for their lives. In tribal languages around the world, the name a tribe uses for itself is the closest word it has to say "human being." When an Ibo tribesperson in Nigeria or a Cheyenne Indian in the western plains says "Ibo" or "Cheyenne," they mean "people." In tribal thought the group says, "We are people; the others are not people as we are. We know the spirits and where the mana-powers are. Others do not. We know how to please the ancestors, make the moon rise, preserve the truth about the rivers. Others do not. We live as it is correct for people to live in this place. Others do not." The primitive person holds to traditional patterns, comfortable to belong. This is all religious, we would say. But for the primitive person the religious element is not very distinct from life as a whole. There is usually no word for "religion."

Archaic Religious Community

Like primitive societies, archaic cultures offer the individual a sense of belonging through identity with a social order given by the ancestors or gods. Devotion to the gods in an archaic society is the same thing generally as devotion to the city, territory, or ruling family in the land. The highest form of patriotism in ancient Rome, for example, was called *pietas*. The religious connotation of the word still exists today in "piety," referring to devotion to God. Roman *pietas* was indeed devotion to the gods, especially to Jupiter and to Janus, gods of war and peace. But this devotion in practice consisted of fidelity to Roman customs. A person who upheld the traditional social and family order was the one who was called *pius*. Even today, people often equate patriotism with religion, saying that God wants people to support their nation and its law and morality.

In general, archaic thought stresses the differences between peoples of different cultures and religions. Each archaic culture emphasizes its own worth and value and disdains others. The "others" are seen as mere barbarians if they are less advanced culturally. Or the "others" are seen as weak and decadent if they are highly civilized. One's own gods and the customs they provide and protect are superior to all others.

This attitude, of course, does not exist only among archaic cultures. In historic and modern times, many people still think in parochial (local) rather than universal ways about the status and value of other people's thought, culture, and religion. It is a normal human tendency to assert that our ways are better than their ways, whoever they are. We all easily tend to be archaic in this way.

Many archaic societies grew very large, uniting what originally had been smaller and more primitive localities into a large cultural group. This occurred in China, India, and Mesopotamia in the second millennium B.C., and in Egypt before that. In all these places the same tendency showed itself. The problem was how to achieve social unity among the various localities. People of different villages could be united politically only if their customs, beliefs, and values could be united. Only a unification of the gods could achieve this.

The conquest of the Shang by the Chou in ancient China (c. 1100 B.C.) is an example of this. After the conquest, the Chou king had the problem of how to consolidate his rule over the kingdom of the Shang, how to win the approval and acceptance of the conquered people, who had a sense of belonging to their own land, family, ancestors, and gods. When the Chou arrived, bringing strange gods and customs, there could have been continuing conflict between the two groups. The Shang had the difficult choice of how to maintain a sense of belonging by allegiance to the old ways, without setting themselves at odds with the new rulers. With political astuteness the Chou king proclaimed that the Shang people could maintain devotion both to their god, Shang-Ti, and also to the new king. It was Shang-Ti, the Chou king said, who had empowered him to overthrow the Shang dynasty because that dynasty was corrupt and no longer taking proper care of the people. The Chou king proclaimed also that his high god, T'ien (Heaven), was the same god as Shang-Ti, but under a different name. Therefore, all the peoples of Chou and Shang territories could join together in allegiance to one and the same high god. All who lived in the new unified kingdom could share a common sense of belonging.

The caste system of India provides one of the most monumental examples of complex social organization and unity based on religious belief. The caste system originated in archaic times, beginning perhaps in 1500 B.C., when the conquering Aryans imposed their rule on the people of the Indus valley, and later on all of India. It was absorbed into the historic-style religion of later centuries and has lasted up until recent times.

There were four basic castes. At the top were the Brahmins, the priests in charge of the rituals. Because they dealt with sacred things, they were not supposed to make contact with anything unsacred. The next were the nobles or warriors (the nobility around the world were originally military leaders strong enough to grab territory and rule it). Third were the merchants and landowners. At the bottom of the four castes were the peasants, those who labored on the land. Below all the castes were the untouchables, those without status. They collected garbage, did sewage work, killed animals for food.

As centuries passed, each caste subdivided. The most exalted Brahmin family might be twenty stages above the lowest Brahmin family group. None would think of being on casual terms with any person more than ten subcastes below his or her own. None would allow marriage to anyone more than four or five subcastes lower. Every person by birth belonged to a very precisely defined level of society with its rules, dietary customs, social privileges, and obligations.

For centuries the people of India cooperated in maintaining this social structure. In every generation there were many individuals who tried to elude the restrictions of the system by pretending to belong to a caste higher than the one they were born into. The sacred writings of India predict severe consequences for those who dare to rebel in this way against the rules that assign them to a specific place in the social order. Every person by birth has a basic dharma (duty, set of obligations) to accept his or her place in society and fulfill the role appropriate to it. This dharma is not just a social rule; it is part of the cosmic order. For one born a merchant to seek to become noble is a grave offense against dharma. The person who rebels against the place assigned by birth will thereby deserve to be born the next time to an even lower caste or as a dog or worm. The only way to rise to a higher caste is to perform one's social role so well in this lifetime that it merits rebirth in a higher caste in the next lifetime, in accordance with the cosmic justice called karma.

Historic Religious Community

Primitive, archaic, and historic societies alike all provide the people with assurance that the social order they belong to is correct for them, because that order comes from the numinous power or powers that guide them. Historic religion, however, gives a special interpretation to this.

Historic religion tends to universalize. It proclaims that there is one underlying unity behind the various aspects of nature, and one supreme cause of that unity. There is but one Brahman, one Tao, one God. If there is a divinely-approved way, or a way that fits the nature of the supreme numinous reality, there is only one such way. There is but one ideal social order, one correct way to be human, one valid and morally proper behavior pattern, one true human identity.

If there are people in the world who do not follow that one true path, historic culture has two basic ways to think of them. One way is to believe them to be less than fully mature or even fully human. This is easy for any culture to do, historic or not. We have seen how the Ibo and Cheyenne think of themselves as people and others as not quite people. The Chinese always believed foreigners to be inferior barbarians. The Europeans who first invaded South and Central America were so startled by the strange ways of some of the more primitive tribes there that they debated whether those tribespeople had souls as full humans do. Once you have decided that the strange people are naturally inferior, you can then justify conquering and ruling them. After all, God or some power made them inferior. Thus it is divinely established that they are fit to be ruled by their superiors; or else some enormous sin of theirs merited them this lowly and flawed condition, and such great sinners do not deserve much concern.

The other alternative that historic religions have before them is to judge that all people are in fact equally human. This belief is more consistent with the universalizing attitude of historic religion, and is the actual position most take. It means that all people should live by the one true way for human beings. They should, for example, all worship the one true God, follow the one universally valid set of moral rules, and adapt themselves to the customs of those wise and virtuous people who have already accepted the one true way.

There is obvious arrogance in ideas like these, but there is also a kind of logic. If in fact there is one Tao and one Yang/Yin order throughout the universe, or if the only real salvation for anyone is dissolution in Brahman, then it would be very wise and most practical for everyone to share these beliefs. If polytheism is true, there is no single unifying order or truth to all reality. If atheism is true, there may be no order of any kind to human existence. But if monotheism or its equivalent is true, then there must be one, true, all-encompassing plan or order to reality.

If monotheism or an equivalent is true, then logic implies that there is one basically correct vision of life that is valid for every human being. On these grounds the Roman Catholic Pope Boniface VIII declared in 1302 that because the pope is head of the church and the church contains the sole truth for all humankind, therefore all people on earth were subject to the authority of the pope, whether they knew it or not. A claim like this strikes us as strange, but it has its own logic.

There is sometimes not only logic, but compassion behind the universalizing claims of historic religion. If people believe they possess the truth that can set all humankind free from estrangement and give them salvation, it would be ungenerous to keep that truth to themselves. Buddhist missionaries went forth through centuries to gently preach the wisdom of the Buddha, out of compassion for all people. Islamic forces have waged jihad, holy war, to overthrow the kings and armies that oppose Islamic belief, in order to "encourage" people to accept the words of Allah written in the Koran. It would be a great benefit to the whole human race, a Muslim believes, to have all people submit to the holy and divinely wise laws of the Koran in a worldwide house of Islam. Christian missionaries have traveled the world to bring people what they feel is the means to eternal salvation for all people. In all of these cases, the outsider may perceive an arrogance and even a religious imperialism, but the believer can do no less than share what he or she takes to be a true blessing for all peoples.

A further consequence of the logic of historic religion is to maintain an alliance between church and state. We who live in contemporary industrialized societies are accustomed to think of religion as private and separate from the public structures of government and civil laws. This is a rather modern notion. Pope Boniface VIII would have said it is a foolish and evil idea. If the religious authorities have God's sole and universal truth, including divine laws governing all aspects of life, then of course the government should be guided or ruled by the church or by the religious authorities. This is known as a "theocracy."

In China, Confucian thought was the basis for all governmental patterns, though Confucian thought is only vaguely religious. In the Roman Catholic church, belief in a separation between government and church was not officially accepted until after 1960. In many Islamic countries it is still maintained that the government must follow the rules laid down in the Koran. The ayatollah Khomeini in Iran agreed emphatically with this. He worked hard in his lifetime to establish a theocracy in his nation, and recommended doing so to other nations.

Some religious groups in industrialized nations also still insist that the governmental laws should uphold the basic moral laws established by God about sex or marriage or abortion and so on. This does not constitute a full theocracy by any means. But it does represent at least a limited belief that civil matters cannot be fully separate from religious ones.

Holiness Communities

In various cultures there are those whose religious affiliation calls them not only to belong to their culture but to a special holiness community within the culture. If the whole culture will not live perfectly, at least these few will try.

From early archaic times, priests or prophets were sometimes set aside from ordinary people and lived as a holiness community within the larger community. The historic traditions have produced the greatest number and variety of holiness communities. Here the historic ideal of perfection finds an appropriate style of life. The core of one form of Buddhism, for example, is the life of the sangha, a community of monks. Buddhism teaches that the cessation of all desire and attachments is the way to salvation, but the ordinary lives of people distract them from salvation by involving them in countless concerns for family, job, friends, entertainment. So life in the sangha is an excellent way to achieve release from desire. The monk leaves all possessions behind, except simple clothes and a bowl with which to beg for food each day. Avoiding all attachments and physical comforts, and especially the great distraction of sex, the monk devotes time to meditation on what alone is eternal and worthwhile: release. In the traditional Orthodox and Catholic communities of monks and nuns, the details of dress and food gathering may have been different, but the rest has been the same. The goal is to step aside from the distractions of worldly concerns, to leave behind the world, the flesh, and the devil, and to devote oneself entirely to God.

The explicit goal of a traditional monastic life has been to prepare for an eternal salvation: nirvana or heaven. But this life also provides the person with an ongoing sense of belonging. The monastery is a community of people who share the same vision of life and confirm one another's lifestyle. They pledge themselves to live in harmony and mutual kindness. And as the community is one that is thought to be close to the divine or numinous, it is especially uplifting to be able to belong to it. The lifestyle of holiness communities also prepares a person to enter into mystical contemplation of the Ultimate.

SEPARATION OF SOCIETY AND RELIGION

The human desire to maintain a unified sense of belonging to family, culture, and religion all at once is a very strong one, but no person will find total belonging in all aspects of life. There is always some disjointedness, some estrangement. Religion usually helps to overcome such estrangement, but occasionally it is a cause of estrangement from some aspects of family or society. Sometimes religion demands that a person make a choice between belonging to the family and society that have nourished that person, or belonging to a religious movement that challenges the family values and societal order.

Possibilities of Separation of Society and Religion

In general, all aspects of life—politics, economics, medicine, family, social class, and so forth—have been intricately tied up in the threads of religious beliefs and values, so much so that any distinction between religion and society is an artificial one. The cultural context provides each person with religious beliefs that become so familiar as to appear to be the obvious and only truth. The religious beliefs, in turn, provide the justification for the various cultural patterns. That, at least, is how things most often have been.

Modern experience has made us more aware, though, that religions and culture can diverge or contradict each other. We live in a pluralistic society where many religious traditions exist side by side, and none of them is totally in harmony with all aspects of the culture. From this vantage point we can look back in history and around the world and recognize various modes of separation between religion and society.

Primitive and archaic religion   A primitive religion cannot be separated from its social context. The social rules on marriage, for example, are religious rules. The religious beliefs about food are the tribe's dietary customs. Religion and society are one. To lose attachment to one is to lose attachment to both simultaneously. As was mentioned, the primitive person's world is a "one-possibility" thing. The person must belong to this social- religious pattern, or belong nowhere at all.

Archaic societies also see their social order and their religion as one, but these societies are internally complex, offering each person alternative roles to play. Archaic societies segregate the roles of priest, king, merchant, landowner, and peasant. The gods are somewhat segregated from daily life also, to the extent that they are more distant than local spirits and mana-powers. All of this creates the possibility that one aspect of society can be in explicit tension with another. The power of the king, for example, cannot simply exist; it must struggle against the individual powers of landowners, who do not always want to support the king. Each side in a struggle may claim that the gods are on its side.

An example from ancient Israel is an instance of religion providing moral criticism of society. In the 8th century B.C., a man named Amos felt called to speak in Yahweh's name against social injustices. Amos saw abuses all around him. He saw widows and orphans in poverty; he saw rich people and religious leaders condoning oppression of the poor; he saw people bought and sold into slavery. Amos shouted out that Yahweh rejected these customs and would punish all who "sold the innocent for silver." He declared that the standard religious offerings in the temples were useless; what Yahweh desired was compassion and justice.

Conflicts between religion and society are highly noticeable because conflict is more striking to the eye than quiet, untroubled times. It is nonetheless still true that society and religion do not usually conflict. The same people who constitute society are also the religious believers. People have a strong desire for peace, a sense of unified belonging. They usually expect religion to support their social patterns, not attack them.

Historic religion   There is a special element of separation between religion and society introduced by historic religion: other-worldly perfectionism. This element does not usually create conflict between religion and society. Hindu thought supported the caste system. Islamic law forbids carved or painted images. Christian tradition declared chaste celibacy to be superior to married life. In each of these cases, religion formed the culture and vice versa, so that they blended into a unity a person could belong to without inner division. Yet the otherworldly perfectionism of historic religion contains within itself the element of separation from society.

We have seen that historic religion arose when the human mind became accustomed to thinking about the universal and the perfect. But this world is highly imperfect. For some Hindus it is maya—illusion. For traditional Christianity the world is a vale of tears, made good by God but so corrupted by sin as to be no longer a fit home for humankind. The result of such thought is to make a person feel he or she does not belong to earth or any part of it, not even to earthly society and culture. All earthly things pass away. In comparison with eternity, they are neither lasting nor of value in themselves. A sense of detachment is the proper attitude. Belong to heaven, to the eternal, to the otherworldly. Do not put your trust in princes. Do not store up treasure where it can rust. Do not belong to earthly things. Join a holiness community perhaps.

This otherworldliness can separate a person from society. Ordinarily the religious believer will feel enough at home in the society not to reject or criticize it; it is still true that social and religious belonging usually merge together. After all, it is usual that the society a person grows up in provides and even reinforces religious beliefs. But when a time of conflict comes, when a person becomes angry at a certain rule, is uncomfortable with a social pattern, cannot fit in with a cultural value, then religion provides one way of justifying a separation from earthly society. It is not one's true home; it is not where one really belongs.

In principle, then, a historic religion is always somewhat separated from its social context. Even while it is part of society, it can also be society's critic. The religion preaches perfection as the ideal; society is never ideal. Every time people take to the streets today protesting in God's name against injustice, they are demonstrating the kind of tension that inevitably exists between historic religious ideals and society. Archaic religions can do this too, but historic religions by their very nature, by their ability to dream of perfection, are built to be social critics.

Some sociologists use a handy threefold division of how historic (and sometimes archaic) religiousness can function in relation to society. The first form is labeled "church."

Church   A church is an organized body of religious believers that has its own distinct leaders and forms that are not identical with the political, economic, and social structures of the society in which it exists. Like any historic religion, it has some sense that its patterns of belief and practice belong to the divine order rather than to the earthly. Yet every religious group is made up of people and people make up society. So the normal state of affairs is that the same religious people who feel that their practices, morals, and beliefs link them to the eternal are the people whose practices, morals, and beliefs are actually closely linked with society. The word "church" is used by the sociologists to label this normal condition, that of conformity between religion and culture.

We see this conformity every day. For example, as long as a culture says that only men can be leaders, no women may function as priests. When the culture changes to admit women to leadership, religious groups conclude that it would have been right all along to eliminate any discrimination against women. For years some religious bodies in the West have insisted that capitalism is the economic order God prefers. But a Roman Catholic pope raised in Communist Poland is sympathetic to certain elements of socialism as more in line with the justice he believes that God desires. Religious beliefs affect society and vice versa. People who have a sense of belonging to their own society and culture as well as to a historic religion, one that supposedly represents the one universal way of things, will ordinarily find ways to integrate these two forms of belonging. Religion and society blend together on the whole, with moments of tension passing into some workable accommodation. Most religious people today find it easiest to belong to a church in which there is a blend of social and religious belonging.

Sect   Not everyone feels at home in society, though. Some individuals discover that they are not comfortable with the social reality they have learned from family and neighbors. Some find society to be too immoral, too chaotic, or too uncertain about its beliefs. Others find regular churches to be much too casual and lighthearted about basic matters of rules, roles, and purposes. In some traditions a monastic holiness community is the answer. In other traditions there are movements that preach strict and clear principles and that tell a person exactly who to be, how to live, and what to live for, in order to provide the stable and exact security that society and the churches do not. These are known as "sects." They form a kind of non-monastic holiness community.

The sociologists define a sect as a religious movement that derives many of its ideas from the same dominant religious tradition as the churches do. The difference is that a sect adds significant variation that separates itself from society and ordinary church style. In particular the sectarians see themselves as the truest and most strict believers. They adhere more fervently to their beliefs than the average church member does. At times a major church may find it has some sectarian movements within it. The Pentecostal or Charismatic movements within mainline Protestant or Catholic churches are examples of this today. The holiness communities in Orthodox and Catholic Christianity have functioned all along as sectarian elements, practicing the religion in its purer and stricter form, apart from the general society.

In the United States there are a number of strong sects. The Seventh Day Adventists believe firmly in the Bible, as the other Christian churches also claim to do, but they are strict observers of a code of behavior that includes a ban on the use of tobacco, alcohol, and even meat. Their rules separate the Adventists from the rest of society to some extent. They reinforce a sense that the real purpose of life is not to conform to society but to prepare oneself for the end of this world. Likewise, the Church of Latter Day Saints (Mormons), Jehovah's Witnesses, Christian Scientists, and others derive many of their beliefs from the larger Christian tradition, but add further interpretations and usually expect a more exacting adherence on the part of believers than the churches do of their members generally.

Cult   In addition to the church and the sect, there is the cult. A cult is a group that defines itself in terms that are quite foreign to its cultural context. Those who find their own society, family, and culture unsatisfying, may end up repudiating them entirely. They feel so little at home, so dissatisfied, that only a strongly different perspective appeals to them.

Cults such as the Church of Scientology, the Hare Krishnas, or the Krishna Consciousness movement appeal to many people. The Hare Krishna movement invites people to live in a strict community of believers who give up ordinary earthly attachments in order to devote themselves to praise of the Lord Krishna, whom they believe to be the major form of the Ultimate divinity. In clothes, food, methods of prayer, and a dozen other ways, the Krishna follower abandons Western culture and absorbs the belief and lifestyle of a devotee imbued with a form of Hindu-inspired ideas. In the community house, the ashram, the believer finds a sense of belonging in a new identity and social pattern.

Other cults are only half-foreign. Scientology has been influenced by Freudian thought, by a European adaptation of Buddhist ideas, and by modern technology. This religion uses electronic E-meters to determine where mental blocks are inhibiting the release in the person of the basic spiritual or mental power we possess. Overall, as the next chapter will show, Scientology's beliefs are un-usual or "foreign" enough to call it a cult in the sociological sense.

A complex case is that of the Unification church ("Moonies"), which teaches a system of thought that is somewhat Judeo-Christian. Jesus tried to initiate the ideal human family, the Rever-end Moon says, but failed. Now it is up to the Unification church to create the perfect worldwide family and bring unification and total peace to all. In time this movement may be thought of more as a sect than as a cult. It aspires to transform society eventually ac-cording to its beliefs, and in so doing, to be no longer a cult or sect, but a mainline church in a society made compatible with its beliefs. In all these cases the lines of distinction are hard to draw. From your own knowledge of some of those mentioned you may want to categorize them differently. The differences between categories of church, sect, and cult are often blurred in reality, but they pro-vide useful guides, nonetheless, for perceiving patterns of religion.

Belonging as a Source of Intolerance

The great human need to find a home in a social community has a dangerous side. The need to belong can produce a fierce sense of loyalty to one's own group that goes beyond loyalty and passes over into intolerance and hatred of what is not one's own. There are various causes of bigotry. One is a fear of anything that calls into question the rightness, the validity, the true worth of the community a person belongs to.

Whatever is different from our own community, clan, nation, or race might be accepted simply as something different, some-thing good for other people. People are often tempted, though, to see such differences as a challenge. If our ways are correct, why should anyone refuse to follow them? If other communities do not follow our ways, are they suggesting that our ways are wrong? The more a person feels insecure about the validity of the group he or she belongs to, the more that person may be tempted to at-tack anyone or anything that threatens it. Intolerance, hatred, big-otry, even murder can result, as we see in the history of the Ku Klux Klan, Nazis, and other such groups.

Even when they are not bigoted, community members easily fall into patterns of mutual reassurance in which they praise their own ways and make demeaning jokes or comments about outsiders. At times this takes the more charitable form of condescension. If the community has the truest and best pattern for human life, then one of its members may speak sympathetically of the depraved, ignorant, or misguided outsiders who must still suffer the lack of what believers have been blessed, wise, or humble enough to accept. Of course, this is all perfectly logical. Jews see themselves as God's chosen people. Christian tradition has insisted that outside the church there is no salvation. Islamic faith declares that only members of the House of Islam can expect to reach paradise right after death. Such beliefs can tempt the believer to look down upon the outsider.

These religions, like all historic religion, assert that all people are of equal worth before God or the Eternal. All people share in one human community. We are all brothers and sisters. We are all equally deserving of compassion and love and support. But it is hard to maintain that sense of universal human community if we constantly divide humankind into "us" and "the others." The others with their strange ways and odd beliefs do not look and behave the way we want them to. Sometimes they are even our competitors or enemies.

Occasionally a great leader inspires people to see through differences and to cherish everyone. In this century the religious leaders Mohandas Gandhi and Martin Luther King, Jr., each led a crusade for freedom and justice. Yet both insisted firmly and repeatedly and at great personal risk that even the oppressor must be protected against harm. Both required nonviolence from their followers, on the grounds that all people, even the oppressor, are to be loved. Both tried to maintain a sense that Indian and British, black and white, all people, are part of one human family. This is the ideal that historic religions preach, but we humans have a very hard time learning to accept it and live by it.

Summary
This chapter has described ways in which feeling of belonging is itself a kind of salvation. As an answer to a feeling of being adrift without a true home or acceptance, religions can offer a God to belong to, a natural order to conform to, or, most especially, a community of companion believers in whatever form such a community takes. Usually, society as a whole has been the religious community people belong to. But in historic cultures, sects, cults, and holiness communities may stand aside from the main-

stream of life and provide a special group to belong to. (We will speak later about the religious pluralism of modern culture.)

When we have found where we belong, though, we might still feel uneasy about ourselves. Are we truly all right, secure in our selfhood and truly worthy? That is the topic of the next chapter.

FOR FURTHER REFLECTION

1. Do most people find it very important that there is a God who understands, loves, and forgives them? Why do you think this is so?
2. Would you find it comforting to feel that you are part of a cosmic unity? Why? Why not? Is it true that whatever is natural is good?
3. Identity the community of people you feel most thoroughly at home with. Do you belong to many communities? Which of them are religious communities in any sense?
4. Have you ever supposed that your community's way of life is the best one for all humankind? Why? Why not?
5. Are there standards for life that are or should be the standards that all people everywhere live up to to make us all one community? What are they?

SUGGESTED READINGS

Steven T. Katz, *Mysticism and Religious Traditions*, 1983.

Moses Maimonides, "The Practice of the Presence of God" in Jacob Needleman, *et al.*, *Religion for a New Generation*, 1977 (2nd ed.), pp. 471-479.

Robert Bellah, *et al.*, *Habits of the Heart*, 1985; contemporary reflections on community and the individual today.

Milton C. Sernett, "Religion and Group Identity," ch. 13 in T. William Hall, ed., *Introduction to the Study of Religion*, 1978.

Rodney Stark, "Churhc and Sect" in Phillip E. Hammond, ed., *The Sacred in a Secular Age*, 1985.

Bryan Wilson, *Religion in Sociological Perspective*, 1982.

Jacob Needleman, *The New Religions*, 1987; informed analysis of Asian-inspired new religions in the United States.

A True
and Worthy Selfhood

Identity as Salvation

Religious salvation is freedom from estrangement through relation to a numinous reality. The salvation achieved by attaining some heavenly condition is the kind of religious salvation we most often think of. The salvation from aloneness that comes from belonging to a divine being or a sacred community is not quite so obvious, yet it is plain enough once it is described. The salvation that is least obviously religious is salvation from confusion about one's own identity. The topic of identity sounds more like a matter of psychology than of religion. Still, estrangement from selfhood and self is a basic problem for every human person, and there are fundamental ways that religiousness has entered into this problem as it has into others. Our identity has an intrinsically mysterious dimension to it, and so the question of who we are is one that religions address in one way or another.

THE PROBLEM OF IDENTITY

We may have felt a need at some time to get to know ourselves as individuals better, to get in touch with our feelings, to find ourselves, to learn who we really are. Goals such as these have become commonplace in this psychological age. Perhaps we have had only an occasional restlessness about our inner character and feelings. Or perhaps we have stumbled upon some deeply upsetting desire, attitude, or habit that sets us apart from others and makes us worry about our own normalcy, worth, or sanity. We all can experience unsettling moments about ourselves because we are born without identity and must learn who we are to be as we grow. As we grow, we also continue to change, so our identity is always changing in some way.

Born Without Identity

We are unfinished animals, said sociologist Peter Berger in his book, *The Sacred Canopy.* He was not trying to be insulting; he was just pointing out a contrast between us and all other living beings. Every dog, kangaroo, and monkey is programmed thoroughly enough by its genetic make-up that the offspring of each species has minimal need to be taught how to be an adult.

A puppy is born with an array of specific directions inside its cells telling it how to become a full-grown dog, not only biologically but also behaviorally. A puppy raised apart from all other dogs has only a limited need to learn at the appropriate age how to bark, how to mark off territory by urinating in the right places, how to catch food if necessary, how to recognize when it is time for mating. It will not have to be taught any doggy thoughts or doggy values. The same is true, generally speaking, of all species on the planet, except for us human beings.

We are born with few instincts and those we do have are relatively weak. We must slowly learn how to become functioning human beings. We are born genetically inclined to learn, to soak up language skills, to imitate others, to be curious. But we are incredibly open to variation in what we learn, what language we speak, what behavior patterns we follow, and how we interpret our experiences. We do have a number of inborn behavioral tendencies, but our personality, values, opinions, biases, roles, and so forth, are mainly learned from people around us. Each person develops a somewhat unique personality, but one which is largely made up of the values, ideas, and patterns that the social context has made available.

As far as we can tell, most of the various components that make up our identity were invented at some time by other human beings. In prehistoric times the human race (or its prehuman ancestors) began to shift from dependence on instincts to dependence on learning. Over many thousands of years, with some prodding from residual instinctive tendencies, the cultures of humankind built up such vast reservoirs of ideas about family life, food gathering methods, mutual defense, land use, possessions, stages of life, mysterious powers, the use of tools, making music—all the categories and structures of human life—that even an encyclopedia could barely list and describe them. Because these are invented rather than inborn, they have to be learned. We have to spend many years learning and practicing how to be a human being in accordance with the norms our society has provided for us.

Because these norms are invented rather than inborn they are often also somewhat arbitrary, varying greatly from culture to culture. In many cultures, daily nudity is so customary no one thinks to notice it. In North America's warm summers, on the other hand, few businessmen notice how strange it is to wear a suit and tie designed originally to keep people warm in England's cool climate years before central heating was invented. Modern military groups often exclude homosexuals, yet the homosexuality of the fierce military units of ancient Thebes in Greece was thought to be a help to increase the soldiers' devotion to duty and steadfastness in battle. North Americans feel oddly uncomfortable talking to someone who stands too closely face-to-face. Latin Americans, Arabs, and others think that North Americans are cold and distant because they stand so far away when talking with them. Fat white worms that grow in rotten logs are nourishing and tasty to many people. Others enjoy the flavor of well-aged eggs, but think that the rotten milk product known as cheese is disgusting. A cup of warm blood taken directly from the neck of a grazing cow is a main part of some diets.

Clothing, sexual values, conversational styles, and dietary customs are only examples of the kinds of things we humans have invented and pass on through generations. There are some genetically controlled influences at work among these, but they are not too many and do not act very strongly, it seems.

In becoming an individual personality with a complex array of elements and characteristics, each of us drew upon all the inventions that constitute our culture. This happened gradually, so the "I" that was coming into selfhood interacted with the culture to produce each next bit of selfhood. It is not a completely passive process, therefore. Yet 90 percent or more of the specific personal characteristics in each of us is the cumulative product of the inventiveness of our ancestors now encoded in our culture.

Our everyday impression of our customs and identity is contrary to this. We do not think of our social manners, our notions of success, our sexual roles, our musical chords, our hours of sleep, our family structures, our methods of law, as merely human inventions that could easily have been different. We are accustomed to them. They collectively make up our consciousness of what life is like and how we fit into it. We think of them as natural. We do not remember how we carefully watched, imitated, practiced and became persons in the way our culture defines a person. We forget the troubling years of early adolescence when we watched each other, adopted the right habits, laughed at those who diverged from approved behavior, and reinforced one another's conformity to the restricted range of behavior that we learned to know as normal, natural, sane, and acceptable.

We humans want to develop in ourselves some conformity to others in order not to be alone, but the motivation is deeper than that. Even if we found ways never to be alone, always to belong to others in some way, we would still have a further need: to feel we are worthwhile and valuable, to feel we have an identity that does not merely fit with that of others but is praiseworthy in some way. We need to feel fully at home with our own identity.

Our identity, however, is doubly precarious. First of all, it is vulnerable to attacks from those who think we are individually inadequate, odd, abnormal, silly, insane, corrupt, or perverted. Each of us is under constant pressure not to deviate too far from accepted norms. Each has some fear of being embarrassed, looking foolish, not being accepted. Each avoids association with people our culture considers deviant, inferior, or strange. These are all signs of how precarious our individual identity is. We are not quite secure enough simply to be who we are regardless of the social standards, or to accept others for who they are in spite of social pressure. We achieve our security by adhering to the standards.

Second, our identity is precarious because the social standards themselves are largely human inventions. The social norms we use to measure ourselves and assure ourselves that we are all right are largely invented, rather than inborn. Anyone who manages to develop an identity fully in tune with the culture may then feel secure because the culture accepts and praises that identity, but the culture's standards can be doubted, challenged, and changed. Then the old identity that was once secure may now be mocked by others and rejected. For example, the "housewife" was once praised above all other women. Now her identity is less secure because women have opened up more options for themselves. There are people whose sense of importance is still based on a racism that assures them that their race is better than others. Fortunately, this norm is changing. On a more prosaic level, those who smoke cigarettes once were thought to look relaxed, or sophisticated, or tough. Now they just look foolish and hooked. Because social patterns are precarious, so are the identities built on these patterns.

Religion as a Support for Identity

In human cultures the major source of support both for the individual's sense of worthwhile identity and for the security of the social pattern that much of that identity is based on, has been the religious traditions of the cultures.

Both the section on the sociological function of religion in Chapter Two and the discussion in Chapter Six on the interpenetration of religion and culture indicate how important religion has usually been in supporting social patterns. Every culture has inertia of its own and would tend to maintain itself for some time, presumably, even if religion were weak. At times religious groups oppose aspects of their culture and try to change it into something they can support. By and large, however, most societies have been quite confident that their ways are precisely what God, the gods, or the ancestors established, or are in conformity with the numinous forces.

The belief that numinous powers stand in support of the culture works in two ways. First, it provides assurance that the customs are correct because they come not from confused human opinion but from the power and wisdom of the numinous. If anyone rebels against them, that person is simply and obviously wrong. Second, the numinous powers often can be expected to enforce their rules. The rebels are not merely wrong but are doomed to be punished. In fact, because the rebels are certainly wrong, they must be either mentally crippled to stray so far, or else maliciously evil. This justifies any actions by the rest of society to restrain or punish the rebels. The security of the individual's identity can be bolstered by the power of religion to maintain the social customs the identity is based on. There are numerous specific ways in which religion supports individual identity and the social order on which identity is usually based. The rest of this chapter will describe a number of these ways.

WORTHWHILE IDENTITY AND RELIGION

The Special Religious Status of a Few People

Every culture has some people whose significance depends on their special connection with the numinous, whether officially or unofficially. Such persons can feel that their lives are worthwhile, therefore, in a special way. Each is a somebody, because he or she is in touch with what is truly powerful and worthwhile.

There are many official roles. It may include magicians and sorcerers who know how to manipulate mana-power, as well as the shamans who deal with the spirits of disease and death. The priest, official performer of ritual, has special status. So also do the official augurs and prophets of the temples. A later chapter will speak of those who are official religious leaders.

Many people have unofficial ways of achieving worthwhileness or significance through religion. Numerous people today find themselves possessed by a divine spirit who gives them wonderful powers of healing or speaking in tongues. These Christian charismatics or pentecostals believe they have received these powers as gifts (*charisma* in Greek) from the Holy Spirit, as the Christian Scriptures say the apostles once did on Pentecost in Jerusalem or the Christians of Corinth did a few years later.

Among religious believers with special roles or gifts, there are inevitably a few who are consciously eager for high status in society or a feeling of importance. Most presumably are intent on genuinely religious devotion for its own sake. Nonetheless, whether intended or not, to achieve special religious status is also to achieve a sense of being right and being worthy. Even if no one else were to know that a person received special gifts from God or was able to deal successfully with spirits, that person would have some added sense of worth from this special relation to the numinous.

Special Status for Everyone Through Religion

It is not only the special individuals such as priests and charismatics who get a sense of clear and worthwhile identity through relation to the numinous. In most cultures all people receive their identity in some ways through religious beliefs or practices.

Religious rituals are a main way most cultures give identity a clear form. This is especially true of the "rites of passage," those rituals by which a tribe, culture, or religious tradition marks off the main points of a person's life. (A later chapter will deal more fully with ritual.) Birth rites acknowledge that a person has been born and passed into a specific identity as a member of this family, its tradition, and its gods. Infant baptism, for example, is a naming ceremony in which the child is officially made a member of the religious group. The child's identity comes from belonging to the group.

Puberty rites, when childhood is left behind, are important rites of passage in many cultures. The notion of adolescence as a period between childhood and adulthood is a recent invention. For most societies the young person who is old enough to be a parent is an adult. There is no formally recognized in-between status. Puberty rites mark this very important passage into adulthood. Some Australian aborigines, for example, bury their young men in the belly of the earth mother. When they are released a few days later from their hole in the earth, they have been born again as adults. There are puberty rites still in our society today, though we rarely think of them as that. For Jews, it is the bar Mitzvah ceremony. For Christians, it is confirmation or adult baptism. By these rituals a person is asked to take on personal responsibility as a young adult member of the religious group.

Puberty rites highlight the growth of identity. Every child, adolescent, or adult has a need to grow into a specific identity, to adopt specific ways of thinking and behaving, to achieve a sense of being a specific someone who fits somewhere in particular. Puberty rites tell the young person when to leave behind the child's behavior and begin to take on an adult's. The rites can cut down on the fumbling trial and error of adolescence by assigning specific behavior patterns to anyone who has gone through the rites. The girl who played with brothers and male cousins could do so until her puberty rites. After the rites she must avoid the company of male relatives until she is married. The boy who lived at home and addressed his mother with respect becomes a man through the rites, moves into the men's lodge, and treats his mother as someone who no longer has authority over him.

It is not only through rituals that religions establish identity; the moral code also dictates how people are to act, think, and feel. Those who adhere faithfully to the moral rules can feel they are good persons. A religion that tells people it is immoral to dance, drink, or play cards, may be depriving them of occasional fun, but it is providing them with a clear set of standards that define a good person. The sense of worthy selfhood achieved by obedience to the code of behavior can be more important than a game of poker, a glass of beer, or an evening of dancing.

Religious beliefs generally help establish basic human identity. They can tell us we are animals, or the offspring of the ancient heroes, or the children of gods, or made in the image and likeness of God. They can tell us we are part of nature's patterns, or belong instead to a spiritual realm, or that we do not really exist as individuals at all. Each of these beliefs influences how we think of ourselves and one another.

Our Secret Identity

There are a number of religious traditions that teach that we are not who we think we are. Plato and the Gnostics held that we are not so physical as we might think. We are really pure spirits merely trapped temporarily in this bodily form. Hindu and Buddhist beliefs go a step further and tell us we are not even as real as we might think. Neither the body nor even the inner self is of any significance; the self we believe we are is a mistake. The only thing in us that is truly real is that which is identical with the eternal and incomprehensible Atman, that which is not individual at all.

Children have fantasies of being a royal foundling, that is, a prince or princess found by the parents in a basket on the doorstep with a note: "Take care of this baby until the time comes to reveal its true identity." The me you see, a child dreams, is not the whole me or the real me. I am like Clark Kent or Diana Prince. Under the right circumstances I will be revealed as Superman or Wonder Woman. The Rosicrucians have the message that we have untapped mental powers within us, that we are more powerful beings than we know. New Age writers today propose that each of us may have lived many prior lives, perhaps as important individuals in history, and have a chance to be born yet again in the future, perhaps, in roles of great importance.

The system of thought known as Scientology makes even more impressive claims. According to one report, L. Ron Hubbard, founder of Scientology, has declared that we are all Thetans, members of a race of superbeings who have lived for millions of years. By the power of our minds alone, we could leap small galaxies at a single bound, travel faster than a speeding photon. But it was all too easy for us, Hubbard explained, so we began to set limitations on our powers in order to make our existence more challenging. The greatest limitation we chose was loss of memory that we are Thetan. All the frustrating limitations we now experience in life, therefore, are self-imposed and artificial. With the proper training we can become "clear," our memories restored and with them, our superpowers.

Beliefs such as these promise many kinds of salvation. They offer power that people can use to overcome the estranging limitations of earthly physical life. Through such beliefs people can achieve a great sense of belonging. They also can provide a third form of salvation: a sense of individual worth. After all, we are truly Thetans!

Reassurance for a Threatened Identity

The importance of achieving a meaningful identity is most visible precisely where it is most difficult. Most of us grow into our identities with a vague sense that we are what people are supposed to be like, but we all have some doubts, some problems about who we are. Many people live a socially and psychologically marginal existence. They live on the margins of society, as it were, and often look to the numinous powers for a sense of personal significance.

A vivid instance of this is the snake-handling sects in the United States, made up mainly of people who are poor and powerless in society, who have little education, and who have the most reason to wonder about their own worth. They are Christians who have been told that God loves them, but their lives mark them as outside the patterns of success and competence that other people enjoy. On certain occasions they assemble in simple churches to show concretely that they are actually people God has blessed with wondrous powers because they are strong in their faith.

After prayers and hymns and perhaps a simple sermon or testimony, the leaders will open up a box of snakes, the more poisonous the better. According to the Acts of the Apostles in the Christian New Testament, the apostle Paul was bitten by a viper when he and others were temporarily stranded on Malta. The inhabitants concluded that Paul must be a murderer who was being punished for his crime in this way by a numinous power. They expected him to swell up and die, but Paul shook the snake off of his hand into the fire and remained unharmed. (The inhabitants then decided he must be a god in disguise.) Christians have taken Paul's immunity to snakebites as a sign of his great faith and divine protection. So the modern Christian snake-handlers prove to themselves that they are people like Paul, specially blessed and protected by God, by picking up poisonous snakes and passing them back and forth. Only rarely are they bitten. The risk is worth the reward, apparently, of feeling that they are approved by God, regardless of how they appear in society's eyes.

Sects and cults in general have the power to transform social rejection into self-affirmation. Those on the margins of society are susceptible to the leader who comes along and tells them that their exclusion from social acceptance is a sign they are special. It is not because they are unworthy that society does not appreciate them; it is because society is ignorant, foolish, or sinful. By joining the sect or cult a person not only achieves a sense of belonging; the beliefs of the cult or sect also give the person a sense of individual significance, of worthy identity.

Through many forms of religious affiliation, people find significant selfhood. In ecstatic visions, in priestly status, in rites of passage and rituals of power, in discovering their true and awesome identity in belonging to a special group of true believers—in any or all of these, religious believers discover a way of seeing themselves as significant. The unusual cases draw our attention most, but it is the everyday patterns that are most influential. The set of beliefs we take for granted about our human identity have the strongest effect on us precisely because we do not think to question them. Our ordinary beliefs about childhood and adulthood, male and female, what is natural and what is unnatural, are the beliefs that make us who we are. To repeat: throughout human history, religious traditions have been the repository and support of these patterns of identity. Today that may be changing, but that is a topic for the chapter on modern religion.

IDENTITY IN THE STAGES OF RELIGIOUSNESS

We live in a culture that is an accumulation of ideas from primitive, archaic, and historic times. We also have an individual accumulation of ideas collected from childhood, adolescence, and later years. Each of us individually—as well as our society, therefore—

is a mixture of identity-patterns from different stages of individual and cultural development. Once more the standard warning about neat categories: they are rough approximations, not the simple truth; there are exceptions to each of them. Yet, it is worthwhile to divide identity patterns into various stages for the sake of any insights these descriptions can provide.

Identity in Primitive and Archaic Religions

As with the issue of our place in the universe and our sense of belonging, the issue of identity does not become an explicitly profound one until historic times, after the axial age. Primitive people are apparently the least self-conscious about who they are; they take it for granted that it is right for them to be as they are, to do as they do, to maintain their traditions. In various matters such as relations between wife and husband, parent and child, cousin and cousin, neighbor and neighbor, the primitive person is aware of a need to learn the proper roles and rules, and thereby achieve what we would call the correct identity. But the primitive person does not do this in a conscious attempt to discover his or her true inner selfhood. The correct identity ideas are learned for a practical reason: correct behavior earns a person the continuing right to share in the food, the common hut, a religious dance, and so forth. Correct identity is learned simply as the external pattern of behavior suitable for a human being as part of tribal life.

Primitive people often do not seem to have much language to identify their inner selves. They often attribute even their own inner emotions to a particular spirit acting within them or to a part of their bodies: "The spirit gave me anger"; "My kidneys grieve." We still do this today when we say, "The devil made me do it," or "My heart is sad." But we are more apt to recognize these explicitly as figures of speech.

By the late archaic stage, at least some people seem to be more conscious of the problem of identity. They can see that there are different lifestyles in other cities. Life is no longer just a one-possibility thing, so it is easier to wonder why this identity, out of many possible ones, is the one to take on as one's own. They are better able to wonder about who they are and how they should behave, and why the group's roles and rules should be followed.

Too much wondering about identity would cause a great deal of personal confusion and social chaos. If too many people question their roles as warrior or mother or prophet or servant, soon everyone might be doing whatever she or he feels like doing and everything would be disorderly. The religious beliefs often help to prevent such chaos. The beliefs explain that the social rules and roles are assigned and upheld by the gods. Other rules and roles might have been possible, the believer knows, but the gods have settled the issue for the group. There is no use protesting it.

Archaic civilizations exhibit greater conscious concern about identity than primitive people do. Both primitive and archaic people have concern for explicit social status, for honor and even for public glory. Their sense of identity is not merely a practical matter of earning enough acceptance to maintain a full share in the city's life, possessions, and food; it is also a matter of personal status. But in many archaic societies there is a highly developed sensitivity to insults. Honor has become an explicitly important standard. Heroism in battle is said to be admired even by the gods and may earn for the hero a blessed afterlife instead of the more usual boring one. All this is largely, however, a matter of external status, not inner worth. The external power, honor, and wealth a person commands is the measure of the person's importance. Obviously every culture, including our own, retains this archaic tendency to value people according to their external success. Historic culture and consciousness add additional standards of worth that are based more on the inner qualities of the person.

Identity in Historic Religions

The axial age gave birth to the historic forms of religion, when humankind had developed a new form of self-consciousness. Some individuals may have arrived at this self-consciousness hundreds, or even thousands, of years before the axial age, but around 600-500 B.C. the new way of thinking became common in poetry, drama, philosophy, and religious writings. It was the age when people learned to stand back from the world they experienced and ask ultimate questions about it. So it was also the age when people became more skilled at standing back from themselves and at asking ultimate questions about selfhood. How can I judge myself and others by what they really are, instead of by what they possess or their external successes? In fact, what does it really mean to be a person? they asked.

The beginning of such questioning appears in the experience we have all had of an awkward or embarrassed self-consciousness over a period of time. The person who is moving toward historic consciousness can most truly be embarrassed. It is not the embarrassment as such that is significant here; it is the ability to imagine ourselves through the eyes of others, to picture a "me" that is not the one I am inside myself, but the "me" that others see or think they see. We can wonder, "What am I really like to others? How do they really see me?" Such questions can lead to the questions of historic thought. "What am I really like inside? Who is the real me?" This implies further related questions: "Where do I belong in the scheme of things, and what is my purpose?"

These questions in turn contain, at least implicitly, the ultimate question about identity: What is the human person in the context of the whole universe? What is the purpose of any person or all people together? These questions hold the possibility of full estrangement. Where primitive and archaic consciousness discovers individual problems and specific mysteries in life, historic consciousness discovers an awesomely large overall threat, namely, that we might ultimately not fit anywhere, have any ultimate purpose at all, or any ultimately meaningful identity. Historic consciousness discovers that the mystery of human identity is potentially infinite.

In order to find a secure and worthwhile identity, the historic culture has to discover ultimate answers to the problems of identity. That is to say it must find out how the human person relates to the infinite scope of reality. We do not worry about this on a daily basis. We live out a practical identity as persons who need to live, work, enjoy friends and family, and deal with our daily problems as they come. Yet, we live in a culture where the ultimate mystery of life has become an explicit part of the religions, the philosophies, and the literature that tell us who we are.

In response to ultimate questions, historic religions offer ultimate answers about who humans are and where we fit. The Hindu says we are not who we think we are, but we are of infinite worth because the true reality within us is Atman, which is Brahman. The Taoist says we are enfolded in the eternal ways of Tao and must learn to accept our humble status in relation to the eternal. The Jew, Christian, or Muslim says we are beings in the likeness of the infinite God or destined for eternal union with God. Each of these answers relates the identity of the individual to whatever is Ultimate.

There is one practical result of this type of historic thought worth mentioning here, though a later chapter will say more about it: historic religion conceives of the individual identity as being of special value. The extra consciousness of selfhood—"Who am I really?"—that is part of historic thought leads to a deeper concern for every individual self. The self-conscious self can dream of a perfect self, can aspire to infinite perfection. That means it can also feel more frustration, be hurt more deeply, despair more thoroughly. The historic religions find in this awareness of our self-consciousness a motive to be compassionate toward every human being. After all, we are all fellow sufferers and dreamers, all companions in the enormous mystery of life and selfhood. Each historic religion in its own way recommends that we treat every person as of equal value. Historic religion preaches concern, care, and compassion for every person. It grants to every person an identity of intense worth.

That is not enough, though, to eliminate our human feelings of anxiety about our identities. Every person is still liable to suffer some lack of purpose, some loss of self-esteem, some self-doubt. Among the best-selling books today are those that tell us how to get ahead, make friends, get rich. Selling equally well are the books telling us how to become better persons. They tell us how to change our thinking, educate our emotions, gain self-confidence, create a new self. The religions might tell us we are of immense worth but we do not find that enough. We continue to look for ways to improve not only our external social and economic status, but also our inner self. There is nothing new in that; the historic religions have been doing it since they began. There are many traditional religious texts giving instructions on how to transform the self. In the course of many hundreds of years, the historic religions have developed and tested some basic means to achieve a new, lasting, and basically valid selfhood. One thing the historic religions agree on is that this is not easy to do. Transformation of self is a long process.

PROCESSES OF SELF-TRANSFORMATION

Many new religious movements try to offer instant salvation from insecure identity. They let us in on the truth about "the real you." They accept us lovingly into a community of people who tell us we are valuable. They perform rituals to give us special status. But life goes on. We keep thinking and dreaming and worrying. Uncertainties recur. The same weaknesses and faults remain in us; the easy answers are not enough. Something deeper and more enduring seems to be needed. Over generations of trial and error historic religions have developed long-term methods of self-transformation.

A branch of Buddhist thought now known as Zen Buddhism is essentially a method of self-enlightenment. By meditations and instruction over the years a person comes to perceive that the structures and things of reality as we see them are all caught in self-contradiction and meaninglessness. When we truly come to perceive this, these Buddhists say, we will finally be close to release into nirvana. Similarly, the Confucian sage spends years in study and practice, imitating the wisdom of Confucius and generations of scholars until finally the sage achieves an ideal balance in life in conformity with li, right order. Likewise, Muslim and Jewish mystics spend years learning to contemplate God. Jewish and Muslim scholars devote lifetimes to absorbing the sacred laws imparted by God; they hope not merely to learn the law but to become one with it in their inner beings. These are long processes of inner transformation that integrate certain values, habits, or attitudes into the person's continuing identity. To give a clearer idea of how such processes can work, here are two further examples from two greatly different, yet somehow similar, historic cultures and religious traditions: Hindu yoga and Christian mysticism.

Hindu Yoga

The word "yoke," the collar joining two oxen or horses, comes from the same ancient word as yoga. A yoga is a means to achieve union with the supreme reality. One simple classification divides yoga into three types. Bhakti yoga is union through devotion, through special worship of a god or goddess who will help a person achieve union with Brahman. Karma yoga is the path of morally good action in conformity with the cosmic law of justice. By good behavior a person earns rebirth into a higher life, one close to attaining union with Brahman. The third type of yoga is jnana yoga, the way of contemplation.

The most widely-esteemed method of jnana yoga is one developed in the 2nd century B.C. by the Indian holy man Patanjali. His method is sometimes called raja or "royal" yoga because it is thought to be a noble way to achieve enlightenment and release into moksha, eternal salvation. The goal is to meditate on reality, self, and eternity until one truly recognizes that the real self is Atman-Brahman, and that this means there is no individual self. This yoga is a means to come face to face with one's true identity as not-self but Self (Atman). Anyone who achieves this recognition has already achieved union with Brahman-Atman, a unity that will become complete when the person dies. Through discovery of true Self, therefore, a person achieves eternal release from the self.

Patanjali's way is arduous and complex. It begins with learning moral goodness. When we have put aside all anger and jealousy and greed, we are ready to begin. Then we must release ourselves from even lesser attachments, all the little pleasures and irritations in life. This begins with a conscious asceticism, a deliberate denying to self any particular pleasures or comforts. After some years of practicing moral virtues and asceticism, a person will begin to lose all attachment and desires. The yogi, the one following the path of yoga, will become utterly indifferent to all pleasures and pain, all comfort and discomfort.

Meanwhile, as the yogi learns detachment, he or she also begins the practice of meditation. Detachment from pleasure and pain makes it possible to give oneself over to meditation more fully, but there are still other obstacles. A person's body can be a major source of distraction. Bodily cramps, a lack of oxygen, gas in the bowels, can all interfere with the yogi's concentration. A person must learn techniques of posture and breathing and bodily control that will eliminate internal distractions. The senses also must not be distracting. With training, the yogi will learn how to allow ears and skin to still function, perceiving sounds and pressures and heat, but in a way that does not distract the person. The yogi remains aware of the outside world, but his or her mind no longer pays any attention to it. The techniques of physical self-mastery are called hatha yoga.

There are yogis of sorts who have apparently mastered many of the techniques of controlling the body or ignoring pain, and who demonstrate their skills for the sake of attention or money. This is entirely contrary to Patanjali's advice. Anyone who still needs to receive attention, praise, or physical rewards is still obviously attached to this worldly maya that keeps us from our true eternal identity. The serious yogi will not be seen in the streets lying on a bed of sharp nails or walking on hot coals; the yogi who does such things has not yet begun to understand what true self and reality are.

The serious yogi will have learned moral goodness, detachment, and bodily control. Years of meditation will reveal the limits of self and the world. The meditation thereby leads eventually to insight, a clear recognition of the truth that the self and the world are maya. In time the insight will produce an inner experience of self as not-self but Self (Atman). The experience of Self is a moment of union with the infinite Atman, which is Brahman. This moment of union with the infinite will completely consume all the tiniest webs of desire, attachment, or illusion that might remain floating in far corners of the yogi's consciousness. When the yogi opens his or her eyes again after the moment of union has passed, he or she will still live on until natural death but will have no attachment of any kind. Family, home, and personal name will not exist for the yogi. When death comes, the inner emptiness of the yogi and the total lack of attachment assures that he or she will merge completely into Brahman's undifferentiated oneness, never to be born again. This is moksha, salvation. It is true Self, which is non-self.

Christian Monastic Mysticism

The previous chapter presented a brief description of the mystic who achieves a sense of belonging to God through union with God. To achieve this union with what is eternal, the Christian mystic must endure a training process and an inner transformation just as the Hindu yogi does in seeking a union with the eternal Brahman.

Near the beginning of the Christian era, some people decided that in order to be a perfect Christian and achieve salvation in this wicked and useless world, only thorough asceticism would be sufficient. In the deserts of Egypt there grew up small colonies of solitary ascetics. In Greek they were called *monachoi*, loners; from this the word "monks" evolved. Influenced perhaps by Gnostic dislike of the material world (see Chapter Five), the desert loners decided they must give up all physical pleasures. They ate and drank and slept very little, through hot days and cold nights with little protection against the climate. Through trial and error over generations, certain practical rules developed and were handed down on how to regulate one's own life in order to be morally good, undistracted by earthly concerns, and attached only to God. Eventually many of these rules were incorporated into organized bodies of regulations followed by whole communities of people. Individual people became organizers of such communities and the solitary ones of the desert became less solitary, as they banded together into homes for *monachoi*, known now in English as monasteries.

Like the yogi, the monk is supposed to practice morally correct behavior. The monk is to strive to avoid all sins. He is to practice kindness toward all the people he meets, but he is also to avoid too much contact with people. The main goal is holiness through an attachment only to God. The monk learns to avoid excessive food, drink, sleep, conversation; he learns to fill every idle moment with prayer rather than trifling conversation; he learns to see every event and person and thing as a form of the presence of God. Even as he learns to do all these things, the tradition warns, he will be tempted to become proud of his accomplishments, to be smug about how holy he is becoming. Such temptations are a sign that the person has only begun the long process of achieving holiness and has a long way to go.

A major goal that more and more monks as well as their feminine counterparts, the nuns, came to cherish was mystical union with God in prayer. They practiced what is usually called a life of prayer; but it is not a prayer that asks something from God; it is not even a conversation with God. While it is traditionally called prayer, it is more accurate to think of it as meditation. It requires years of training before a person can achieve mystical union in this way.

In one classic formulation, a person must first go through purification, a process of losing all attachment to pleasure, to one's own desires, to pride and self-love. Then a person has begun to enter the second stage, that of illumination. In this the potential mystic begins to discover that the God whom the monk or nun seeks in meditation is awesomely great, the infinite and eternal One. This involves realizing ever more clearly that God is not imaginable, not even conceptualizable. Illumination thereby turns out to be, in one famous metaphor, darkness. John of the Cross, a 16th-century Spanish mystic, proclaimed that a person reaches God only through a dark night of the soul. In this a person knows that even the powers of the human spirit are too limited to grasp God. This mystic proclaimed God's brightness to be so great as to utterly blind a person's mind. Those who say they can conceive God in their minds are therefore deceived. By this time the potential mystic may be entering into the third stage, the stage of unity, in which all desires and selfhood are left behind and the soul is so filled with the Infinite God that the person is as nothing. For a moment the person has become united with God, transformed and overwhelmed.

In the mysticism of the West, unlike that of India, the individual self retains his or her own identity. Jewish and Islamic mystics share this notion with Christianity, although all three sometimes speak as though the individual is completely dissolved in God. In the West, unlike in Hindu thought, a person does not have to become a mystic in order to achieve final salvation. Paradise or heaven or the kingdom of God are open to all morally good believers. Moral goodness alone, however, is difficult. Monasticism, even for those who are not mystics, is a way of life involving self-transformation through a long developmental process of moral growth, asceticism, and meditation.

For the Christian monk and Hindu yogi, the ultimate goal is to unite oneself with the infinite. In this union all forms of estrangement are eliminated because now the person is perfectly at home, united to the eternal truth, fulfilling the ultimate purpose of every person, achieving the fullness of what a human person can aspire to. But even as they work toward this ultimate goal, they are already achieving a sense of salvation. By dedicating themselves to the process of transformation, they already can feel they are giving their selfhood over to what alone is truly worth belonging to.

The Continuing Need for Long Effort

The two examples of long processes of transformation are centered on the concern to achieve inner union with the Absolute. In general, any and all attempts to establish inner transformation of one's selfhood involve long processes.

In primitive and archaic societies, only external behavior patterns require long conscious effort. Inner identity is taken for granted. Thus, the primitive hunter knows that only long practice with a spear creates real skill, but having an identity as a tribesperson is automatic. An artisan of an archaic culture knows it requires years of training to become an expert silversmith, but worthwhile identity is mainly a matter of being loyal to one's family and society.

When historic consciousness appears, it includes a more explicit inner self-consciousness, and with it the notion of perfect selfhood, an ideal self without any failings or unworthiness, a happy self without any fears and frustrations. Even if a person sees that no one manages to be perfect, the image of perfection, nonetheless, remains present in the culture. All this conspires to make a person restless to develop a better selfhood. Then experience begins to teach a person that such development requires years of effort.

This has remained true in modern times also, as we will be seeing. Modern thought is more this-worldly and does not seek mystical union with an other-worldly absolute. In the quest for ideal selfhood, however, modern thought still acknowledges a need for a long process of personal development, accomplished through hard effort, through an asceticism that includes a willingness to face years of reflection and experience.

The modern person, like people in all types of cultures, will still look for the quick fix. The primitive and the childish in us will expect that reading one or two insightful books, or finding the perfect philosophy, or engaging in a series of seminars by psychology experts, or joining the new cult with the answers to everything, will finally make us all right. Then it turns out that even the leaders of the cult or the new psychological advisors expect that only years of disciplined community life or years of seminars, analyses, and training will lead us to the sense of worth and belonging we seek. It is not easy to achieve the salvation that is the sense of ideal selfhood. In modern thought, in fact, a different idea will appear: one can be at peace even with one's imperfect self.

Summary
This chapter has surveyed some aspects of identity and religion. Identity is a problem because we are born without one. The question of identity was not explicitly asked in primitive cultures. Archaic cultures answered it by loyalty to the local gods and nations. Finally, historic cultures asked who we are *ultimately* in relation to the universal power or order behind all else, and even came to provide programs of growth toward our ultimate fulfillment.

END OF PART II

There are patterns running through the quest to achieve salvation through the numinous. One pattern is the set of observable stages of development from primitive to archaic, historic, and eventually, perhaps, the modern. This is a progress of awareness from local to universal, from home-ground awareness to a cosmic consciousness.

This is also a progression toward more and more self-awareness. The primitive sees little of his or her interior self, attributing even unwanted emotions to the actions of spirits. By historic times, humans learned how to mentally stand outside of self in order to look at self as this individual with certain needs, hopes, and fears. Consequently, the progression from primitive to historic times has also been a movement toward an ever deeper questioning of self. Where the primitive person need only look around to find the one natural (local) way to live, the historic person may have to connect together in one universal and coherent picture all the ways of life with ultimate justifications of it all.

All this means that the kind of salvation offered by religion, at each stage of religious and cultural development, must be adequate to the scope of awareness of people. A primitive person who is told that salvation consists of achieving nirvana or the beatific vision may worry whether there will be plenty of pigs and chickens there. A historic person who is assured that after death there is a pleasant valley for spirits to live in may want to ask whether there is any ultimate purpose to that.

Another pattern is the ongoing threefold dimension to the mystery we humans all face. These three are the questions of who we are, where and how we belong, and how the world we exist in can be made right for us. Problems of selfhood, relation to others (and the universe), and the conditions of our universe have constantly challenged people and made them wonder whether it makes sense (is intelligible) and has a purpose (is worthwhile). A consistent part of this pattern of human behavior has been the faith that, in spite of the mysteriousness, in spite also of confusion and evil, our existence is indeed intelligible and worthwhile. This is religious faith.

Primitive, archaic, and historic stages of culture have all included a firm religiousness, assured that the mystery is the realm of a numinous reality that provides a good world (here or to come), a proper and worthwhile place to belong, and a secure and worthy identity. Modern culture, as we will see, looks at times as though it is the first culture to lack this assurance. We live in an age when it is possible to doubt the existence not only of the spirits and gods, but even of God or any other such Ultimate. It is as though the modern segment of humankind is going to see whether it can face the mystery without religion.

Something like this has happened before, however. One of the charges on which Socrates was tried and condemned in Athens in 399 B.C. was the charge of atheism. His universalizing way of thought seemed to call into question belief in the gods. Jews and Christians were sometimes called atheists by the authorities of ancient Rome, because they refused to worship the gods. The axial age had introduced the idea of a God in the West as far back as the 6th century B.C. But it took many centuries before historic religiousness became so strong that it dominated politically. It then turned out that atheism, in the sense of disbelief in the gods, was actually a step to a new form of religious belief.

The modern way of thinking may also well be as Bellah describes it, not irreligious but a new stage of religiousness. Even in these somewhat skeptical times there is still endless mystery, there is still the need to discover who we are, where we belong, and how life can be made whole; and there still seems to be the underlying faith that even in the presence of mystery, somehow life does make meaningful sense. Even the modern era, as we will see, still has some lingering inclination to treat the infinite mystery as numinous and not as emptiness.

The most obvious kinds of salvation are concrete and limited—having a helpful God, for example, who can also provide life after death. Equally obvious are the human needs for various kinds of salvation, needs that arise out of our experiences of helplessness before death and life's unfairness, of being lost and alone, of lack of self-worth. Less obvious is the infinite depth of these needs. The mystery of where we are, how we fit in, what our purpose is, and where our happiness lies is an endless mystery. If none of the answers of historic religion is fully satisfying or fully convincing to some people in these modern times, they may nonetheless find that only a modern form of religiousness, not unreligiousness, is what they will seek.

All these ideas, however, have to wait upon later chapters for a fuller and clearer explanation concerning modern religiousness. Before that, there are other aspects of the religions of humankind that have to be surveyed to provide a better description of the ways we humans live our lives in the presence of mystery.

FOR FURTHER REFLECTION

1. Can you identity any particular patterns of human behavior that are clearly natural (inborn or conformed to nature) and not just invented? What are they?

2. Do you see it as good and valuable that people can establish a sense of worthy identity through their religion? Why? Why not?

3. What are the main social forces or groups or individuals that tell you who you are? Which of them are religious, if any?

4. Is there an ideal self you can imagine you might become through long effort? Is religion relevant to this? Explain.

5. What are your plans to develop your own selfhood in the years to come? If this strikes you as an odd question, explain why.

SUGGESTED READINGS

Margaret Mead, *New Lives for Old*, 1956; identity and belonging change in primitive or archaic groups.

Denise L. and John T. Carmody, *Ways to the Center*, 1981; see the sections of each chapter in Parts II and III entitled "Structural Analysis . . . self."

Robert S. Ellwood, Jr., *Introducing Religion from Inside and Outside*, 1978; ch. 1, Scenarios for the Real Self.

John Powell, *Why Am I Afraid to Tell You Who I Am?*, 1969.

Leonard Biallas, *Myths: Gods, Heroes, and Saviors*, 1986.

Robert C. Neville, *Soldier, Sage, Saint*, 1978; religious stages of individual identity.

John Hick, *An Interpretation of Religion*, 1989; chapter 3 on salvation as human transformation.

PART III

GUIDES TO LIFE

To the extent that we are unfinished animals, as Peter Berger says, we need to learn patterns for living; we need ideas and practices to guide us. Throughout history, religion has been the dominant source of guidance, at least up to recent times. Even in the relatively less religious modern culture, religion is often one of the strong sources of guidance in most people's lives. Religion does this in many ways. In the next four chapters we will survey some of them: moral rules, sacred texts and leaders, rituals and symbols, and rational reflection about beliefs and practices.

Those who are committed to a specific religious tradition will normally follow its moral rules, respect the traditional texts and leaders, participate in symbolic rituals, and learn the formal religious thought. They will do these things because it is expected, because such practices together seem to make up the religion. A person does all these things because that is what belonging to the specific religious tradition entails. Jews observe the Sabbath, Christians the Lord's Day, and Muslims do the same for Fridays. Hindus do not eat meat, while Jews and Muslims do not eat pork.

What is less obvious is that participation in all these practices has an educational function. Together the symbols and rituals and texts and leaders and moral rules and religious reflection constitute a guidance system. They sum up an interpretation of what life is in relation to the ultimate mysteries. They explain the origin and order and purpose of things. They offer an understanding of where estrangement comes from and how to overcome it. By participating in all the practices and forms of a religion, people take on its world-view as their own, often to an extent they do not realize. The world is "mediated" to them by religion; that is, the reality of things is presented to them in a certain way through the medium of religion. Religion thereby guides them in how they understand themselves and their relations to others and to the universe.

Religion is not the only source of interpretations which guide life. There are non-religious moral visions, leaders and texts, rituals and symbols, and rational analyses of things. Some are informal and unorganized. Thus we all learn pieces of how to interpret life from television programs, the common prejudices of school friends, a favorite magazine or comic book. Other interpretations are more thoroughly formulated, as in non-religious philosophies like those of The American Humanist Association's Manifestos. Not all world-views are constructive ones. The crude, distorted, and angry world-view of the Ku Klux Klan is an example of a destructive one, though it presents itself as a religious perspective.

Whether reality is interpreted for us by religious or non-religious sources, organized or informal ones, we must learn some interpretation of reality on which we can then build more of our own life, in full harmony with what we have learned or in opposition to it to some degree. We cannot construct a whole universe of ideas and meanings and values for ourselves all alone. Even when we feel that we are rejecting our tradition and our upbringing, we still reproduce much of it in our own lives. In the next chapters we will see some of the ways this happens, especially through religion.

CHAPTER EIGHT

What Should I Do and Why?

Religion and Morality

THE PROBLEM OF MORALITY

One of the great mysteries of life is knowing what makes something good or bad. We do not usually experience this as a mystery because there are various human drives and many societal standards that tell us what is good or bad to do. Inner drives such as hunger tell us to eat; external standards tell us to wipe our noses and not to beat on our neighbor's head. Yet everyone experiences some confusion sooner or later about what is really good or bad.

Any discussion of morality is soon tied up in a thousand complexities of religious tradition, individual reasonings, societal prejudice, personal psychology, and so on. It is notoriously difficult to sort out not just what is good or bad, but even what "good" basically means. Each religious tradition will have its ideas on this, and its own code of behavior, one related in some way to a numinous reality.

To help sort it out, this chapter will rely on some developmental theories concerning moralities, theories that fit fairly well with the theory of cultural and religious development proposed by Robert Bellah. The theories of moral development used here are those of the French philosopher and psychologist, Jean Piaget, and the later work of an American, Lawrence Kohlberg. Aspects of these theories are disputed and some of the ideas in this chapter are further speculation based on those disputed theories, so caution is wise here. The theories, however, do provide a useful and illuminating way of sorting out the complexities involved.

Different Types of Morality

To some extent, the type of morality varies with the stages of culture and religion. Primitive culture and religion have dominant notions of what makes something good or bad that are different from the notions dominant in historic or modern cultures. Each of us individually also goes through stages of personal development, with different standards of morality dominating in the different stages. Our notion of good and bad at the age of seven is quite different usually from what it is at the age of seventeen.

To make it all even more complex, each of us retains our past standards to some extent, so that as we mature we end up with a collection of different moral standards operating in us. Thus sometimes like any seven year old, we avoid lying only because we are afraid of getting caught in a lie, but other times we do it out of a more adult conviction that honesty is something that people owe to one another. Cultures are more complicated than individuals, so they also have many different moral standards operating in them at once.

There are four different types of moralities that will be described here, in the order that they seem to appear in the development of each person's life. The first is called "taboo morality," an egocentric concern for one's own pleasure and which defines as "bad" only those things for which a person gets punished in some way. The second is called "acceptance morality," based on a seemingly natural human desire to be approved by and to fit in with a certain group of people as one's own group. A third kind is "universal laws morality," based on a supposition that there are certain objectively valid moral norms which all people everywhere ideally ought to follow. Finally, there is a "basic value morality," which claims that the best foundation for any moral judgment is whether in the long run it will best serve the basic value of general human well-being, whether it helps people rather than hurts them. Each of these four kinds of morality has been part of religious traditions.

TABOO MORALITY

Taboo Morality in General

Psychologist Lawrence Kohlberg characterized our earliest childhood morality as "egocentric." A morally egocentric person is one who calls things good if they feel good to that person, and labels something bad only if it causes pain or discomfort to that person. Stealing is bad, according to this attitude, only if you get punished for it when you get caught at it. If there is a way to steal that results only in profit without pain to the person doing the stealing, then stealing is good for that person. There is no morality except to discover the list of things that earn punishment, and then to figure out how to avoid that punishment but still get as much pleasure as possible.

This is a morality that is a collection of specific rules, learned one at a time, about what feels good to do and what results in pain or punishment. It is similar to the list of "taboos" that a primitive person learns, or to the list of "no-no's" that a child learns.

This taboo morality is one in which intentions do not count. If a person breaks a rule, violates the taboo, does a no-no, then punishment follows. The exception to this is that the taboo moralist sometimes learns that *other* people think that intentions are quite important, and uses this knowledge to try to avoid punishment. "I didn't mean to do it" is a plea that the taboo moralist can use in order to manipulate others, even when in fact the taboo moralist definitely did mean to do it but just hoped to be able to get away with it.

Taboo morality provides some support for the social order by threatening lawbreakers with punishment. If a society has many people who seek personal pleasure, regardless of what the effects are on other people, society will be a jungle of competing desires. Rules for social order enforced by threat of punishment will counterbalance individual pleasure seeking. This way of upholding social order is limited, though. If people are motivated only by personal pleasure and not by any concern for others, they will seek ways to break the rules without getting caught.

Taboo Morality in Children

As young children we all lived by a taboo sort of mentality. Up to the age of five or six, we defined "bad" simply as whatever we would be punished for. Even when the rules did not make any sense, they were simply to be obeyed. A four-year-old child knows it is wrong to lie, without understanding very well what a lie is or why it is bad. Grown-ups get upset when you say things that are not true, so do not do it.

Little children do not believe in the value of good intentions. Piaget told a story to little children about two little girls who played with their mother's scissors and some cloth. Alice wanted to help her mother but cut a large hole in the cloth by accident. Jane knew she was not supposed to play with scissors but did it anyway just for fun and cut a small hole in the cloth. When Piaget asked little children whether Alice or Jane should be punished, the children said that both of them should be punished. Alice's good intentions are irrelevant. In fact, the children agreed that Alice should be punished more because she cut a bigger hole in the cloth than Jane did.

Social order among small children would dissolve into chaos were there no adults. Children are short-term pleasure seekers, willing to make deals with one another at times, but not too reliably. Two of them exchange toys, but one of them tries to end up with both toys. This basically egocentric impulse is evident in the common technique parents use for dividing a piece of pie or cake. One child cuts the cake; the other gets first choice. The one cutting will cut with tongue-bending precision, sure that whoever gets first choice will of course choose the bigger piece. The one cutting does not want to give away a single crumb more than necessary.

Some children learn from their context to think of life as full of dangerous forces that punish you. Children beaten by their parents grow up to experience the world that way. So also do children who are punished and rewarded inconsistently by parents who are moved easily by moods of anger or irritation. Like primitive people, children assume that events have causes that make sense and that the world is supposed to work right if you follow the correct order. Children reason that if they feel pain it must be due to something they did wrong. If something really bad happens, such as a divorce or the death of a parent, the child tends to feel that this is a punishment the child has some-how deserved. Not yet able to tell themselves that maybe the world is wrong or that the parents are wrong, such children be-gin to feel that there must be something basically wrong with them as persons.

Primitive Culture and Taboo Morality

Because all human beings begin their lives as children, all of us have taboo morality as part of our life-story. Primitive people are no exception to this. Because primitive and archaic cultures do not have *explicit* universal laws morality or basic value morality, as we will see, the other two kinds of morality stand out more clearly in these cultures. That makes primitive culture especially a good place to look to see what taboo morality would look like if it were a dominant morality in a culture.

All of us are inclined to think that things that please us are good, and things that harm us are bad. The primitive person agrees. "Good" is what feels good, earns a reward, receives praise. "Bad" is what hurts, what you get punished for. If stealing from a neighboring tribe does not cause you any harm, then it is all right to do it. If being kind to a stranger results in sickness in your house, then it is bad to be kind to strangers.

Just as primitive cultures live by collections of folk tales that describe the pieces of reality, they also live by collections of rules that have to be learned one at a time and obeyed one at a time. The primitive person has an overall concern to live correctly and thereby make life go smoothly. What constitutes living correctly is contained in a set of customs and stories handed on from the days of the ancestors. The story of the man who slept with his sister and was then turned into a goat is a story that instructs about the dangers of incest. The traditional saying that those who light their neighbor's cooking fire (meddle in their neighbor's affairs) will carry their neighbor's sores (will be the one treated meanly by spirits who are actually angry at the neighbor) is a saying that in-structs people about good social behavior. (It is also a saying as obscure as many such sayings are, even to the tribespeople them-selves at times.)

There are various motives at work to make primitive people observe the customs. An obvious incentive to keep the rules is threat of punishment from a person's neighbors. If you kill a man, his relatives may seek to kill you or members of your family in re-turn, or demand repayment in the form of some cattle and will threaten to kill you if you do not pay up. This concern to avoid personal punishment is a taboo type of morality.

There are also often punishments from the realm of the numinous that visit those who break certain rules. Sometimes it is a mana-power that is triggered automatically by violation of the customs. Belief that breaking a mirror brings bad luck is a modern form of this. Other times it may be the spirits, especially those of the original ancestors, who punish people for violations. Fear of punishment by the numinous is a more explicitly religious form of taboo morality.

Some acts carry their own punishment in an obvious everyday way. Sticking your hand in the fire hurts. Punching your neighbor in the nose is liable to earn you your own bloody nose. But most of the harm that comes to a primitive person does not result from such obvious causes. You stumble and break a toe. A bag full of berries breaks, scattering them all over. Your skin erupts in sores; your children are crippled by disease; your tribe starves in a drought. All of these are bad because they hurt. The primitive tribesperson does not believe that they can be random accidents. There is a reason for everything that happens. If the cause is not an obviously visible one, then it must be a mysterious numinous power at work. If harm comes to a person in any form, the primitive person reasons, then some spirit has done it, or it has been caused by dangerous mana-power that someone has misused. When the numinous is dangerous, as it often is, it is labeled "taboo."

In fairness to primitive people, it is important to note that another motive they have for keeping the rules is their social value. The rule that forbids killing a fellow tribesperson is useful to keep the tribe functioning well, gathering its food harmoniously, and defending its territory. Primitive people recognize the need for social peace and harmony in the tribe rather than anger and fights. They recognize that the customs help to preserve this social order and they will support the customs for this reason, and not just out of fear of punishment by the numinous or from each other.

Nevertheless, the primitive tribes that have had firm belief in the numinous forces behind the customs or in the punishing power of the spirits may be more likely to survive. The spirits can see who cheats on social rules and can make sure that no one really escapes punishment. The person who has cheated will worry that the spirits will soon inflict harm. Within a few weeks, of course, some harm is bound to befall the person. That will confirm the belief that the spirits uphold the tribal order and thereby give people an extra reason to conform to that order as the right way to live. (This also illustrates the ideas in Chapter Two about how belief in the numinous supports the social order and also provides greater security for the identity of the person who has learned how to act as a human on the basis of that social order.)

Life gives concrete evidence to primitive people which suggest that intentions are not very important to the invisible powers. A person tries to save a child from drowning but is drowned in the process. A person who goes out in the rain to help another is killed by lightning. People who steal and kill but do not offend the spirits, live long healthy lives. There is much evidence to primitive people that the numinous powers that run things and cause things to happen do not really care about our intentions.

Many rules of taboo morality are externally imposed restrictions that the primitive person does not usually expect to be able to understand. The rules exist. If it were clear that they served some higher purpose, then the intention to achieve that purpose might count—even when the person failed or did something wrong by mistake. But the rules often are just there. They represent how life is and what is dangerous to do; that is all. Laws, morality, and codes of behavior are one and the same thing: part of the collection of instructions on how to behave in order to avoid getting hurt, especially by the numinous powers, and to keep social peace.

Archaic Culture and Taboo Morality

Archaic cultures are more complex than primitive ones are. Their stories include long myths that explain how the world came to be long ago through the great actions or struggles of the gods, and how the gods now rule the world, establishing the kings and laying down the rules that people must follow. But taboo fears remain as a major motivation to observe the rules. In the days of King David of Israel and Judah, for example, about 1000 B.C., archaic times for these people then, a man named Uzzah tried to save the sacred ark, the throne of Yahweh, from injury when it was about to fall. As a result of this well-intentioned act, Uzzah died. The throne was taboo to ordinary people. In touching it, Uzzah had touched mana-power too strong for him. The people thought that Yahweh had struck down Uzzah for daring to touch the sacred ark. Rules are rules, not to be broken, regardless of intention or purpose.

The great literate archaic civilizations used their writing abilities to create a detailed body of laws. The laws were codified, put into formal lists that could be used by judges for deciding legal cases brought to them. To some extent, this removed some of the laws from the control of religion and made them mainly secular or civil matters. Yet civil contracts were still signed in the temple of a god or sworn to in the presence of a god, with offerings made to the god to be a witness to the contract. Whoever violated the contract would thereby incur the anger of the god at having his or her name used in vain. This insult to the god would result in punishment to the offender. So the motive to be honest would still be taboo motivation, fear of punishment, and one based on religious belief.

Taboo Morality in Adults Today

It is not just children and primitive and archaic people who live by taboo morality and motivation. Everyone probably follows some rule or other for no other reason than out of a fear of punishment. Many sexual rules have functioned in this way. The religious ban on masturbation was long supported by nothing more in many people's minds than threats of punishments. It will cause pimples or insanity, some said; others declared that God would send a person to hell eternally for such a deed. Some rules imposed under the threat of punishment might be good rules, but if a person obeys them for no other reason than fear of punishment, that is a taboo morality motivation.

There are also a good number of people in places as diverse as prison, the United States Congress, and neighborhood used car lots whose basic moral sense is to do whatever is rewarding as long as they can avoid getting caught and punished. "Fast-buck" operators who swindle the elderly out of their savings seem unmoved by the suffering they cause. They even seem unembarrassed at getting caught and publicly exposed. Avoiding prison or a fine is all that is important to them. They believe others would do the same as they did, if only the others felt they could avoid getting caught. Everyone is looking for a self-serving angle on life, the taboo moralists figure. They do not seem to be able to recognize that other people have a moral motivation that is not so selfish. Many of these modern taboo moralists can be rather intelligent, as is true also of primitive taboo moralists, but somehow their life's context has kept them confined to a moral vision that is scarcely moral at all, just a desire for personal gain, regardless of others, as long as they can avoid any punishment.

Even among religious people today, there are taboo moralists who obey God or the gods only because the divine beings have power to reward and punish. Their formal beliefs may be drawn from a historic religion, but their way of understanding those beliefs can be primitive or childlike. A punishing God who passes laws to be obeyed regardless of whether they make sense is a God who fits well with taboo morality. Those who believe that society can be held together only by belief in a God who punishes offenders may be taboo moralists who do not expect anyone to obey moral rules for any reason except to avoid divine punishment.

ACCEPTANCE MORALITY

The Need for Acceptance

Another type of morality is that which is based on our human need to be accepted by others, to be approved, cherished, praised, or honored. This need for acceptance can be part of taboo morality in that it may function as just an egocentric desire to get attention or to avoid the irritation of being mocked. But the need for acceptance also leads a person to get beyond such narrow self-interest and to find some fulfillment through participation in a community of people. We give a group of people our loyalty and expect to receive their support in return. At times this motivates us to sacrifice our own individual interests for the good of the group. It can produce great heroism. It can also, however, lead to bigotry and mistreatment of those who do not belong to the group, and especially to those who are perceived to be the enemies of the group in some way.

There are many kinds of groups. We all tend to have a strong allegiance to our families, feeling protective toward them even if they are wrong in disputes with other. In many cultures the clan is the basic unity of society. All those who are related to you, even if they are your uncle Abner's grandchildren or second cousin Bertha's husband, are to receive some degree of special treatment. Patriotism is also a form of group loyalty. So is loyalty to the members of your street gang. In each case the need for acceptance has its corresponding price of loyalty to those who accept us and make us significant by giving us a worthy group to belong to.

Where the need to find acceptance through allegiance to a group is strong, leaders and heroes will be unusually important. Stories told of heroes will exemplify the virtues of loyalty and courageous defense of the group and its ways. Certain individuals will provide a focus for the group, promoting its beliefs and values, bestowing approval on this person or that as a valued member of the group. The nation has its king or president; the street gang has its leader; a religion has its authority figures. (See the next chapter for more on religious leaders.)

Forms of the Need for Acceptance in the Individual

Kohlberg describes a stage in the moral development of the individual in which a child seeks to be accepted by the people around the child, primarily the parents but also adult relatives and teachers. This is the "good boy and girl" stage in Kohlberg's language. We have already talked about this need for acceptance in the chapters on belonging and on identity. Children need to know that their parents will not give them away or abandon them, that their parents love them even while the parents beat them. Children also become confused and angry when people make fun of them. Primitive people also, like all of us, have a strong desire to be accepted by others in their group, to be praised rather than mocked. Sometimes this need for acceptance will manifest itself only in the self-centered concern typical of taboo morality. But at other times it will lead to a much greater concern about the whole group of people to whom we belong.

In early adolescence our need for acceptance becomes more consciously important. We feel a desperate need to conform to group standards in order to be one of the crowd, in order to be thought normal instead of weird. We experience the common human need to achieve a sense of self-worth through acceptance by others around us. Perhaps we are mainly self-centered in this; but perhaps we also begin to feel some sense of greater devotion to others, of loyalty to the group.

The need for acceptance and the impulse to give our loyal support to those to whom we belong remain part of a person throughout life. Acceptance morality is, therefore, part of every person and of every culture. But it may be outweighed by other types of moral motivation such as those that emerge in historic and modern culture, as well as in later stages of individual development. Acceptance morality is more clearly visible in archaic cultures, before other forms of morality take on the explicit importance they will achieve in later forms of culture (or in later stages of individual development).

Acceptance Morality in Archaic Cultures

Among archaic people as among adolescents, the virtues that are considered praiseworthy are the group virtues of loyalty to one's own people, dedication to the causes of the group, and trustworthiness and honesty in dealing with others in the same group. To be found disloyal or a traitor brings shame and dishonor. To look out for only selfish interests is ignoble. While acceptance morality is by no means confined to archaic cultures, it stands out in such cultures as a dominant morality. These are cultures of loyalty and heroism and honor.

A stress on honor is a major manifestation of acceptance morality in the late archaic style of culture. Honor even becomes a sacred thing, to be guarded and protected against anything that might profane it. The purpose in going off to battle is to gain honor. Those who die in battle receive the greatest honor, because they have sacrificed themselves for the good of the group. On the other hand, to be dishonored is the greatest evil. No person is worse than the coward, who places personal safety above the needs of those to whom he or she should be loyal. To be thus dishonored is to be shamed or to lose face. In some cultures only suicide can clear a dishonored family name or resolve the tension incurred by loss of face. Whether a person dies a hero or by suicide in shame, this kind of moral motivation may require great sacrifices by a person. "Death before dishonor."

Archaic cultures (or the archaic element in any culture) will look to a leader. Primitive culture has no formal leader. Tribespeople sit and talk and come to a consensus, albeit with some individuals more persuasive or stronger than others. Historic cultures, as we will see, suppose that there is a body of law that is superior to individual leaders. But the archaic style of culture knows no good way to make society cohere than to find a strong leader to whom people may give their loyalty and who will reward them with special attention when it is earned by devotion. This style of thought thinks that it is legitimate to break the law in service to one's leader. Laws appear to them only as taboos, of less moral value than loyalty and honor. It often does not occur to them that laws may deserve more reverence than a leader. The section on historic culture and universal laws morality will explain more about this.

Loyalty to the Group

Unlike taboo morality, acceptance morality tends to value good intentions. A person who means well is one who is loyal and supportive, one who can be trusted. The loyal person may make mistakes or prove to be not very competent, but that person's good intentions are enough to compensate for most other failings. Taboo moralists are not too surprised by the neighbor who falsely pretends to be friendly or the trader who cheats. After all, who wouldn't do such things? Acceptance moralists are upset by such double dealing; it is a sign of untrustworthiness. The liars, the hypocrites, those whose intentions do not match their masks of honesty and innocence are bad people. Of course, it is often all right if one of the group or clan lies and cheats to outsiders, because outsiders do not count for much.

The acceptance moralist gives over much of his or her identity to the group. This person can feel worthwhile only if the group is worthwhile. In defense of his of her own belongingness and identity, therefore, the acceptance moralist does not merely praise loyalty above all virtues, but also praises his or her group over all other groups: "We are the noble, the true, the sacred band; others are inferior, mistaken, or evil." This is the original meaning of "chauvinism," believing that what belongs to one's own group or kind is naturally superior.

Every group has members who promote, either maliciously or thoughtlessly, a kind of bigotry that derides others simply to bolster their sense of the value of their own group and of their identity with it. Acceptance moralists are also most likely to feel threatened by any member of the group who seems to place some other value before blind loyalty. The person who criticizes some aspect of the gang or tribe or religion or nation is a threat to the person who is strongly driven by a need for clear standards of what the group wants and lives by.

Motivated by a need for acceptance, a person tends to feel that right and wrong, the very standards of good and evil, are identical with the group's identity and customs. Many rules of the group might be ones an outsider would judge as wise or practical, but that is not the motivation behind acceptance morality. Whether the rules are wise or foolish, practical or impractical, easy or hard, humane or cruel, matters little. The rules and standards are felt to be correct because they are those of the group. If an outsider challenges the group values, the group will draw together in self-defense, regardless of how reasonable the outsider's claim is. Only if there is a consensus within the group for some change, if the leaders or heroes whom the others use as their model recommend some change, will the group be able to adopt new ways. The motivation for this to maintain a sense of belonging and acceptance.

Acceptance Morality and Religion

The person whose main desire and value is to achieve acceptance can find it very fulfilling to belong to a religious group. The group's beliefs and rules will provide clear standards for the person on how to remain worthy of acceptance. Ordinary churches will not be so attractive as sects, cults, or some select clique within a church. A sect or cult more clearly defines itself by contrast with other religious groups or with people in general. The sect or cult thereby provides a more sharply defined group to give loyalty to and to receive acceptance from.

Religious ties based on acceptance morality will tend to focus on religious leaders and heroes as symbols of the group's standards and as focal points of the group's authority. Wherever the leader takes them they may follow with fervor, even to their deaths. The acceptance moralist will most likely join a new religious group or become part of a heretical or schismatic group not because of abstract beliefs, but because the group has a leader upon whom a person can focus as the bearer of truth and godliness.

The allegiance toward a certain religious movement may include intolerance toward other groups, such as a firm conviction that all nonbelievers are going to damnation. This belief also serves to fortify a sense of belonging; to praise one's own group as the source of true salvation is act of faith and loyalty to the group.

Among the various numinous powers, it is the personal and attentive gods or God who will be of greatest interest to the person who values mainly acceptance as a standard for knowing right and wrong. The acceptance moralist turns to a God or gods who love people in spite of their mistakes, provided only that they are loyal followers of the authority of the religious leaders and defenders of the beliefs of the group as the unchangeable truth. If there is still some fear of punishment for mistakes or sins, a fear continuing on from an earlier life-stage when taboo morality dominated the person's thoughts and feelings, this fear may be balanced by a loving trust in the care the gods or God is bound to show toward a devoted follower.

The acceptance-minded person will expect that good intentions, sincere faith, and feelings of devotion are important enough to earn acceptance, forgiveness, and love from God or the god.

Pure Land Buddhists in Japan say that merely to invoke the name of Amida-Buddha in an act of trust in this divine being is enough to earn life in paradise after death. Catholic Christians trust to the loving help of the saints, especially the Blessed Virgin Mary; many Protestant Christians emphasize a trusting faith in God as basis of salvation. The bhakti yoga of Hindu thought says that acts of devotion and praise toward the god, whether Krishna, Shiva, Kali or some other, can compensate for lack of moral exactness in behavior. One would expect to find such ideas especially strong in a person who sees loyalty and devotion to be the highest moral values (though these religious ideas may also be part of a more complex belief-system).

Acceptance Morality Is Both Good and Bad

Acceptance morality is a normal kind of human motivation. We can guess that over the last fifty thousand years of human development any innate impulse to loyalty to one's own kind and kin could be a powerful help to preserve the lives of the people of the group. Sociobiologists, who investigate how much our behavior is guided by our genes, claim that we may have born into us some inclination to help out those who are like us or those with whom we have been raised. Whether this is so or not, we certainly act with passionate loyalty at times when our family or friends are threatened.

Acceptance morality has much that is good in it. The loyalty that motivates a person to sacrifice pleasure or safety for the good of others seems praiseworthy. Dedication to a God who is loving and accepting rather than vengeful seems to be a humane way to live.

But acceptance morality also has its bad side. It may sustain the tendency to see outsiders as inferior or dangerous. This tendency is a source of antagonism that manifests itself in ways ranging from petty bigotry all the way to war against the evil enemy. Like many human things, acceptance morality is both good and bad.

But if you agree with that statement, it raises a question: how do you know what is good and what is bad about acceptance morality or, for that matter, about taboo morality? What standards of good and bad are you using to make that judgment? One of the possibilities is that you have learned and grown accustomed to another basis for making moral judgments, one that does not clearly appear in history until historic cultures develop. That is the morality of universal laws.

THE MORALITY OF UNIVERSAL LAWS

Taboo morality is self-seeking and self-centered. Acceptance morality has a concern for self also, but it achieves acceptance through loyalty toward others. A third kind of morality also achieves a sense of self-esteem, but it does this by measuring self against what it sees as a set of objective and universally valid moral standards. It is a morality which is worked out explicitly for the first time in historic cultures, the cultures that begin to reflect systematically on the universal structure and order of things.

A sign that a culture has developed a strong historic element is the development of a moral vision that seeks perfection. Thus historic cultures tend to look outside of this world for salvation because they want something more perfect than earthly existence could provide. Similarly in ethics there is a tendency for historic religions to propose a morality of absolute laws that everyone in theory should always obey, even though in practice people can never fully adhere to such laws, as we will talk about when we consider the disadvantages of universal laws morality.

The Idea of Universal Objective Norms

Truly objective and universally valid moral norms would be standards that are valid whether anyone agrees with them or not. If such moral standards exist, a person could use them to judge whether a given group, even the person's own clan, nation, or religion, is right or wrong. In theory, therefore, these standards can overrule the standards of acceptance morality.

Universally valid standards apply to everyone, everywhere, in all situations; they show no favoritism to one group over another or one person over another. Every person's moral rightness could be measured by such standards. We live in a time when belief in such standards has diminished. We are accustomed to hearing that every person has his or her own morality. Universal laws morality insists, however, that regardless of what people think, there is as a matter of fact just one true and universal set of moral laws, which all people ought to obey.

Universal laws morality does not necessarily include any specific laws different from what taboo morality or acceptance morality might impose. The basic difference lies not so much in which laws are to be obeyed as it does in how universally the laws are said to be applied. A law against cannibalism is not a universal law if it forbids eating only your neighbor but allows for hearty meals whenever strangers stumble by. It is common enough in history for a group of people to try to forbid killing and stealing among themselves but to allow wholesale plunder and murder of outsiders for pleasure and profit.

At some point in a culture's development, however, it may extend its basic moral rules to all people. The ancient Hebrews, for example, in their archaic days were not surprised that their god, Yahweh, insisted on a set of laws and rituals that were not the same as the ones that followers of Marduk had to obey. But by the time of the Babylonian exile many of the Jewish prophets interpreted some of the laws given by Yahweh in a new way. The laws against killing, stealing, and lying, the laws demanding justice and honesty in human affairs, were recognized as laws that all people everywhere should follow. What had been only the tribal laws of an archaic society became the universal laws of a historic religion. The prophet Isaiah dreamed of a wonderful social order, with justice and equal protection for all people, that would result from obeying the universally applicable laws of God. Because the Jewish people could share those laws with everyone, Isaiah promised that Judaism would become a light to all nations.

The Advantage of Universal Laws

Universal laws are supposed to be obeyed by everyone, everywhere, under all conditions. Most people have some familiarity with this kind of morality. Many people have been told at some time that it is always wrong for anyone to steal or that no one should ever tell a lie. Most people today usually believe it is legitimate at times to make an exception to the rules, but a totally universal morality supposedly does not allow for exceptions. Once exceptions are tolerated in any cases at all, the principle has been established that the laws are not fully universal, that exceptions are possible. There is then the practical problem that more and more exceptions may be granted until law and order breaks down. Strict adherence to universal law can be a strong defense against anarchy. The rules are supposed to be followed, though, because they are objectively right and not just because they are means to preserve law and order.

Universal laws promote equal justice. Everyone is to be judged according to the law and not according to social status or political influence. This is the principle that allows the poor and the rich equal rights; not even a king or president is above the law. It is not easy to enforce this principle. Money and power can bend rules. But the principles of equality set the standard to live up to. Where archaic style of thought is willing to make exceptions for the powerful or the famous, for the leaders and the heroes, historic cultures seek to establish the primacy of law over status, promoting the ideal of equal justice for all under the law.

Universal laws morality functions as a challenge to a culture and its people to be always better than they have been, simply because no culture has lived up to such a morality perfectly. No matter how necessary it might seem at some time to lie or steal, universal laws morality stands as a constant reminder that all such things represent a failure in human existence, that such things can never be simply accepted but must always be regretted, that there must be an unending search to find ways to avoid violation of the ideals expressed in the universal laws. Universal laws morality can be very difficult to apply, but attempts to follow it can have a good effect on a culture.

Universal laws are expressions of some basic insights about human life. It is always a bad thing when someone is killed by another. Even a person favoring capital punishment can say that each time a criminal is executed it is genuinely bad that such an extreme solution is necessary. In each case it is a terrible part of life that one person's life is sacrificed. Likewise, it is always a bad thing when someone steals, no matter how valid the justification. Even if it is necessary to steal in some situations, it still is true that there is unjust loss to one person, that more mistrust has been created, that it is sad such stealing should ever be necessary. The basic insight of universal laws morality is that such things as killing and stealing are always bad in some respect. A universal laws morality takes this insight and transforms it into a set of laws. If killing a person is always bad in some way, then it should always be forbidden, the reasoning goes.

With the shift to a historic style morality of universal ethics comes another change, to a different definition of the individual person. The egocentric kind of individualism of taboo morality is a primitive one, where each person simply does what he or she has to in order to avoid pain and find pleasure. This is followed by acceptance morality, which subordinates the individual to the group. Universal laws morality develops a new kind of individualism, wherein the individual person can now measure her or his own identity and value by comparing self to the universal standards. Each of us, in a universal laws morality, can choose to adhere to the high ideals the laws present, ideals of not cheating, lying, stealing, or killing, and take some measure of individual pride in ourselves no matter whether anyone else knows or praises us or not. Each of us can then stand as an individual, guided by principles that transcend our culture, presumably, against the egocentrism and against the crowd-pleasing inclinations in and around us.

Universal Laws Morality and Religion

It is when a religious tradition reaches its historic stage that universal laws morality is most likely to flourish. In many cases ideas from archaic times were the base upon which the later morality was built. Belief in a Yang/Yin order in nature goes back to archaic times in China. Perhaps so does belief in the right order called li. The idea of karma existed in India before the axial age. Egyptian belief in maat, the proper order to all things, is very ancient. Greek belief in a fate that rules everything predates the axial age. Such beliefs provided a basis eventually for a more historic formulation.

In late archaic cultures around the world, need for some explicit basis for law and order and overall social coherence became greater as the cultures became more complex. The great kingdoms of China, India, Mesopotamia, and Egypt all had to find ways to unify diverse elements of vast populations with different traditions. Sheer force works only for a time. Human beings can grow restless unless someone makes sense out of the order of things by showing why things are, and should be, just the way they are.

We can speculate that perhaps this practical need to articulate some basis for overall and unifying social order gave cultures the drive to discover universals. Perhaps the need to provide justification for the laws, customs, and morality that an empire imposes on various people pushed them into the axial age and into universalizing consciousness. Perhaps. At any rate, out of archaic beliefs in the will of the gods, fate, li, and karma, there materialized the historic moral systems of universal laws.

By the 3rd century B.C., for example, the ancient Stoics discovered a morality built into nature. They perceived a divine pattern in nature, a cosmic structure that included human life. They called it the divine *Logos* (word or rational order); sometimes they even called it "Zeus," although they did not think of it as really being the anthropomorphic sky-god. To conform to the *Logos* of nature is to live naturally, they said, and therefore wisely.

Stoic thought is still influential in some forms of Christian morality today. To Stoic thought Christians added the belief that God created nature. To behave naturally, therefore, is to act in conformity with God's will. The Catholic church still reflects a somewhat Stoic "natural law morality" in its rules about sex. By its very nature according as God made it, the reasoning goes, sex is for the purpose of producing children. Therefore any sexual activity that deliberately excludes the possibility of pregnancy is unnatural activity. God made nature, so unnatural activity is contrary to God's will. What is against nature is always intrinsically wrong. Therefore, the Catholic church concludes, artificial contraception is contrary to the nature of sex and is always intrinsically wrong, as are masturbation and homosexuality for the same reason.

The full force of universal laws morality, though, is not found just by looking at particular conclusions. By itself each law is just a law; but in the historic religions it is part of a universal harmony. To adhere to one law can be to put yourself in touch with what you believe to be the order of the cosmos. To build a life upon the set of laws may seem to integrate your life into a vast unity of all things. When universal laws morality is part of a religious vision, it is a way to create an identity and a belonging that unites the person to the all-encompassing supreme Reality, to the infinite and numinous Source of life and nature, of their order and purpose. To conform to a universal laws morality is not merely to be good, it is to belong to God or to the Eternal.

Difficulties With Universal Laws

In spite of the advantages cited, there are problems with any universal laws morality. One is that rules and attitudes from taboo and acceptance morality tend to get mixed in with the universal laws. Every historic religion is made up of a mixture of people, some of whom operate more on the basis of taboo and acceptance motivation. Every historic religion is also the continuation of some culture's tradition and retains within it many ideas and values from archaic and even primitive times. The universalizing tendency of historic religion produces some basic insights about the harm involved in every act of killing, stealing, and so forth. That same universalizing tendency, however, often leads people to make supposedly universal laws out of what actually are no more than the local customs of the group or culture. Is it true, for example, as Islamic tradition insists, that charging interest for loans is always and everywhere wrong? Is it true, as some Christian missionaries tried often to insist, that public nudity is intrinsically immoral and therefore always wrong? A universalizing religion often interferes with its own claims about the objective and universal nature of moral laws by insisting that its whole set of culturally-produced laws and customs are all universally valid.

A severe problem in all this, as you may have noticed by now, is how to tell the difference between a universally valid law and one that merely happens to have been maintained in a given culture. Whatever a person is most used to automatically seems objectively correct. A person taught to fear God's punishment for masturbation, or to fear being rejected from the group for allowing divorce, may really act out of taboo or acceptance motivation in claiming that divorce and masturbation are intrinsically and objectively wrong. Our motives are often mixed. The motivation behind a genuine universal laws morality is not fear of punishment or rejection, but a sense that there are standards worth following simply because they are intrinsically valid, whether or not they are accepted by others or rewarded.

The greatest problem with universal laws morality is that each law appears to have some valid exceptions. The same religious traditions that insist that certain laws are always valid often allow exceptions. They say that a person may steal food if that is the only way to feed a starving child. A person may lie if that is the only way to prevent much greater and long-term harm. A person may even kill if that is the only way that can be found to save innocent lives. To forbid any exceptions at all would create a cold and sometimes cruel legalism, the law for law's sake, not for people's sake.

Casuistry

Historic religions can say that universal laws could always be obeyed if there were a perfect world, but since this is not a perfect world there is a need for guidelines that are more applicable to it than laws that may never be broken under any circumstances whatsoever. There has been a practical set of guidelines on how to apply the universal laws to fit an imperfect world. These guidelines make up what is called "casuistry," a name derived from the fact that they are guidelines about difficult *cases* in applying universal moral laws.

Casuistry has a bad name for those who believe firmly in absolute universal laws morality, because it consists of ways to soften the rules in their application. Casuistry is thought of as hairsplitting and quibbling because it produces complicated justifications for not giving simple obedience to some universal law in a given case. Supporters of casuistry value it, however, as a way to deal realistically with the complexities of life.

Universal moral law has been taken to command, for example, that no killing is ever allowed, not even of one's own self. Therefore suicide is also wrong. But what if a person is trapped on top of a twenty-story burning building, asked one textbook, and the only way to escape a painful death by flame was to jump to what seemed to be also a certain death? Jumping would be suicide and therefore immoral in itself—unless (and here is an answer given by casuistry) you intend to jump not to kill yourself but only to avoid the flames. You jump; you just do not intend to land. (This is called "the principle of double effect.")

That sounds a little silly to our ears. But it points out something worth noting. That is that sometimes we do something that in fact has harmful consequences, not because we intend those consequences but because there is some other harm we want to avoid. Are we then being immoral because we do that which in one way is harmful but in another way is helpful? Not necessarily, says casuistry. Life is complicated.

There is in fact a major principle of casuistry that sums up all the others fairly well. That is that it is always legitimate to do the lesser of two evils when it is inevitable that you will have to end up doing at least one of them. This is often summarized in the expression "the principle of the lesser of two evils." Telling a lie to save a life is an instance of this. It is an evil to tell a lie, but it is also an evil that someone should die. Real life usually consists of complicated trade-offs between different evils and goods. Casuistry acknowledges this and tries to give guidance on how to deal with real life as it is.

Casuistry was originally a set of rules attached to universal laws morality, rules used by people who wanted to maintain universal laws morality but be flexible in their application. Others have used the insights used by casuistry to construct a different kind of morality. Here we can call it "basic value morality."

BASIC VALUE MORALITY

Human Well-Being as the Basic Good
When confronted with conflicts among moral laws, casuistry tried to discover the option that did the most good and the least

harm. In doing this it was following a very general moral norm, much more general than the specific universal laws. The general norm is this: do good and avoid harm as much as possible.

But this begs the question: how does a person know what is good? Taboo morality calls good whatever satisfies a selfish concern for one's own pleasure even at the expense of others. Acceptance morality calls good whatever is part of the person's group norms and whatever promotes the good of a person's group. Universal laws morality breaks out of group loyalty in order to offer objective and universal standards of what is good or bad. But when even universal laws are not adequate for defining what is good, then what does it mean to say that a basic moral norm is to do good. What is "good" and how does a person know?

Basic value morality can offer only a vague answer to that. This morality proceeds on the basis of concern for the well-being of every human person as much as is possible. But there are many arguments about just what this well-being is. Is the invigorating challenge of a free capitalistic world better for people, or is the humane security of a socialist state? Would we all be best off if we lived in a world run by robots who protected us from all possible physical danger and all confusing choices and all disturbing surprises? Or would that make life too boring and make us too immature? But then what is it about maturity, whatever that is, that makes it part of "human well-being?" The questions can be endless.

In the 19th century some basic value moralists called "Utilitarians" defined "good" as individual pleasure. The goal of all moral decisions, they said, should be to increase the sum of individual human pleasure in the world as much as possible. This approach was labeled a "hedonistic calculus."

Other basic value moralists disagreed. Some said that pleasure is not an adequate good for human well-being. Other words like "happiness" or "fulfillment" would come closer to describing it. Others added that the original form of utilitarianism paid too much attention to individuals as such and needed to learn to appreciate love and loyalty and devotion to family and community life as part of human well-being.

Some ethicians have tried to solve the problem of defining human well-being by side-stepping it and focusing instead on the intentions behind our actions. The way to achieve the basic value of human well-being, they have said, is to act always out of love, to do whatever is most loving of all people. In every situation, act lovingly. (The name "situation ethics" is sometimes used for this approach.)

But this emphasis on intentions can actually be very harmful to human well-being. People who act out of good intentions may yet be ignorant, incompetent, or impulsive, and cause great harm. It may be personally very gratifying to be able to say that you acted out of love. But personal gratification is not the goal of basic value morality; actually achieving what is helpful to others is the goal. For this reason some forms of basic value morality are called "consequentialist ethics," in order to stress that it is the consequences of our actions that counts the most.

This brings the question back to the nature of "good." If a person acts out of love in order to produce good consequences in the lives of others, just which consequences are good ones instead of bad ones, and how do you know? Having a loving intention will not solve this alone. What criterion does a person use to evaluate whether the consequences have in fact been good instead of bad?

Basic value morality can partly say what is harmful and what is good by appealing to the insights of universal laws morality. Universal laws express the recognition that certain kinds of acts or events seem always to include some degree of harm to people. Lying and stealing and killing and torture and slavery and many other things are all found to be greatly harmful by those who are on the receiving end of these actions. Basic value morality does not abandon the insight of universal laws morality that some actions always do some harm. Rather, it adds the idea that the goal to avoid harm is the basically important goal behind the laws. That is why even good and insightful laws can sometimes be broken.

In practice, people also seem to be able not only to build upon the insights of universal laws, but also to agree on what is harmful in any of the other kinds of morality. We say that the selfishness of taboo morality seems bad because it is willing to harm others for personal gain. The group loyalty of acceptance morality extends its concern mainly to its own and not to outsiders. The outsiders may all be harmed. Universal laws seeks to treat all people equally, but could harm people if the laws are applied as strictly as they seem to demand.

Although none of this provides a fully clear answer yet about the nature of human well-being and therefore of what is "good," people can nonetheless usually agree on what is opposed to human well-being. Pain and suffering, fear and despair, deformity and death all seem worth avoiding whenever possible. We can also usually agree that love and friendship, accomplishments and good health, hope and long life are all desirable, at least as long as they are not overburdened by all the things worth avoiding. While we continue to struggle to learn more about ourselves and what is good for us and each other, we know at least a great deal about how we can already help rather than hurt each other.

Other Characteristics of Basic Value Morality

Basic value morality is a universal law morality. It is a single moral law that applies to all situations everywhere and always. It says one thing: always do what best promotes human well-being. There are no valid exceptions whatsoever to this single law in basic value morality. This is the basis of all other laws and all valid moral judgments. Nothing is good or bad except to the extent that it serves this basic value.

Basic value morality is also very demanding. It can appear to be easier than universal laws morality because it allows exceptions to the rules. It softens hard legalism and subordinates it to a concern for human welfare. But it is not easier, because it makes everything a moral matter. All our thoughts and acts affect people eventually in some way. We are always responsible for all the ways we affect people, because every effect could be good or bad; it is up to us to worry about that and do our best to make it good. Even doing nothing, leaving things undone, is a choice open to us and therefore part of our moral responsibility. The burden of basic value morality is to put a person under a constant moral responsibility for all the person's actions of all kinds. There are limits on what we can reasonably be expected to do, but to the extent we fall short of helping others, we fall short of doing good in basic value morality.

Basic value morality can be both dangerous and frightening. It can be dangerous because it is vague. When people are given very specific rules of what to do, then good and bad seem clear. When the rule is only the general one to help instead of hurt, it is open to misuse by all sorts of people who use this as an excuse to do whatever they want. They can argue that there are no unbreakable rules. Basic value morality and the casuistry on which it is based has established that, they say. But they ignore or fail to understand that basic value morality says that the rules can be broken *only* to help people and avoid harming them, not broken in whatever way a person wants for any reason. Morality is confusing enough, however, that once moral laws seem no longer unbreakable then some people will allow themselves to do as they please. Such people tend to do as they please anyway, however, so perhaps the danger here is no greater than what already existed.

Basic value morality can also be frightening because it hands over so much responsibility to the individual person. Sets of specific rules, whether taboo rules or group rules or universal law rules, are at least fairly clear most of the time. All that a person needs to do for the most part is to memorize them and follow them. Basic value morality says that this is only a useful beginning, that a person must also then reflect on and take personal responsibility for whether this rule or that should actually be obeyed or broken. While some people enjoy this responsibility, others flee from it.

Finally, basic value morality extends and modifies the notion of the individual. We saw that universal laws morality allows a person to define self clearly and as worthy by building a life based on the universal laws. The person who does not steal, cheat, kill, lie, and so forth can feel assurance that she or he is a worthwhile person, living as a person ought to, regardless of what others may say or think. Basic value morality similarly offers a way of defining the worth of one's selfhood, but now by a general standard instead of through many specific laws: whether the person is one who works effectively to help others rather than hurt them or ignore them.

The Motivation Behind Basic Value Morality

Basic value morality says that the well-being of each person should be the guiding purpose behind every act. But how does the basic value moralist know that this is so? It is tough enough to decide just what human well-being really consists of; how can anyone know that it is really the most basic value? A way to approach this is to ask about the motivation behind it. Discovering the motivation for accepting human well-being as the most basic value, in fact, can shed light on the nature of morality in general.

It is possible to affirm that human well-being is the most basic value on the grounds that God or society or neighbors will reward the person who affirms this and punish the person who denies it. In that case it is a taboo morality motivation at work. Or a person could support human well-being only because that is one of the commandments of the group to which the person belongs and is loyal. This is acceptance morality motivation. A universal laws morality is built on a kind of conformity also, but in this case to the supposedly objective and universally valid laws of the universe. A person can achieve a sense of true and valuable identity by making his or her own character conform to this universal set of laws. Evidently there can be more than one motivation for upholding the basic value of human well-being.

There is one more motivation that may in fact be the strongest one at work in a true basic value morality. That is a sense of sympathetic compassion for others. There is a kind of compassion for others that exists in most people from a very early age. A child sees a puppy hurt and cries with it, imagining the puppy's hurt as its own. This compassion is not very deep. The same child may torture a bird out of curiosity. An adolescent has a compassion for some people that is sometimes intense: a friend or classmate in trouble, a person's suffering reported on the evening news or described in a work of fiction. This compassion is also often limited, though; not all people will be able to earn the adolescent's sympathy. Most adults also have some inclination to shallowness or restriction of compassion for others.

Basic value morality usually represents a fuller compassion, one grounded in a sense that we are all human together. We are all confused, limited, frustrated; have hopes and dreams, needs and aspirations; look for love and are lonely. We all search for happiness but learn to accept less than what we imagined we would have. The person next to us is like that too. As we become increasingly sensitive to the humanness we share, we can begin to feel a personal pain from other people's pain and a personal happiness from other people's happiness. Every person, no matter how much a criminal or a sinner, no matter how boring, obnoxious, disappointing or weird, is you and me; partly who we really are, partly who we easily might have been. We all hurt in various ways. We all need the same understanding and acceptance.

This compassion still does not solve the problem of exactly what is good about human well-being, or even what this well-being fully consists in. But it takes people much closer to being helpful to one another instead of harmful. And some of the answer to why we should be good and what goodness consists of lies in the realm of the mystery of the human person, as the last section of the chapter will discuss briefly. There may be no better answer than that of basic value morality.

Basic Value Morality and Religion
Basic value morality has been most explicit in historic and in modern forms of religion and culture. The great historic religions

of the world have often proposed the one basic value of human well-being as the foundation of all morality. The idea of subordinating all specific laws to the one basic value appears in the Christian New Testament when Jesus declared, "The sabbath was made for man, not man for the sabbath." The great rabbi Hillel had already proposed that the whole law of Moses could be reduced to two precepts: love God, and love your neighbor as yourself. This sense of concern for every human person shines through in the endless variations from around the world, but it often takes a familiar form known as the golden rule: "Do unto others as you would have them do unto you." Give to them the same compassion and patience and acceptance that you yourself would want to receive. They are human just as you are human.

In every religious tradition such sayings are repeated more often than they are practiced. For some people, "doing unto others" only means making deals to scratch each other's back, a form of self-serving taboo morality. Some feel that the neighbor who deserves their loving concern is only the one who acts properly and earns a decent place in society or shares the "one true religion." This is a form of acceptance morality. Others are sure that there are some God-given laws to be obeyed no matter who gets hurt, a form of universal laws morality. The basic value of human worth has often been buried under the universal laws, the need to conform to the accepting group, or to narrow self-interest. Nonetheless, various traditions have acknowledged that service to all one's fellow human being, including explicitly the lowly or the outcast or the "sinner," is the highest morality in this world and the guide and foundation for all other moral precepts.

The strongest form of basic value morality, though, is probably the insistence that every human life is sacred, that in the people around us we are seeing in concrete and limited form the best clue to the inner nature of the infinite God or Self. In the familiar Western religions, each person is said to be special to God. Each person, in fact, is special because to be a person is to convey something of what the divine Mystery is all about. In the words of Hebrew Scriptures, God made people in the divine "image and likeness."

People turn to religious moral guidance because religion is a source of clear and secure direction. The kind of morality a person desires is bound up with the kind of religion a person prefers. Sometimes religion provides clear lists of rules about many aspects of life, and appeals to people who enjoy receiving firm and clear guidance about life from the numinous. At other times religgion offers only a more general inspiration and ideals, and leaves it to the individual to work things out. It is the modern forms of religion that come closest to this through their emphasis on basic value morality.

The difference here exists often within a single religious tradition. Thus Muslims disagree among themselves on how strict they should apply some Islamic rules. Jews disagree among themselves on how literally and exactly they are to follow the law of Moses. Christians range from very strict to very liberal in their interpretation of moral rules about sex and marriage.

The difference of interpretation of moral rules by religious people is also a difference of interpretation concerning the place of the human person in the universe. Some religious people presume that people are meant to listen and to learn and to obey. Morality, then, consists primarily in receiving moral instructions and carrying them out. Other religious people think of the human person as created to be intelligently free and responsible. Morality is, then, something that people are supposed to create themselves as they learn more about life and about human needs and possibilities. Most people probably do a little of both in their lives.

Morality and Mystery

To arrive at basic value morality is to arrive at the edge of mystery because it raises the question of why anyone should value anything at all. We live by the half-conscious faith that life makes sense and is worthwhile. But our minds still have the capacity to ask how it makes sense and why it is worthwhile. The taboo moralist knows it is worthwhile to enjoy life and avoid pain. So do we all. But we would give up some enjoyment and endure much pain under the right circumstances. One purpose is what we have in common with every acceptance moralist: to be accepted, appreciated, loved. For this we would suffer much. Yet we admire the person who would sacrifice fame, acceptance, even love, for a great cause and a noble principle. We admire a person who sacrifices his or her life to obey a principle that forbids killing another. We might even do it ourselves. But why? Because God will reward us? Because people will admire us then? Because it is objectively the right thing to do? Because there is something sacred about life? But what is that and how do we know? The question is the universal and ultimate one: What finally is the purpose, the value, of anything and everything?

There are pragmatic answers to ultimate question: Eat, drink, and be merry, for tomorrow we die; live and love and grab all the gusto you can get. There are more inspiring but vague answers: Live a worthwhile life so that when you are about to die you can feel satisfied that you have not wasted your life. Pragmatic answers and vague but inspiring answers can be satisfying, but the human consciousness has the capacity to seek better answers. Only an ultimate and universal answer could provide a complete solution.

What this means is that morality is inevitably a religious question. That does not mean it is inevitably a matter of receiving divine commandments or obeying religious rules. Morality is deeper than rules and commandments. It is the question of precisely what the ultimate value or purpose is to anything and all things. The kind of answer it requires will connect moral values to the ultimate truth about God, the Tao, Brahman-Atman, nirvana, the cosmos, or whatever it is that is the ultimate truth about human existence in this universe. The answer might not be a religious one. An atheist can offer a non-religious interpretation of the ultimate meaning or value of human life. But the question is religious in its scope.

Summary

This chapter has described four different stages of moral perspectives and made some general connections of these with four stages of cultural and religious evolution. Primitive religion and culture seem to hold on to a taboo perspective more than other cultures do, though this perspective can be found in all cultures. Archaic religion and culture, with its heightened sense of honor or pride, gives a stronger emphasis to the need for public acceptance, though this is a need common to all people. Historic religion and culture is the first to construct clearly universalist ethics, usually by means of many laws. Modern religion and culture have made more explicitly focal the general notion that loving one's neighbor, helping others, is the basis of all morality. People find guidance in religion not just through moral tradition but in many other ways. The next three chapters describe some of these ways.

FOR FURTHER REFLECTION

1. To what extent is fear of punishment by God needed in society today to maintain good social order and morality?

2. Do people you know find it easy to go against their family's and neighbors' opinions in order to do what seems objectively right in their own eyes?

3. How do you know what is really good or bad? Is it just a matter of individual feelings with no objective validity at all? Explain.

4. When others seriously hurt you or your friends or the weak and helpless, on what grounds can you say this is really wrong?

5. How would you feel if you had to admit to yourself that you are one of those who are careless about hurting others? Explain why you feel that way.

SUGGESTED READINGS

Ronald M. Green, *Religion and Moral Reason*, 1988; a developmental and evolutionary interpretation.

Mary M. Wilcox, *A Developmental Journey*, 1979; a good general introduction to the ideas of Piaget and Kohlberg.

James W. Fowler, *Stages of Faith*, 1981; see the end of the chapters of Part IV for comments on changes in moral perspective.

Stephen M. Tipton, "New Religious Movements and the Problem for a Modern Ethic" in Harry M. Johnson, ed., *Religious Change and Continuity*, 1979, pp. 287-312.

H.T.D. Rost, *The Golden Rule: A Universal Ethic*, 1986; traces the golden rule based on compassion through many cultures and religions.

CHAPTER NINE

The Process of Tradition

Leaders, Texts, and Interpretations

RELIGIOUS TRADITION AND CULTURE

The introduction to Part II noted that we all must learn how to be human, and that it is our culture that teaches us this. Another word for culture could be "tradition." The word "trade" comes from the same root. Tradition is whatever is passed on or handed over to someone. Our parents, teachers, community, and whole culture pass on to us a way of seeing life and living life. That is tradition. It teaches us a way to be human.

Religion has normally been at the heart of every cultural tradition. The basic religious beliefs, values, and practices are part of the cultural air each person breathes, so much so that people do not consciously take note of this any more than of their own breathing. In our modern situation we sometimes exaggerate the private nature of religion. We are used to the idea that every person has the right to determine privately which religious tradition to follow, if any. We think of religion as a matter of a person's conscience, between that person and God. Because of that, we do not always see the influence that religion has on culture. Even in modern times, culture is given certain forms and directions by the presence of religious ideas in the air and by leaders and texts that our culture presents to us as respectable, authentic, or sacred.

Just as religion influences culture, culture also conditions religion. It is formed by the social context we draw from as we become who we are. Every culture and society is formed over many generations. It is the product of historical processes, of the pattern of human behavior and choices in an ongoing development, generation after generation. It is human inventiveness at work, over thousands of years, discovering endless possibilities of language, law, custom, value, roles, rules, all the things that go into making us who we are. All of this has a great impact on religious tradition because religion and culture are usually intimately intertwined.

We are not inclined to think that way about our own religious tradition. We tend to believe that the Law of Moses or the Bible or the Koran is to be accepted not because culture says so, but because it is truly God's word. We believe in the authority of Moses or Jesus or Mohammed, we say, not because society tells us to but because these people spoke for God. And yet it is also clear that much depends on where one was born and to what family. Few Americans worship Vishnu or seek nirvana. Few Japanese pray to Allah and read the Koran. There is individual human choice involved, but choices are guided by society and culture, by a person's historical context. What most of us do is trust that our religious tradition, the cultural heritage of our people, authentically represents the numinous reality as it really is. We implicitly trust that the cultural process that has led us to accept certain beliefs and values and practices is a process that has been in touch with the reality of the numinous, with God or the Tao or the gods or the ancestors.

People do change religions, even against the current of their culture. That is why cults exist at all. People also adhere to minority positions within a larger culture. The presence of Jews in largely Christian and Muslim lands, of Parsees (Zoroastrians) and Christians in India, attests to this. In each case certain people

maintain an allegiance to a tradition that is not strongly supported by society as a whole. Even these traditions, though, exist within a social context and are affected by the currents of ideas and
values flowing about them. Religious traditions have identifiable
roots in the broader cultural traditions and historic patterns.

There are degrees of conformity and variety among people in
every society, which is true also in religion. We will talk more
about people's reasons for choosing to accept or reject their culture's tradition in a later chapter on knowing and believing. For
now, though, we can see some of the ways tradition is formed,
passed on, and interpreted.

THE LEADERS

We are normally very interested in finding out about mysterious powers and how to deal with them, or in discovering answers
to life's ultimate mysteries. Anyone who has any claim at all to be
able to understand, interpret correctly, or deal successfully with
the mysterious and invisible powers in life is likely to be accorded
special status and respect. There have been a few people in history, people like the Buddha and Lao Tzu and Moses and Jesus and
Mohammed, who have had enormous impact. There are many
more people who are less noticed but are still very influential.

Every culture has numerous religious leaders of various kinds,
who learn the tradition and pass it on, or who live it with special
vigor, or who modify it and gather a following for their new version of it. People readily look to special leaders for guidance and
help in their relations with the numinous. Here are a few of the
kinds of important religious leaders.

The Technicians of the Sacred

In any primitive society there are two main religious tasks that
are performed by part-time specialists: medicine and augury. The
medical specialists, called shamans (in English sometimes labeled
witch doctors or medicine men and women), are often also accomplished at augury, though many people might share in this skill.

In archaic societies the roles of shaman and augur are usually
made more formal full-time jobs. The shaman's work is done by a
full-time priest who works in the temple or who roams about
looking for ritual work. The augur is now a full-time professional
prophet, in the temples or shrines or on an independent basis, in-

specting the entrails of goats and chickens or interpreting the skies and stars for a basic fee.

The ancient Brahmin caste in India is a good example of the professional priesthood. As far back as archaic times in India, the young Brahmin boy would be assigned thousands of poetic chants to be memorized exactly. Countless ritual details had to be mastered until, after years of training, the Brahmin could function in the village or town as a priest performing the rituals to end drought or cure the sick. In cities the Brahmins also maintained the constant rituals that helped to preserve the universe and keep it running smoothly. It was usually thought best to hire three priests at once, who would repeat the ritual chants and practices together. If one should make a mistake, the other two would correct him so that the ritual would not lose any of its power.

Historic religions have often found a continuing value in the priestly function. Christianity, Buddhism, and the Hindu tradition still include major groups whose leadership is in the hands of priests. Usually they are no longer considered just technicians and ritual practitioners, but learned guides also. Even in historic religions, however, what identifies a priest is still the ancient function of the technician of the sacred: a careful and proper performance of the ritual to control or influence various numinous powers.

As a rule, the role of the augur is not part of historic religion. The usefulness of augurs lies in the fact that a clear prediction of the future allows a person to avoid bad events. If the goat's intestines reveal that tomorrow is a dangerous day for a journey, then a person can stay home and be safe. Historic religions tend to consider this ability to manipulate one's own future and fortune an affront to an ultimate and universal supreme Being or cosmic Power. Trust or submission is the proper attitude toward God's unavoidable will or the Tao's ultimate influence. Nevertheless, people belonging to a historic tradition find it comforting sometimes to employ prophets or soothsayers anyway. Trust in God, they may say; but for greater safety yet, read your horoscope and consult your palm reader.

Wise Ones and Enlightened Ones

Confucian tradition has high respect for the sage, the wise one whose learning and insight and well-balanced perspective produce a life worth imitating and wisdom worth learning. Kung Fu-Tzu (Confucius) himself is held in highest reverence because of his wisdom. He received no revelations, was not divine, did not practice any particular austerities or devote extra time to worship of the gods. He was not a prophet nor did he perform rituals. He was simply wise, so wise that China was able to build an entire social order on his thought and maintain it for two thousand years.

Taoism, the other great native tradition of China, is also based on wisdom. Ancient Taoism had its beginning supposedly in the brief writings of the legendary Lao-Tzu. His name translates roughly as "the old man," implying that he probably was one whose age had taught him wisdom worthy of reverence. Lao-Tzu was stopped at the border of China, the story goes, by a guard who would allow him to depart from China only on the condition that he write down his wisdom so it would not be lost. Lao-Tzu quickly composed a few pages that became known as the *Tao-Te-Ching*, the Book of the Way. About 250 B.C., Taoism was strongly influenced by Chuang-Tzu, whose great wisdom guided generations of Taoists. Neither of these two, Lao-Tzu and Chuang-Tzu, was said to be inspired by the ancestors or given a revelation by the gods. Their authority lay simply in the wisdom of their words.

Buddhism also has its origin in wisdom. In this case it is the insight or enlightenment of Siddhartha Gautama in the 6th century B.C. Buddhism has its many priests and its holiness communities, but it was begun not by priests or monks but by the prince who turned to reflection and achieved enlightenment, thus earning the title of Buddha, "Enlightened One." At first, Siddhartha Gautama followed the path of Indian yogis and ascetics of his time, training himself in meditation and then fasting until his stomach met his spine. This did not provide release from sufferings. He was learning by experience. Finally, he sat one night in meditation under a tree and broke through into full enlightenment. He moved on then to teach others about what he had learned, giving his first lesson to others in a deer park. Many followed his teachings. His insights into life somehow matched the experience of many who listened to him. Soon his teachings on life's suffering and on release into nirvana through detachment became the core of one of history's great religious traditions. (Not too many years later, that tradition began to describe the Buddha not as a wise man only, but as the earthly form a divine reality had taken in order to provide guidance to humankind out of compassion for our suffering.)

The Learned Interpreters

The Chinese sages and the Indian Buddha had all been influenced by ideas that were part of their culture. Lao-Tzu knew about the Yang/Yin of the Tao, because everyone in China knew about it. The Buddha knew we are all condemned to be reborn into suffering countless times, because that was an accepted belief in India. Even the wisest and most learned have to start with some ideas and values from their cultural tradition. Sometimes the role of wise and learned religious leaders is explicitly acknowledged to be that of interpreter of the religious tradition. The Jewish rabbi is one such interpreter. So is the Islamic imam ("leader") and the Protestant preacher.

After the return of many Jews from the exile in Babylon in the 6th century B. C., the priests in Jerusalem were the religious leaders and custodians of the tradition. Since the law of Moses often needed recopying, work done by hand, the writers ("scribes") who did the copying came to know the law in detail. They often helped to interpret it. The role of the priesthood ended with the destruction of the temple in Jerusalem in A. D. 70 by the Romans. Without a temple in which to offer ritual sacrifices, there was no need for priests in Judaism, so the learned interpreters of the law took over as the leaders of Judaism. They were addressed as "rabbi," meaning teacher or leader. Their authority to this day comes from their learning. They know the law and the great body of interpretations of the law that accumulated and were gathered into a collection known as the Talmud ("teaching") by the 6th century A.D. The major religious leadership role in Judaism is that of the learned person, the interpreter of the law.

Continuing what began with the Jews in the West, Christians and then Muslims also compiled their own sacred texts. For centuries the leaders in Christianity were the priests. Then, with the Reformation in the 16th century in Europe, many of the Protestant Christian churches eliminated priests and gave the leadership role to those who knew the sacred texts, the Bible, very well and could interpret it and preach its message. In Islam religious teachers, called imams, who are learned in the Koran and can help others in interpreting and applying the will of God written there.

Rabbis and preachers and imams, Confucian sages and Taoist philosophers and Hindu thinkers, and even the priests of many traditions are all called on to know the religious tradition and guide others to better understanding and application of it. At times in all the religious traditions, there are also those who claim great learning without having it, without even understanding what learning really is. Others equally unlearned will listen and not know the difference. Every tradition has some movements within it, claiming the authority of the tradition but which actually depart from it, sometimes without even realizing it. The problem of interpretation is one we will return to later in this chapter.

The Messengers: The Great Prophets

English-speaking people are accustomed to use the word "prophet" to label individuals inspired by God to speak for God and, sometimes, to predict the future, even if somewhat obscurely. The function of predicting the future is one that primitive and archaic prophets had, inasmuch as these prophets were really augurs, soothsayers, readers of omens. The best-known prophets are not soothsayers, however, but messengers of God who deliver to people information and guidance from God. Isaiah, Jeremiah, Ezekial, Hosea, Micah, and Amos are some of the messengers of God in the Hebrew Scriptures. As a messenger, the primary prophet in the Jewish tradition is Moses. The instructions from God transmitted through Moses provide the foundation of Judaic thought. In the New Testament, Jesus is portrayed at times also as prophet, a new Moses bringing to the people a new understanding of God's will.

In Islamic belief, Mohammed is God's final and supreme messenger. His teachings are written in the Koran, though they are not really Mohammed's teachings. They are the eternal will of God given by God's angel Gabriel to Mohammed so that he in turn could transmit them to all people. According to Islamic belief, the teachings of God delivered to Mohammed are the fulfillment of the teachings God gave to Moses, Jesus, and other prophets.

The Appointed Agents of God: Messiahs

As we have seen, the name "messiah" is from a Hebrew word meaning "anointed." The ancient semitic practice (still observed in a few cases today as in the Catholic ritual of confirmation) was to anoint with oil a person who was appointed to a special role. The kings of ancient Judea were anointed. The future king many Judaeans hoped for is thus the anointed one, messiah. Christians are familiar with the Greek translation of the word. "Anointed one" in Greek is *christos*, shortened in English to "Christ."

As far back as the 7th century B. C., the prophet Isaiah had offered hope for an ideal king to come. This was associated with the "Day of the Lord" when Yahweh would bring about a peaceable kingdom, the ideal life without war or bloodshed. Subsequent generations continued to hope that God would send a leader in times of troubles. Most hoped for a king, a royal messiah. Others thought Yahweh might anoint a priest, a prophet, or a teacher to be the agent who would usher in God's kingdom. Some Jews speculated that perhaps it was not an individual person but the whole nation of Israel that was to be anointed by God to bring peace and happiness to all the world in a glorious millennial Day of the Lord. One result of all this was the growth of the apocalyptic thought described earlier. Another result was the birth of Christianity, originally a Jewish sect adhering to Jesus of Nazareth as the agent appointed by God to inaugurate the apocalyptic coming of the Day of the Lord and the Kingdom of God.

The notion of messiah belongs also to Islam. Some forms of Islamic tradition have looked forward to the arrival of a person sent by God to order things the way God wants them. This messiah will not reveal any new truths or instructions. The Koran is the last word on such things. But there is still need for a leader who has the authority to propel people toward accepting God's will and living their lives properly. The majority group of Islam, the Sunnis, look forward to a mahdi, one who is divinely guided. He will appear on earth near the end of the world. Other Islamic groups expect that God will send a very special imam (leader) to restore all things in the end. In various religious traditions it is possible to find messianic ideas. Perhaps the Buddha and other figures who bring salvation in some way can all be called messianic figures. Anyone who claims to function as the agent of God and lead people to salvation can now loosely be called a messiah.

Holy Ones

Some individuals become authorities in a religious tradition because they are thought to be very holy. They are not appointed by God or the gods to this role. It does not necessarily even require insight or wisdom or learning, although this is a deficiency that can make holy people very dangerous.

Holiness is a difficult attribute to define. It usually consists of an intense devotion or dedication to the service of the divine or numinous. We often think of holiness as a moral quality. In that case, holiness is firm obedience of all moral laws and a superior measure of virtue such as patience and compassion. But holiness appears in other forms also. Some people are considered holy because they give up pleasures and practice great asceticism. In primitive and archaic societies especially, holiness is identical with sacredness; anything that is the presence of the numinous is sacred. This means that all strange or mysterious persons are holy, because it is the strange and mysterious that is the numinous. Epileptics are holy, for example. The words they say before or after a seizure are to be listened to as words from the spirits. Even the insane or mentally retarded are considered to be touched by the numinous and are to be treated as sacred. Religious leaders who have charism, a powerful personality and style of presenting themselves, may be treated with special reverence or followed blindly.

There are people who institutionalize holiness. The monks and nuns in Eastern and Western religions seek holiness in this way. On the other hand, there are holy people who devote themselves to the divine in very individual ways, living as hermits. There are many who cross back and forth across such lines. St. Francis of Assisi (1181-1226) was an individualist who devoted himself to God through a simple way of life, prayer, and kindness. But he also assembled others into what became the Franciscan order of friars and nuns in the Catholic church, although Francis himself did not remain very comfortable in his own order. In India there are gurus (teachers) who have schools of disciples, but when the guru dies the disciples move on. In the lifetime of the Buddha, one of his followers, a cousin named Ananda, took the Buddha's ideas and helped make them the basis of a religious community. Holiness is sought alone or with others, in different ways around the world. Those who are considered holy, for whatever reason, are often respected as guides to the right way to live and to deal with the numinous.

Incarnations

The word "incarnation" literally means enfleshment or embodiment. It is used to indicate those persons who are not merely human but are in some way actually a god or God living somehow as a human person on earth.

Kings have sometimes been considered to be the incarnation of a god. The king of the Shilluk people along the Nile in the Sudan is actually the god Nyikang. When the king dies the god moves on into the body of the next king. The pharaoh of ancient Egypt was Horus, divine son of the god Osiris. Upon the pharaoh's death, he became Osiris and the new pharaoh became his son, the new Horus. For many generations the ruler in Tibet has been the divine priest-king, the Dalai Lama, the chief priest of a form of Buddhism in that country. When one Dalai Lama dies, the other priests go throughout Tibet looking for the omens that tell them which young child is the new reincarnation of this god, the new Dalai Lama. The sacred and awesome power of the gods who control reality and society is present physically in the person of the king, pharaoh, or ruler-priests in these cases.

In other traditions it might be the relatively powerless who are incarnations. The guru of India is a person who is both wise and holy. The guru whose yoga training is far advanced can guide others in the path of salvation because the guru has already achieved the insight or enlightenment into ultimate truth. As a person approaches the ultimate truth, he or she discovers that the only true reality is the Atman or Self; this divineness somehow lies within a person. The guru is one who has discovered the inner divinity we all have and are, insofar as we really exist at all. In that sense we are all incarnations of the divine, but only the guru is close enough to this inner reality to truly grasp it and guide others to a realization of their own inner divineness.

A more usual instance of what is meant by incarnation is the Hindu belief in avataras. This word implies a descent from godly status to human existence. According to one Hindu tradition, the god who has most often thus descended is Vishnu, worshipped by his followers as the supreme form that divinity takes (though it exists in other forms in other gods also, and ultimately is Brahman, beyond all the gods). The first avatara or incarnation of Vishnu was as a fish. Vishnu has been incarnate nine times so far, in fact. The avatara of Vishnu that is most important to many Hindus is his incarnation as Krishna. According to Vishnu's worshippers, the Buddha was another incarnation of Vishnu. There is still a tenth one to come called Kalkin, who will appear at the end of the world.

The Christian use of the word "incarnation" is the most familiar one in the West. The fourth gospel in the New Testament declared that the divine Word of God became flesh in Jesus of Nazareth. In its rather complex doctrine of God, Christianity came to assert that the one God has within itself three distinct aspects or "persons," one of which is called the Son. This divine Son is also called the Word (*Logos* in Greek). It is the Son who is incarnate in Jesus, but through the Son the whole divineness of God is said to be incarnate in Jesus. (As was said, it is a complex doctrine.)

Both Jews and Muslims reject this Christian belief on the grounds that it makes God into a mere god. A god like Zeus could beget a son on earth and did so a number of times. A god like

Vishnu could become enfleshed as Krishna. But God is absolute, infinite, and unchangeable, both Jews and Muslims say. God is not anthropomorphic like Zeus, nor finite and changeable like Vishnu. So God cannot have a son, except perhaps poetically speaking, nor can God shrink down to a finite size to become human. In response, Christians say that Jesus is not a god in disguise but is a fully human person who is nonetheless also the real presence of the infinite and absolute God. The traditional formulation says that in Jesus full finite humanness and full infinite divinity meet and join, but without any mixing between the two. If this seems hard to understand, the tradition says that is to be expected, because God is truly infinite and incomprehensible, just as Jews and Muslims also insist.

The Significance of Leaders

The list of leaders is long, one that includes shamans and soothsayers, priests and prophets, the wise and the learned, messiahs, holy ones, and divinity incarnate. The significance of the list is that it helps illustrate the fact that a person in any culture turns to other persons and to the culture as a whole for guidance and leadership in religious matters. The numinous is intelligible to us only in ways that our culture has prepared us to grasp. The numinous comes to us in ways others have taught us to perceive and relate to, because this is the way we come to understand any aspects of reality.

Religious leaders are sometimes people with very special gifts of insight, eloquence, or leadership. They are often people who have spent many years in pursuit of the divine or the sacred. Every culture has its significant few, those more deeply perceptive, more compassionate, more dedicated, or even more desperate for religious meaning. But they do not produce their ideas out of air. They plunge deeply into traditions, especially their own, drawing from them the materials from which they form saving insights or build structures of wisdom, morality, community, and contemplation. These will support others in their search for meaningful existence in the face of the mysteries of life. Occasionally, they shift the direction and focus of their own tradition in ways that constitute the beginning of a new religion, a new way of achieving salvation from estrangment through relation to the numinous. The new comes out of the old, however, and there is continuity between them. The few intensely religious people become leaders because their sensibilities and perceptions are human enough, however divine they might also be said to be, to make contact with the needs and hopes of others.

Religious leaders have different kinds of authority over their followers. Some lead by persuasion and eloquence, others by the example of their lives, some by the claim to have divine support. But all of them lead mainly because they were first accepted by a few, and then by many, and then became part of the cultural tradition themselves. All of them spoke out of a cultural context that made them intelligible to others in the first place, and in ways that touch the humanity of others. All of them are significant because they contribute to the flow of human life in its cultural contexts, for better or for worse.

SACRED WRITINGS

Like religious leaders, sacred texts are focal points in religious traditions. Many traditions are based on scriptures of one kind or another. The word "scripture" merely means writings. At some time in the history of humankind, the use of writing was itself a sacred thing. To those unaccustomed to writing, it can seem wondrously magical that strange little markings can convey thoughts and words over a distance and through time. In some societies, writing techniques were used mainly for religious purposes, as with the earliest hieroglyphics of ancient Egypt. As writing became more common for business and governmental records, it lost its awesomeness. Among the many writings in the world, there are some we still call by the special name, "scriptures," to indicate that these writings are treated as sacred.

To be classified as scripture or as sacred, however, it is not enough that the texts deal with the numinous. After all, libraries are filled with books on religion, and rather few of these books are considered sacred. To be sacred scripture, a text must also somehow carry special authority. Those reading it must see it as a text that has a power, status, or authenticity that raises it above ordinary human writings. There are various ways of attaining this status.

The Truth That Is Tradition
Some writings have a special status as sacred truth simply because they are traditional. The world's cultures have usually had great reverence for the past and for tradition. Things handed on

from long ago have a lustre and an authority. They have endured and have achieved respect. What is new is untested and may soon pass away.

Most of the world's scriptures have some additional claim to sacred status besides being traditional. Those who accept a certain text as sacred will tell you that it was revealed or inspired by the gods or God. But if you were to ask how they knew that gods or God had revealed it, the answer would often be simply that everyone knows that; it is tradition that hands on the belief that the text is sacred. As long as everyone has assimilated the belief from prior generations that a certain text is truly sacred, then people will find it normal and natural to accept the text in that light. The longer it has endured as sacred, the more obvious it will seem that it is in fact a true and powerful link to the numinous realities it describes.

Wisdom Literature

The original book of Taoism is the *Tao-Te-Ching*, the Book of the Way ascribed to Lao-Tzu. The book gained acceptance because it was viewed as unusually perceptive and wise in its statements. Chuang-Tzu was highly respected in his lifetime as a very wise person. His sayings were recorded and now form part of the traditional writings of Taoism. Confucius was a great sage; many of his sayings were written down. In time many other bits of wisdom were linked to his name and added to the collection of sayings attributed to him, forming the Analects (sayings and stories) of Confucius.

The authority of the names associated with these writings is part of the reason they gained respect. Ideas attached to famous faces and human personalities achieve a little more "authority" in people's imagination. But the Chinese wise men were famous because they were wise. It is not the fame of the authors but the wisdom that is supposed to be the basis for the authority of these Chinese texts. There are also texts in the Jewish and Christian Scriptures, in Hindu writings, and in the Buddhist tradition that have authority simply because they are considered wise.

Revelation and Inspiration

The most frequent explanation given by religious traditions for the sacred status of certain writings is that those texts were produced not by humans alone, not even by the wisest of leaders, but by a divine being or power. The humans involved were merely the channels for the divine influence. Ideas that have come from a divine source are called either revelations or inspiration. These words do not have clear definitions, but there is a common distinction that is somewhat useful.

Messages directly given by a numinous being are most often called revelations. The avatara Krishna spoke at some length to a charioteer named Arjuna. These words are now recorded in the sacred Hindu writings known as the *Bhagavad Gita*, written in the early centuries of the axial age and still among the most beloved of Hindu texts. Ahura Mazda, the Wise Lord, spoke to Zoroaster. His followers wrote down these revelations as Zoroaster passed them on, recording them in the Avestas ("laws"). In Jewish belief God gave his law to Moses on Mount Sinai and later. Mohammed received the words of the Koran from Allah by way of the angel Gabriel. These were all held in respect not because they were words of a holy and wise person, but because they were words spoken directly to a messenger by a divine being and, therefore, were words of undoubtable validity and importance. When these words were put in written form, they bestowed upon the pages and markings a certain sacredness. Not just the ideas and the words, but even the texts themselves are treated with reverence.

Sometimes the words of sacred writings are not thought of as directly revealed by the numinous being, but only inspired by the god or God in a general way that left the writer or speaker free to choose the particular words and images. The most ancient parts of the Hindu sacred writings known as the Vedas, for example, begin with poems for use in rituals, poems composed by seers known as rishis, who were said to be inspired when composing. Similarly, although the author of the Old Testament book of Proverbs who collected the many folk sayings in one book does not seem to have claimed that God revealed these sayings directly, Jews and Christians have usually accepted the book as somehow the result of divine inspiration and have treated them also with deference.

The Complexities of Sacred Writings
The fact that the authority or sacredness of given texts can derive from tradition, wisdom, revelation, inspiration, or any combination of these all at once, is one source of complexity. The Vedic tradition actually encompasses all of these categories. Similarly, the Hebrew and Christian Scriptures contain direct

revelations (God's words to Moses), inspiration (Paul's New Testament letters), wisdom (as in the book of Ecclesiastes), all mixed together, though Christians have usually said that it was divine inspiration that led to the particular compilation of traditions, prophecies, stories, and so forth that now comprise the sacred texts.

The historical nature of many texts is the main cause of this complexity. Religious people can mentally lump their own scriptures together as sacred texts produced "back then" when God spoke or inspired certain people. But "back then" can cover many centuries. The earliest words of the Vedic tradition may go back to 1500 B.C., but this tradition includes writings from the 6th century B.C. and perhaps from even more recent times. The Jewish tradition began taking written form in the 10th century B.C., but received major additions, including a large body of interpretative writings up, until the 6th century A.D.

Even texts put together in a relatively short time have a history. The Christian New Testament texts were produced in about sixty years time (A. D. 50-110?). But the first texts were based on sayings and stories that had been in circulation for over twenty years. For a long time Christians were not sure which of the many early writings should be counted as authoritative. There are lists of scripture used by Christians in the 2nd century that include books like "The Shepherd of Hermas" and "The Epistle of Barnabas." It was not until after A.D. 150 that there was significant agreement on just which books should be called part of scripture and which not, although arguments continued for many years.

The Koran was delivered more quickly by the angel Gabriel to Mohammed over a period of a few years. But then another historical process followed. Mohammed transmitted verbally to people around him the various sayings that make up the Koran. These others had to write them down, a process that continued after Mohammed's death. For a while there was more than one list of these sayings, in different order. Then a single collection was compiled. Most of the sayings were put in order of their length and not in chronological or topical order, making it difficult at times to know how to interpret them. Then they had to be applied, from then until now, to life's varied and complex situations. A tradition of interpretations as well as methods of interpretation had to develop to guide people.

INTERPRETING THE TEXTS

A Desire for Certainty

People who live by a religious tradition like to be able to feel that the basics of their tradition are well-settled and clear. Religions fulfill very important human needs. They make sense of life in the face of suffering, injustice, and confusion. They provide a sense of belonging and identity. They give help, comfort, and security. All this is possible, provided that the religious tradition can speak clearly and authoritatively. When people turn to religious leaders and sacred texts they usually do not want to hear conflicting voices and changing opinions. When they do hear of conflict and change, they either try to dismiss it as peripheral and insignificant, or they attack it as serious error. On the whole, religious believers manage to maintain some sense that what they believe is the unchanging and firm truth.

This sense of stability and certitude, however, must be won by continuous effort, especially by the historic religions. Primitive religion takes stability more or less for granted in its one-possibility universe (sometimes changing, nonetheless, without much fuss). Archaic religion is open to a variety of beliefs. With so many gods and powers about, there is always a new one to learn about. Historic religion, though, contains what it believes to be universal and all-inclusive truth. The one God or supreme Reality rules all things at once. All aspects of life must be integrated into one all-embracing religious story of reality. (We will see more about this in Chapter Eleven on reason and faith.)

The historic belief system expressed in some leader's words or in sacred scripture is therefore adequate only if it spells out the basic and final unity to everything. This will include a description of the ultimate numinous reality, ultimate salvation, including identity and belonging, the moral requirements of life, and all other necessary means for relating to the numinous. It can be difficult, though, to maintain such a complex unity. Life goes on. Ideas change. New problems arise. Stability and unity of religious existence is maintained only by a constant effort at interpreting the tradition and applying old meanings to new contexts.

The Necessity of Interpretation

The actual use of the Koran by Muslims is one example of this. The Koran is the set of instructions on life given by the Almighty, ordained from all eternity as the final and full truth for human beings. The words of the Koran were given to Mohammed over a few years. These words should therefore be able to settle all disputes about religious matters.

But problems of interpretation quickly arose. To this day, there is a dispute over who is to be the major political leader among Muslims, dividing Sunni from Shi'ite to some extent. Other difficult questions had to be addressed. How were non-Arabic people to be joined to an originally Arabic religion? Must even the poorest and most distant Muslim make a journey to Mecca, as required by the Koran? Should the yearly all-day fast during the month of Ramadan be kept strictly, even by Muslims who happen to be living in countries where most people do not observe this fast?

In cases like these, Muslims apply hadith, sayings and practices of Mohammed not in the Koran. In addition, during the early centuries of Islam a body of laws known as the Shari'a (the Way) was articulated on the basis of the Koran and hadith and common practice. When neither the Koran nor hadith nor Shari'a provides answers, then a consensus of opinions of learned imams may be followed. There is no single collection of hadith that is the one authoritative collection. And there are at least four major schools of Shari'a for Sunni Muslims. Interpreting how a good Muslim is to live in accordance with God's will can be difficult. The same is true in any religion. There must be interpretation; it is unavoidable. And once people begin to interpret the tradition or the texts, they may disagree.

Sometimes interpretations of scriptures are collected into a kind of adjunct scripture. In India, Vedic commentaries known as the Brahmanas and the Upanishads took on a sacred character of their own. Judaism treats the Law of Moses (the first five books of the Bible: the Pentateuch or Torah) as most sacred, but it also reveres the words of the prophets and other writings as holy commentary on the Law, and has added to all this the learned commentaries of early rabbis assembled into the collection known as the Talmud. Many Christians rely on the great councils of church leaders in the first five centuries of Christianity as authoritative interpretations of scripture. It was only in 325 A.D. that Christians found formally explicit words to express their belief that Jesus is truly and fully divine, the *Logos* of the Trinity incarnate, rather than only a god or a son of God. It was only in the next century that they found explicit words to say that Jesus is also completely what a human being is and that Jesus' humanity remained fully distinct from the divinity of Jesus. Most Christians, though not all, have accepted these ideas as the correct way to interpret what their Bible says. The complexity of these beliefs illustrates why interpretation is difficult.

There are countless more instances of the complex and historical process of interpretation. It is important to have seen at least a few of them in order to have some concrete experience of the fact of interpretation, because religious traditions sometimes obscure or even hide their own dependence on interpretation and reinterpretation. The reason for this is that the problem of interpretation is not just how to do it well, but that it has to be done at all. Each time it becomes necessary, that suggests that the answers to life and how to live it are still not fully clear, that there is still some uncertainty. Religious people usually seek certainty and confidence in their religious beliefs.

It is here that religious leaders can become especially important. Among the religious believers there can be those who officially or unofficially carry the burden of deciding for others what the best interpretation of the scriptures and the whole tradition might be. Gurus and charismatic leaders, messiahs and incarnate divinities, holy ones and priests, learned interpreters and wise ones, all can give their followers a sense that certainty does exist, that there is some clear and authoritative message people can confidently obey without doubt or confusion. Some religious groups claim that their leaders may even receive ongoing divine guidance in interpreting the tradition and scriptures. Catholics make this claim for the pope under certain precise circumstances; Mormons say this concerning revelations granted their chief elder.

Literal or Loose Interpretation

Leaders and ordinary believers alike often have difficulty deciding how literally to interpret their sacred writings. A strictly literal interpretation can provide a divinely authoritative set of specific and exact instructions, it would seem, on how to live and what to believe. A strict literalism might thereby eliminate confusion and insecurity. Such literalism has become known as fundamentalism.

Early in the 20th century, a number of Protestant clergy, theologians, and believers reaffirmed the traditional fundamental beliefs of Christianity. Among these was the belief in the "literal inerrancy" of scripture. This belief says that the sacred scriptures of Judaeo-Christian tradition are exactly as God wanted them to be. God inspired the writers to record without error all that God wished to be revealed through Moses, the prophets, Jesus, Paul, and others. Every sentence and every word of the Bible, therefore, is to be accepted as the literal and undoubtable truth. Because these Christians called this a fundamental belief, the name fundamentalism has come to be applied to this idea of the literal inerrancy of the scriptures. Among Jews, those who are called Orthodox are rather fundamentalistic about the Torah and Talmud as words to be obeyed exactly. Traditional Islam has been fairly fundamentalistic about the Koran, though there are different schools of interpretation in Islam also. In India there is a Ninsana (interpretation) school that insists that the Vedas are absolutely and literally true.

In every tradition there are scriptural passages, though, that do not lend themselves to literal interpretation. Many Jews and Christians have come to believe that a biblical story about the sun stopping dead in the sky while the followers of Joshua battled with their opponents is not literally true, though once it was taken that way. It seems obvious now that the heaven above is not a hard "firmament" holding back the waters of chaos from descending upon the earth, even though that is what the first chapter of the biblical book of Genesis says.

In every tradition there are also reasons given why even clear instructions in the scriptures should not always be obeyed literally. Not all Muslim nations now amputate the hand of a thief. Few nations with Christian backgrounds are now inclined to stone witches. Every tradition has found some ways of interpreting its own scriptures in new ways when that seems useful.

Careful research has often reinforced this tendency toward loose and more figurative or poetic interpretations. Buddhist texts tell of a virginal conception of the Buddha through his mother's side. A historical analysis suggests that this story was based more on an imaginative writer's desire to offer a strong image of the Buddha's significance than on historical fact. Science's understanding about the age of the earth and about human ancestry suggests that the Adam and Eve stories in the Hebrew Scriptures should not be taken as literal history, but as myth-stories that captured some general truths about life.

The intent behind a loose and more figurative interpretation of scriptures has usually been a respectful one. It is not an intent to destroy the reliability of the scriptures but to get at a broader and more symbolic meaning behind all the specific detail, in order to bring that general meaning into greater clarity for people. If there never was an Adam and Eve, for example, the Jew or Christian could still see in the stories a general truth that somehow humankind has ended up estranged from the ultimate wholeness we need. If there never was a Noah's ark coming to rest on the mountains of Ararat, the Genesis story of the rainbow and the dove with an olive branch could still be a vivid image about having hope in new beginnings.

No matter how good the intent behind these loose interpretations, though, efforts of this kind are seen by many believers as wrong and dangerous. Religious people are people for whom the mysteries of life are real and important enough to make the religious ways of dealing with these mysteries also important. To some extent basic faith in the meaning and value of life carries people on in the face of mystery, but that faith is still threatened by confusion, doubts, and personal trials. Highly literal and unquestioning adherence to religious instructions in scriptures can provide a feeling of security and certitude. Loose interpretations can suggest that the sacred scriptures are just poetic stories or unclear and vague messages that must be interpreted by the already uncertain human mind.

Nevertheless, every reading of scripture, even the ones that are intended to be the most literal, will include a great deal of interpretation and reinterpretation. Scriptures and the words of religious leaders are not passed on to believers on a one-way, perfectly clear course. Instead, there is an ongoing interaction. The sacred words are expressed in a language and a cultural context. That context provides religious leaders and writers with questions to be answered, as well as categories of thought, value, images, and words to be used in answering them. The religious message, whether it comes from wisdom, insight, or divine revelation, has to be expressed in a culture's categories. The message is then passed on to listeners and readers who receive the message as a way of interpreting their own lives and the reality they live in. Since they have their own way of perceiving reality and have their own categories of thought, they add their own interpretations to what is passed on to them, sometimes without noticing that they are doing that.

And so it goes down through the generations: leaders, scriptures, interpreters, commentaries, and readers or listeners all interacting and forming a chain of tradition. It is a living chain, a flowing back and forth of interpretations and reinterpretations that enable people to make sense of their lives through relation to the numinous in the face of the mysteries of existence. The guides of religion are not static signposts, but living currents in the overall human adventure that is religion.

Each generation tends to focus most sharply on the particular leaders and interpreters of texts that its family and recent cultural history have handed to it. Each generation tends to place its faith in the rather specific instructions provided by the religious context it grows up in. Each generation faces the mystery and deals with it by means of the detailed beliefs and moral rules that its historical setting has made plausible. In every case there has been the tendency to overlook or deny that the texts, leaders, and interpretations are in fact part of an ongoing historical process. There is the constant tendency to deny that any real change ever takes place. But no tradition is a package of unchanging beliefs, values, and practices. Tradition is a living process. As we will see, it is modern religion that will admit most fully the fact of ongoing change as part of its own story and life. Modern religiousness will also turn out to be the most willing to live with uncertainty and flexibility about its own specific beliefs.

Summary
Each religious tradition has its leaders and texts that interpret life and reality for people. The importance of interpreters and interpretations is attested to both by the many varieties of religious leaders and sacred texts that exist, and also by the trust that people put in their traditional leaders and texts. What is less noticed, but is an intrinsic part of the story, is that the religious activity of interpreting life is an ongoing process, with each generation guided in slightly new or different ways, so that to trust a tradition is actually also to trust a historical process of human development.

FOR FURTHER REFLECTION

1. List and explain all the ways you can think of that your ideas, values, and personality have been formed by tradition in some sense.

2. Give some examples of ways in which you and others show trust in your traditions, especially in the face of some challenges to them.

3. Which specific leaders have you followed in some way? Moses or Jesus or Buddha? Luther, Wesley, Martin Luther King, Jr., or Mother Theresa? Why?

4. Is there any good way to tell which sacred writings are most worthy to be accepted as truly sacred? How about the Book of Mormon or the Divine Principle of the Rev. Sun Myung Moon or the Tao te Ching?

5. Do you think it is legitimate to select or reject sacred texts on the basis of their rational plausibility? Their moral value? The emotional comfort they provide? On any basis? Explain.

6. If any sacred text is truly revealed or inspired by a numinous being like God, then is not a fundamentalist interpretation of it the best one? Explain.

SUGGESTED READINGS

Robert L. Wilkin, *The Myth of Christian Beginnings*, 1971; chs. 1-3 on the importance of tradition.

Denise and John Carmody, *Shamaus, Prophets, and Sages*, 1985; the role of leaders in the religions of the world.

Ninian Smart and Richard D. Hecht, *Sacred Texts of the World*, 1982; a thorough sampling of scriptures with comments.

Raymond E. Brown, *The Critical Meaning of the Bible*, 1981; chs. 1-3 for general introductory ideas.

J. Benton White, *From Adam to Armaggedon*, 1986; the prelude and chapter 1 offer an account of modern methods of biblical scholarship.

Max Weber, *The Sociology of Religion*, 1922/1963; chs. 2, 4, 5, 10, or 11; for early and influential theorizing on the roles of leaders, texts, and traditions in religion.

Living Images
of the Traditions

Ritual and Symbol

As each religious tradition has developed through the centuries with its beliefs in numinous powers and forms of salvation, in moral codes and religious leaders and sacred texts, it has expressed its beliefs not only in verbal form but also in the language of symbol and ritual. In drawings and carvings, statues and architecture, music and dance, drama and everyday ceremony, the religious visions of reality and life have taken on vivid forms. In their own ways, ritual and symbol are as effective as leaders and scriptures at guiding people in how to live in the presence of mystery.

RITUAL

Ritual is ceremonious or formalized behavior. We think of ritual also as repetitive behavior because most rituals or ceremonies are repeated time after time, but it is possible to invent a ritual to be used only once. It is the ceremoniousness that makes a behavior a ritual. It is also usually not random or spontaneous behavior (though some rituals include these elements) but structured or preplanned behavior. In 1969, Neil Armstrong might have simply hopped from the bottom rung of the ladder of the lunar landing craft onto the moon's surface and said whatever came to mind. Instead, for that one-and-only occasion, he carefully paused, and just before his foot touched the lunar dust he recited, "That's one small step for a man; one giant leap for mankind." He made a small ritual out of that first-ever event.

Ritual is a constant part of human existence. There is something in us that makes us ceremonialize every major element of life and many minor ones. From the simple, formalized greetings of saying hello and asking about one another's health, to the days of ceremony attending the death of a pope or the coronation of a queen, life is filled with ceremonies. Birth has its rituals of "showers," handing out cigars, and baptism. Death is thoroughly ceremonialized in funeral rites. And in between birth and death there are countless anniversaries, holidays, graduations, retirements, toasts and testimonials, formal invitations and thank you notes, rules of protocol, explicit and implicit dress codes that are more symbolic than convenient. In military assemblies and athletic meets, in courtrooms and classrooms, in political conventions and show-business award ceremonies, there is ritual. The list goes on and on. Why do we do this? There are two reasons, to make another simplified division. One is to make reality work right for us; the other is to make reality more real to us.

Ritual Makes Reality Work Right

Ritual is often magical. Since primitive times human beings have been possessed by a feeling that there is power in doing things exactly right. Belief that ritual has magical power is one instance of this. The right words said in the proper way while doing the correct thing with the required objects controls numinous powers. To get rid of warts you must stand in a graveyard at precisely midnight with a dead cat with a rope tied to its tail. Whirl the cat around your head exactly three times and say without stuttering: "Cat follow devil; warts follow cat." Within three days your warts will begin to dry up, provided that you have followed this ceremony's rules exactly.

We have also seen that it is not just small magical rituals that are useful. There are great magical, mana-filled rituals of immense importance such as the Aztecs and the Brahmins used to keep the universe working right. There is a special Taoist ritual of cosmic renewal still performed in Taiwan about every 60 years. This is the Chiao ritual, a nine-day series of ceremonies to renew the power of life. The sun, the highest form of Yang, must be born again each year with the help of appropriate ceremonies. Every long generation of 60 years all Yang-power must be given rebirth also through Chiao. Then babies will continue to be born, the crops will grow, the village will be healthy, and there will be enough good luck for everyone. (This Taoist thought is a popular archaic form rather than a historic form.)

To achieve all this, everything must be done with exact correctness. No one is to wear either leather or wool materials taken from animals. The spirits must all be formally invited so that they do not get upset and disturb the ceremony. Each family, clan, and village must contribute its traditional elements, whether soap, swords, scissors, or scales. The taoist priests will then follow the prescribed forms that have been handed on for generations and create a perfect sequence of ceremonies to renew the cosmic power of Yang.

Belief in the magic of ritual power is alive today in many places. Every little ritual we ordinarily call superstitious is an example of this. The person who spills salt tosses a pinch over the left shoulder to avoid bad luck. Even some historic religious rituals are still occasionally considered as magical. One person administers the rites of baptism with an extreme care to get the words and actions exactly right, out of a fear that if it is not done with exact correctness, then somehow it will not have its effect. Another person is upset because the traditional wording of the Last Supper ceremony or the Bar Mitzvah ceremony has been changed, as though there were a magical power inherent in using the exact words that had been handed down for generations.

There are many rituals with the power to make reality work right not because of magic in them, but because they are well-suited to influence the gods or God who controls reality. In some cases the god has decreed certain rituals. The ancient sky god of the Aryans in south central Asia decreed that only if there is a sacrifice of a horse once a year in the spring will the god guide his followers to victory in battles. In other cases, the ritual is simply well-suited to catch the god's attention. In ancient Canaan the worshippers of the fertility god Baal and his consort Astarte would celebrate annual spring rites that centered on sexual activity, especially in the temples and shrines. Baal and Astarte had to initiate the fertility of the year by sexual intercourse. Their worshippers could catch the attention of these gods and reawaken their interest in fertility by human sexual ritual activity that reminded the gods what to do. In general, just the showiness and ceremony of ritual might impress the gods and flatter them, and the sacrifice offered as part of the rituals adds an extra incentive to the gods to take care of human needs.

The Origin of Ritual

We have already seen some reasons why people have felt that ritual is useful. Water poured on the ground is similar to rain falling upon the ground; thus a water-pouring ceremony might easily appear to be best for producing rain. A voodoo doll made from clothing, hair, and fingernail clippings of a certain person is likely to be able to affect that person in an invisible way. This explains why certain symbols are chosen; it does not explain why the symbols have to be ritualized very precisely.

No one seems to have the final or complete explanation for this. Some have argued that we are born with an inclination to ritualize. Most animal species have some ritual behaviors, especially mating behavior. Perhaps there is a genetic tendency to ceremonialize. Others have noted that children ritualize as a way of learning. They watch adults do all sorts of things with ease: carry water in a cup, trim leaves off a plant, make toys roll across the floor. When children try to do the same, they spill, break, or overturn whatever they are handling. They learn that many things must be done exactly right and with care. Each movement of foot, hand, and eye must be carefully coordinated. From a controlled sequence of acts comes the ability to accomplish things correctly. Perhaps such experiences leave even us adults with a lingering sense that if only a person learns the exactly correct actions in the correct sequences and does them with a ceremonious care, then almost magical results occur.

Ritual serves to make people feel they have techniques for taming the wild powers of the universe. There are many experiences that produce chaotic emotions. Grief over the death of a child is channeled in manageable forms by funeral rites. The powers of madness in certain drugs can be controlled by restricting drug use to religious ceremonial times. The ancient Aryans used the drug soma (or haoma) as part of religious ritual. A native American religious movement uses peyote in its ritual. The controlled patterns of ritual safely contain the awesome power of the numinous.

Other speculation about the origins of ritual notes that dancing and use of rhythms in speech are appealing to all of us as children and even as adults. Maybe patterned and rhythmic behavior came first in human cultural development and eventually had mythic explanations attached to them to make sense out of them. This turned them into formal rituals, the theory says. First people danced. Then they began to tell a story in order to explain why they danced.

Ritual Makes Reality More Real to People

There are many non-religious rituals. Wedding anniversaries have no magical power; retirement ceremonies do not influence the gods. These and countless other rituals are important without exerting any control over numinous realities. These non-religious rituals provide us with a clue that the importance of ritual lies not only in their supposed power to influence external reality but in a different power as well, that of influencing human consciousness.

Human life is not lived as the lives of animals are. Human life is enacted; it is drama that follows the script that culture has written. It is a way of living based on human biological nature in many ways, but is largely composed of themes, styles, patterns invented by the human mind and incorporated into our culture. It provides us with a set of values and larger perspectives that tell us who we are, where we fit, and what our purpose is. The life we live is but one of the many ways that are workable for dealing with reality. This life is our interpretation of how to live, of human existence, of what the meaning and purpose of life are. People disagree on which interpretations are more accurate, which are human inventions and which are based on divine guidance, but they are all interpretations.

As we saw earlier, our life does not seem like an interpretation. Instead, it seems natural, just the way things are and should be. That is a sign that our culture, like other cultures, has successfully performed its function of giving us roles, rules, values, mental concepts through language, and so forth, that we can incorporate as part of our way of being a human person.

One of the ways a culture transmits its interpretation of reality to new generations is through ritual. Primitive cultures rely heavily on ritual because there are no alternatives to it, no schools and no written records. The rituals of birth, puberty, marriage, hunting, and death all contain guides to the tribespersons on how to act and think about themselves. The rituals are occasions to retell and re-enact the folk tales of the ancient figures and ancestors who made reality and its rules. For primitives, in fact, ritual contains reality. The stories told in ritual are real life and not just stories. They are reality-as-it-is, repeated and savored.

For archaic or historic people, ritual is somewhat more distinct from life in general, but it still is a presentation and interpretation of life. On the island of Bali, for example, at the far eastern end of Indonesia, the people have been Hindu since about the 7th century A. D. A central feast day in the Balinese year is the celebration about Prince Rama, the seventh avatara of Vishnu. His story is told in the Ramayana, one of the great classics of Hindu literature. A demon abducted Rama's wife Sita, the sacred story says. Rama joined forces with the king of the monkeys and pursued the demon to Sri Lanka. With the help of the monkeys, Rama defeated the demon and rescued his wife. This story is acted out on Bali in a great live drama in honor of Rama. With special clothing, face masks, and lights, the Balinese bring the demon, monkeys, Rama, and Sita to life before their eyes and those of their children. Through this drama every new generation comes to know about the nature of heroism, about love between husband and wife, about the evil of demons, and about many other things. The ritual thereby tells the generations what reality is like and makes it more emphatically real to them.

In the spring, Jews celebrate the long-ago event of passing over from slavery in Egypt to freedom in Canaan. At an evening meal called the seder, Jews recall this Passover in ritual form. The table is set with special tableware and some unusual food, such as unleavened bread and bitter herbs, in memory of the food the Hebrews had when escaping from Egypt. The youngest child ritually asks, "Why is this night different from all other nights?" The head of the family begins to tell the story: "When we were slaves in Egypt. . . ." The combination of various symbols and stories recreates in the minds of those at table the events of past centuries that made the Jews the people of Yahweh. The story is told not only about ancestors who experienced all these events; it is a story that says, "When *we* were slaves...." It brings the children into an identification with the past. When those children grow up, they will talk to their own children about the times "when we were slaves." Through the ritual every child comes to know what the reality of being a Jew is, and that reality becomes increasingly real through repetition in ritual each year.

Islam structures each day around ritual prayers. Five times daily the Muslim pauses from ordinary activities, ritually cleanses hands and feet and lips, faces toward the holy shrine at Mecca, and prays. It is prayer to praise Allah for his mercy and compassion. Above all, it is prayer that accepts Allah's will. Through daily prayers, through the daytime fast in the month of Ramadan, and through the activities of the pilgrimage to Mecca which every Muslim hopes to make at least once in a lifetime, the beliefs and values of the Islamic tradition are reaffirmed. These rituals confirm the reality of Allah as the merciful and all-powerful God. They confirm the reality of submission to Allah that makes a person part of the Muslim community. These rituals thereby help create the social reality that is the House of Islam.

Christianity has a ritual that explicitly retells the story and purpose of the whole universe. That is the traditional Easter service that recounts the biblical story of God's creation of the world and the first man and woman. It tells of the first sin and the expulsion from the garden of Eden into a world of pain and fear and death. The generations down to the time of the Patriarch Abraham are listed, the story of the escape of the Hebrews from Egypt, and the expectation of a Messiah. The birth and life of Jesus are quickly retold, recalling his trial and death on a cross. Then at dawn the story of Jesus' resurrection from the dead is celebrated. The promise of eternal life for all humankind and the messianic fulfillment of the entire universe are proclaimed with joy. Through rituals like this the Christian comes to perceive all of life in a certain way.

It would take many pages to list the major rituals of the religions of the world, and very many more to explain their significance. Because the rituals, year after year and even day after day, portray reality as the tradition perceives it, they make that interpretation of reality more emphatically real in the consciousness of those participating in the ceremonies.

Ritual sometimes also includes a ceremony of dedication to the reality it portrays. A standard American marriage ritual is a clear example of this. It reminds people of what marriage is, a bond between two persons "until death do you part." This marriage rite also asks whether the two persons promise to maintain this bond. The marriage is formed by the act of commitment in the words, "I do."

The element of dedication or commitment can be less explicit but still real. In the New Hebrides in the Southwest Pacific, a woman has two teeth torn out of her mouth to show she is married. College fraternities today exact a price from their pledges. The applicants for membership must suffer indignities and work hard to earn acceptance. Whether the cost is two teeth, manual labor, or psychological trials, this sort of ritual does not merely keep a person conscious of the new form of reality he or she is entering, but also requires a certain intensity of dedication from the person. This dedication to the reality that is re-presented in the ritual makes the reality more real, and also more important. Whatever costs more seems more precious.

It sounds odd to speak of a reality becoming more "real." A thing is real or it is not, our common sense tells us. The sun rises in the east or it does not; no ritual makes that any more or less a fact, common sense insists. It is not really as simple as that. A sun ritual at dawn every day can make people take note of the reality. The ritual can make people become more explicitly conscious of how reliable the rising of the sun is. That makes the sun's rising more explicitly real in the people's consciousness. Also, a sun ritual will include some interpretations about the sun. The ancient Aztecs and Egyptians both saw the sun as divine. The reality of the sun's divinity was plain to these ancient peoples because, in part, their rituals dramatized this truth to them. Finally, by the act of assembling together at dawn for the sun ceremony, people become more conscious of their unity as those who worship the sun. The ritual helps to create the realness of their mutual belonging and identity. In these ways and others, ritual makes reality real to the participants.

The Separation of Magic from Ritual

When religious traditions become historic they try to eliminate the magical use of ritual. An absolute God or infinite Brahman is totally beyond the power of magic. They cannot be affected by any mana-like power inherent in any rituals. Moreover, in historic religions the universe is controlled by a universal and all-powerful numinous reality. The belief that there are little numinous powers that human beings can manipulate in magical rituals is a belief that might challenge the omnipotence of God, that might suggest there are some things that are not under the control of Allah. For reasons like this, the historic religions tend to oppose belief in magic. Yet belief in magic comes easily to human beings. Traditional rituals, performed with reverence and treated as sacred, evoke a sense of awe in the participants, a sense that there is real power in the ritual actions. Buddhists in Thailand may be tempted to believe that a priestly blessing bestowed on medals bearing the Buddha's image endows those medals with powerful luck. Catholics in St. Louis may be tempted to believe that the baptism ceremony has a magical influence on the inner soul of an infant. If the words and actions are done just right, the divine power flows into the medal or child, the believer is likely to think.

The Buddhist priests of Thailand insist that the medal-blessing ceremony does not bestow special good-luck powers on the medals. It is an educational ceremony, they say, that recalls to people's minds the understanding of life that the Buddha attained in his enlightenment. The Baptist movement in Christianity has tried to guard against a magical interpretation of baptism by making it a ritual for adults, not infants. Adults can participate in the ritual as an act of conscious acceptance of a Christian interpretation of life and as an act of dedication to that interpretation.

There is a continuing struggle by historic (and modern) religion to avoid magical use of ritual. Islam typifies this in its insistence that external observance of the ritual cleansings and prayers does not fulfill the religious requirement. It is the inner intention to acknowledge, praise, thank, and obey Allah that makes the ritual worthwhile. The Catholic church has been emphasizing in recent years that its sacraments (central rituals) are not automatic external routines for producing a kind of divine energy called grace, as some Catholics tend to think. The sacraments are carriers of meaning and have their effect through people's consciousness and faith. They require attention and dedication to have an influence on people's lives. Magic requires only that the external operations be exactly correct. This controls mana-like power. Nonmagical ritual does not control such power; its influence is on the consciousness of the people involved, so their personal involvement is necessary.

Legalistic Ritual

Closely allied to belief in magic is the legalistic use of ritual. Legalism in morality is obedience to the letter of the law instead of its spirit. Legalism in ritual is obedience to the external forms of the ritual instead of participation in the meaning of the ritual.

There are religious believers who agree that their ritual is not magical, but who are still concerned mainly with the external correctness of the ritual rather than its inner meaning. In every religious group there seem to be those who dare not change ritual patterns, or the letter of any religious laws, for that matter, no matter how reasonable it might be to do so. It is a kind of taboo use of ritual, where ritual is done out of obedience to commands and out of a fear of punishment or chaos that would result from doing the ritual incorrectly.

To adhere closely to traditional patterns is not necessarily a legalism. The Amish who retain old-style dress can do so out of a sense of identity with their community. The Orthodox Jewish male who refuses to shave may find this a way of preserving a sense of continuity with tradition. The Catholic who does not eat meat on Friday may act out of a sense that it is good to retain some personal reminder of older ways. Yet among Amish, Jews, Catholics, and all groups of religious people, it is possible to find many who cling to traditional patterns of behavior almost compulsively with little sense of their meaning. The human need for security, identity, and belonging is motivation for such legalism, but it is a way of achieving a secure sense of identity and belonging that focuses on external conformity to programs of dress and behavior rather than on inner meaning.

All this can have the effect of turning the behavior patterns into rituals empty of meaning. Legalism appears to support ritual by maintaining its externals, but legalism can actually kill ritual by depriving it of its inner life. Religious ritual has its strongest effect where its inner meaning is given full attention.

Rituals as Part of the Long Transformation

All of us are tempted to believe that the routine performance of some ritual procedure will give us an easy access to what we desire, as though it were magical ritual. We want to lose weight without dieting and grow strong without exercise. In religious matters too, we want easy and automatic paths to moral rightness or life in paradise. From childhood through adolescence, however, most people slowly grow in the awareness that dedication and effort are needed, that there is no easy shortcut through magic or merely external observances to get what they want. People who belong to historic religious traditions still might like to believe that prayers or rituals will slice through the obstacles to happiness. This is a normal human tendency. But the long-lived historic traditions have ended up saying what every adult may finally learn, that inner development, slow and sometimes tedious processes of training, a gradual transformation of ideas, values, emotional perspectives, and work habits, put a person on the path toward achieving what is worthwhile.

This transformation is supported by rituals that function not magically or merely externally, but as interpretations of life. The rituals describe the worthwhile goals, keeping them before people as incentives; and they reaffirm that there is a path to the goals. They offer encouragement, reminding people of the trials and pains that accompany all developments; they bring people to make the religious vision the guiding center of their lives. The rituals will have these effects to some extent even on people who think of them as magical, but this belief in magic can also distract people from trying to learn from the rituals and from making a personal effort to grow into the reality the religious tradition offers as a path of salvation.

SYMBOLS

To discuss symbols after rituals is a little backwards. Rituals are just one form of symbol. Many symbols and symbolic actions together make up rituals, but symbol is nonetheless a broader category than ritual. Every ritual is a symbol, though a complex one, and there are other symbols besides ritual ones.

In ordinary English, a symbol is something that stands for something else. Those who write about religion like to make distinctions between signs and symbols and other representations. We can overlook all those subtleties here. A symbol re-presents something more than itself. It is a word, picture, gesture, action, object, drama, ritual that brings to people's consciousness something more than itself, something additional that it can stand for in people's consciousness. Like ritual forms of symbol, all symbols are meaning-carriers; they too make reality more real. They are not "merely" symbols in the place of the real thing; they are a kind of presence of the real thing, as various examples here will show.

Kinds of Symbols

There are all kinds of symbols, some rather ordinary. In a sense, each word we read is a set of symbolic marks that represent various sounds. These marks and the sounds they stand for represent to your mind some ideas. Some symbols evoke strong emotional responses: the national flag inspiring feelings of patriotism. Some symbols are as simple as a handshake; others are as complex as the inauguration of a president. The stop sign on the corner is the symbolic presence of the police power of the government. For that matter, the government in a democracy is the symbolic presence of the choices of the people.

Presence-through-symbol can be a limited one: a letter from a friend is a mode of presence of the friend. The friend is far away, yet her thoughts are there in front of you in written form. Her care and humor are present to you in her words. The presence-through-symbol can be a strong and close one: every person's body is a symbol of the invisible personality within. Each of us has an inner self that is always out of view. Yet we can say to one another, "I see you; I hear you; I understand you." That is because bodily motions, such as the sound waves made by voice and lips, all make present to others our inner self. The body is the symbol of the inner self because it really is the presence of that self. The only way any one of us is present to others is in and through bodily expressions. That is why it is worth learning the skills of how to express ourselves well in order to make our inner self present to others, and to be a good conversationalist in order to draw out and discover the inner self of others.

Religious traditions say that there is an invisible numinous reality that influences or controls things. Invisible realities can be perceived only by some visible re-presentations, by symbols. The signs of numinous power are all symbols of the numinous; they are all modes of presence of the numinous. The tree in the forest is a symbol of the wood-nymph that lives in the tree and makes it grow. All green growing things are symbols of the fertility-power of the goddess Demeter. The bright, dry, hot, and lively things of the world are all presences of Yang-power and are therefore symbols of Yang. All dark, moist, cool, and quiet things are symbols and presences of Yin. If the whole universe is created and sustained by God, then the whole universe is the symbol and presence of God's power and creativity. If God is the absolute fullness of what we know as "personness," then every person is a symbol and presence of God.

Everything is or can be a symbol. For an object or activity to function as a symbol, it must be recognized as a symbol. Human consciousness makes things symbolic by relating one thing to another. Water is just water until the human mind links it to other aspects of reality. Then it becomes a symbol and presence of life, of cleansing, of death, or of chaos, depending on how a person views it. For the people of the Nile, the river is the blessed source of life. For those who live near the North Atlantic, the waters of the ocean are symbols of death and chaos because the ocean storms destroy and kill.

Core Symbols

Some symbols are central to their religious traditions, so much so that other symbols revolve around them as satellites. These core symbols re-present most of what is in the tradition. In some forms of Buddhism, the simple sentence "The jewel is in the lotus" is a core symbol. One Chinese Buddhist declared that this saying contained the complete essence of Buddhist truths, and wrote extensive commentaries on it as the "Lotus Sutra" (or lotus saying). Outsiders have a difficult time imagining how these words could contain the whole of any religious tradition, but one who lives by the religious tradition can find a wealth of meaning there. For a Buddhist the lotus, a water lily, is a symbol of human existence because though its roots are buried in the muck and it must slowly grow upward through the murky waters, eventually it breaks out into the air above where it blossoms into its true self. Each person is like the lily growing from muck and through murkiness until released into nirvana.

In Judaism, the Torah is the core symbol. To the outsider a Jew explains that the Torah is the law or teaching given by God to Moses for the chosen people to live by. But the Jew finds in the Torah more than instructions for daily living. The Torah is a symbol of God's kindness and guidance; it is eternal wisdom made concrete in history; it is a call to a covenant with God; it is the presence of a divine promise for an eventual fulfillment; it is the primary symbol of God's presence, activity, and love. All rituals are based on the Torah. All value judgments, cultural forms, and family structures are related to Torah. This law is the center of the relationship of Jew to God.

Other traditions have other core symbols. It is not possible to list them here, but it is worth noting the power they can have. Because symbols are visible and concrete, they give some focus to religious beliefs and feelings. Images, statues, and stories help define the mysterious reality that is the numinous and make it easier to relate to it. The symbols of a religious tradition, in fact, usually control the consciousness of the people who follow that tradition.

The symbols define and interpret reality, and the place of human existence in that reality.

RITUAL, SYMBOL, AND THE NUMINOUS

The numinous is the invisible and mysterious. Symbols, including ritual, give concrete form to the numinous and re-present it. The ways religious traditions re-present the numinous in beliefs, moral codes, rituals, community forms, architecture, and theologies are ways of making the numinous symbolically present so that the human mind and imagination can deal with it. They are all symbols.

The Symbol in Primitive, Archaic, and Historic Religion

In primitive religion little or no distinction is made between symbols and the numinous. The three rocks in front of the cave in Australia are not symbols of the old woman and her daughters who formed the landscape. They *are* the three women themselves turned into stone. When the aborigines perform the rituals that re-tell the stories of the beginning of things in "dream time," these rituals are a way of actually living in the past and doing the original deeds.

Archaic religions sometimes show the same tendency. The statue of the god is the god. The Babylonians used to take the wooden statue of their god out for a walk after lunch and then tuck him in bed for a nap. In the villages of India a goddess mother is carried in procession, decorated with flowers, and given sweet-smelling incense to breathe. But archaic cultures also often believe that statues and symbols are not themselves the numinous power, but rather are representations of the power. The god may make her or his power known through the statue or temple, but actually lives on the mountain top or in the sky above. The Indian villager is comfortable in throwing away an old statue of the goddess; he or she knows that the statue is a presence of the goddess but is not the actual goddess.

Historic religions are much more conscious that what is divine is not identical with what symbolizes the divine. Historic religions believe that there is one all-encompassing power throughout the whole universe, a power that is infinite, eternal, and incomprehensible. But all symbols, including rituals, are part of limited reality. Therefore, no symbol or ritual is divine of itself. No statue can be a God; no ritual can capture infinite divine powers. Symbols are modes of the presence of the divine, but are not the same as the divine. They can only re-present it.

Historic religions have a strong need for symbol. A finite god can be directly present in an appearance to a person. The infinite God always is beyond the limits of any image or appearance. The person who wants to turn toward the infinite God or Brahman or Tao must rely on clues, pointers, symbols. To the Taoist, the patterns of nature are the symbols of the Tao. To the Jew, every person is a symbol of the supreme God. To the Buddhist, silence is a symbol of infinite nirvana. Such symbols are necessary to re-present that reality which in itself is infinite and incomprehensible.

The Problem of Idolatry in Historic Religions

Symbols, however, are not just valuable; they can also be misleading or even dangerous. Symbols like statues, rituals, and doctrinal descriptions of the numinous are more appealing and comfortable to people than the infinite and eternal for which they stand in historic religion. They are concrete images the mind can more easily deal with. In this lies the danger of idolatry: treating something finite and limited as though it were infinite divinity itself, as though it were the actual ultimate and eternal reality that alone is God or Brahman or Tao.

In India, religious leaders recognize that there is a disparity between the religious practices of most Hindus and the belief in an absolute Brahman. The leaders do not worry much about that. Those who worship statues or believe in gods are simply immature souls. After a few thousand more lifetimes these people will begin to appreciate that nothing finite or temporal is of any lasting value or reality. Eventually they will begin to long for true moksha, total release into oneness with the eternal and infinite Brahman. Meanwhile, the religious leaders are indulgent toward the god-worshippers, as wise adults are indulgent toward children who still have much to learn.

The Western tradition is somewhat more strict. The Judaic tradition explicitly forbids worship of any gods but the Lord God, Yahweh. While this may originally have been a form of henotheism, it became strict monotheism. As part of the defense of monotheism, Jewish law forbade the making of any carved images in order to prevent people from falling into worship of such images. Even today the Jewish temple or synagogue typically has no pictorial images. The symbol of God's presence there is the scroll of the Torah kept in each place of worship.

Christianity inherited at least parts of the Jewish law, including the ban on the worship of false gods. Yet early Christians lived in a Greco-Roman cultural context for the most part, one that used many pictorial images in statues, murals, and paintings. Christians used images of Jesus and his mother, Mary, and included also pictures of various apostles and saints. Christian belief has insisted that these images are symbols and are not divine in any way. But not all Christians have adhered strictly to that belief.

As an aid to preserving pure monotheism, some Christians have tried to ban all pictorial images on the grounds that finite images of holy beings such as angels or saints distract people from God, or even lead people to idolatry. In the 8th and 9th centuries in Constantinople there were many iconoclasts (image-breakers) who tried to get rid of all statues and pictures. In the 16th-century Protestant Reformation in Europe iconoclasm became popular again, as the Reformers tried to eliminate the superstitious use of statues, medals, and so forth, simply by eliminating them altogether.

Islam is very strict in its monotheism. Arabian religion before Muhammed had been an archaic religion worshipping many gods, in awe of many spirits and mana-filled springs and rocks and amulets. Muhammed and the Koran outdid the neighboring Jews and Christians in discarding all these distractions from the belief that there is but one God. Like Judaism, Islam forbids all graven images. It also takes great pains to insist that nothing be given religious reverence except Allah. The sole possible exception to this is the Koran, treated by most Muslims as the eternal wisdom and will of God written in human language. Some Muslims (the Shi'ite branch) even warn against excessive reverence for the Koran, lest this distract from full reverence toward Allah.

Islamic tradition warns against any way of treating any limited and finite reality as though it were God. The Arabic word for this is shirk, sometimes translated as "idolatry." But shirk consists of any tendency to take some aspect of reality, whether it be a person's nation or fame or success or power, and to make it the guiding goal in life. Only Allah and submission to Allah is ultimately worthy of a person's full devotion.

The Islamic tradition on this is one form of an idea that occurs in all the historic religions. We humans face endless mystery in our lives. This mystery threatens us because its mysteriousness leaves us confused and unsettled. We want to blow away the mists of mystery and find concrete descriptions of all aspects of what is real. We want specific and fully understandable answers to all the disturbing questions of life. We want to eliminate mystery from even the ultimate questions about the nature and purpose of things. We want a clear and definite meaning to life.

This means that in a sense we are born to be idolaters. We are born to want to take some clear answer and make it our ultimate answer. We want to find something definite we can use, not merely as a clue to the purpose of life but as the ultimate purpose itself. A historic religious tradition will usually offer definite answers, providing a belief system of ideas to be accepted as true and authoritative guides to truth: leaders, scriptures, and approved methods of interpretation; a moral code that gives definite answers about how to behave; symbols and rituals that are correct and valid. Because the beliefs and rituals and moral codes and community patterns and texts are not divine in themselves they too are symbols, ways in which the numinous is represented. But the temptation exists to identify all these symbols as somehow eternal and divinely sacred, instead of as limited ways in which the eternal and infinite is re-presented and made more concrete to us.

Historic religion has a special temptation to do this because this is the form of religiousness that human consciousness accepts when it achieves the ability to conceive of universal and complete perfection. The religious symbols historic religion lives by are not symbols of just limited and imperfect numinous powers, but of infinite and fully perfect Reality. It is possible, then, for historic religious believers to feel that since the symbols represent what is eternal and perfect, the symbols themselves must be everlasting and unable to be surpassed or corrected.

The constant, internal tension of historic religion (and modern also in its own way, as we will see) is to live by symbols that represent the infinite and incomprehensible mystery and give it a face and presence in doctrines, codes, community forms, rituals, and images, without at the same time covering up the mysteriousness that still remains.

In many cases there are no serious consequences of forgetting the infinite mysteriousness of the ultimate. People may pleasantly devote themselves to their own religious symbols as though those symbols were the totally complete, final, and utterly correct ones, but still somehow do so with a comfortable tolerance toward those who do not agree. This temptation to idolatry, however, can also produce severe intolerance. If the symbols are absolutely correct, then perhaps all those who disagree are enemies of the truth, whether they know it or not. One person might then condescendingly try to help the ignorant opponents of truth. But another person might also try to oppress, imprison, or kill them. It has happened.

The historic religion tempted to idolatry can overcome that temptation by reminding itself that its symbols can never be eternal and perfect; only the Ultimate can. There is practical value, then, to the Buddhist use of silence as a symbol for nirvana, or the Western use of the poetic image that describes God as a light so bright it blinds the soul. A famous koan (saying) of Zen Buddhism in Japan is apt: "What is the sound of one hand clapping?" If that question gives you a clue that our language and thought powers are limited in the face of mystery, the Zen master might approve (or might not).

The Death of Religious Symbols

Eventually, we will be discussing skepticism about religion, intellectual doubts about the validity of religious traditions. There is, however, another kind of loss of religiousness that is not so intellectual. That is the death of the symbols, including the death of beliefs and rituals and moral codes because they begin to lose their power to interpret and re-present reality.

Any symbol can die. It might be an image that no longer conveys meaning to an observer. We no longer see cows every day, so we no longer think of them as symbols of wealth or motherhood. A symbol also might die because the meaning it conveys, however strongly and vividly, is no longer acceptable. The image of a king still has some meaning because of all the stories about kings we are used to, but if a tradition pictures God as a king in order to suggest that God is a dictatorial ruler, some people today would find this unacceptable and insist that God should be symbolized more as a loving and creative force. Symbols can also be killed by legalism, which adheres to the use of a symbol but ignores its inner meaning. People who are pressured into external participation in a ritual may become indifferent to its significance and cease to be affected by it.

Any given symbol can be replaced by a competing symbol. A whole set of symbols associated with one community might be replaced by symbols from another source. Most cultures in the past received their symbols from religious sources. Religious tradition mainly passed on the culture's interpretation of who we human beings are and how we are to achieve some sort of salvation in the face of the estranging elements of life. Today, television and motion pictures provide images for interpreting life. Electronic images are replacing scriptural ones.

Symbols can die also when they are not needed at all. Religious symbols stand between human consciousness and mystery; they give form to numinous mystery, picturing it, describing it, or dramatizing it in some concrete way so that a person can relate to it as a numinous and saving reality (or as a demonic and threatening power). All symbols function best when they give form and content to what is otherwise hard to speak or think about. If a person or a culture does not perceive any mystery, something significant but hard to understand, then symbols will be rather useless. If your own sense of life is that there is no significant mystery that needs to be dealt with, then symbolic expression will not be important to you. Only if there is a dimension to life that touches you closely and is disturbing, yet escapes understanding, will you need some way to represent that dimension in a symbolic way.

This discussion of symbols is bringing us closer now to jumping into a topic that is often thought of as of primary importance in religion: religious beliefs. The next chapter will deal with knowing and believing as aspects of religiousness. But this discussion of ritual and symbol comes first in order to make one point plain: the beliefs and intellectual reflections on belief take place in the larger context of religious symbols and all the culture's symbols. The rituals, scriptures, revered leaders, community structures, and moral customs all together form a consciousness-context that people's minds rely on when they try to stop and consciously spell out to themselves their interpretations of life. We are able to think about life because our culture first has represented life to us in many ways, especially religious ways.

Summary

This chapter has described ritual and other symbols. Rituals have been part of human activity since the beginnings, used for their magical powers or to influence spirits or gods, but also because they told the stories of reality in a way that helped people understand how things are or should be. Rituals are symbolic, as are many aspects of religiousness. Symbols represent realities, numinous or not, so that people can have some image of or guide to what might otherwise be obscure or unknown. Thus symbols such as rituals interpret reality and life for people, guiding their thoughts, feelings, and behavior. It often happens that people become more attached to the symbols than the realities they represent, although at other times certain symbols lose their power and are replaced.

Religion is a symbol system that interprets reality for people, so that in the face of the mysterious dimension of reality and its power to cause estrangement, they can find instead the saving power of the numinous as the object of the basic human faith in the meaningfulness of life. That much is true of all religiousness. The next question that religions face is that of knowing how to establish just which symbol system is better for this. That is the topic of the next chapter on faith and reason.

FOR FURTHER REFLECTION

1. Which class of rituals and symbols best represents your particular values and interests? Religious symbols? Patriotic symbols? Family or economic-business or party-time symbols? Explain.

2. Do any of the rituals or symbols you use have magical powers? If not, what is their value to you?

3. Can you think of yourself, your community, or your physical world as the symbol-presence of the numinous, such as God? Explain.

4. An idol is a finite reality treated as though it were divine. Do people ever literally idolize success, money, or power? Explain.

5. Identify any rituals or symbols that now educate you about life in any way. Are any of them religious or provided by a religious source? Explain.

SUGGESTED READINGS

Paul Tillich, *Dynamics of Faith*, 1957; ch. 3 on symbols of ultimacy.

Frank W. Young, *Initiation Ceremonies*, 1965.

Niels C. Nielsen, Jr., *et al.*, *Religions of the World*, 1983; chs. 1 and 2 on symbols in general, their cultural importance, and some concrete examples.

Shirley Park Lowry, *Familiar Mysteries*, 1982; myths, folk tales, dreams, and symbols.

Richard Schechner and Mary Schuman, eds., *Ritual, Play, and Performance*, 1976; many and varied articles.

Nicholas of Cusa on avoiding idolatry, in Hugh T. Kerr, ed., *Readings in Christian Thought*, 1966, pp. 134-136.

Jacob Neusner, *et al.*, *Religion, Science, and Magic*, 1989; describes how different religious traditions have tried to exclude magic.

Believing and Knowing

The Interrelations
of Faith and Reason

Many religious persons today are usually convinced that there is a major difference between faith and reason. People think of faith as a basis for belief precisely when reason fails. Faith is defined as a trust, perhaps, in certain symbols, scriptures, leaders, and so forth, that goes beyond the evidence. Or it is a commitment to a religious viewpoint in spite of a lack of rational justification. Faith says, for example, that there really is a life after death, even if there is no hard evidence of this. Reason, on the other hand, believes in things like gravity precisely because there is good evidence for it. That is how people often think about this, at least.

A classic proponent of this notion of faith was the 2nd-century Christian theologian named Tertullian. He declared that he *be-*

lieved that Jesus had risen physically from the dead precisely because it was not the kind of thing that made sense to reason. If it was reasonable he would not need faith to accept it. His concluding words are often quoted: "I believe because it is absurd." He dramatized his position by asking, "What has Athens to do with Jerusalem?" that is, what does all the rational argumentation of the philosophers and scientists of the intellectual city of Athens have to do with the religious faith that Jerusalem stands for?

Tertullian's position, however, is not the only one. While most people think that faith is what a person relies on just where reason falls short, they nevertheless usually like to think that their faith is at least somewhat reasonable and not totally disconnected from reason. There is such a thing as reasonable faith.

There is a sense, in fact, in which even science is based on faith, although a very reasonable faith. The everyday scientist certainly has some faith that the scientists who have gone before have actually done the experiments they claim to have done and have collected the evidence they claim to have collected.

Even more basically, scientists in general have a faith that the world they study really exists. This is contrary to what some Hindus seem to say, following Shankara. Similarly, the Chinese wise man, Chuang Tzu, dreamed that he was a butterfly; and when he awoke he asked how he could be sure that he was not a butterfly dreaming he was a man. We cannot prove that we are human and not butterflies. But the overall evidence makes it very reasonable to believe that we are, and rather unreasonable to believe that we are really butterflies instead. The belief that science has in the reality of the world is also a reasonable one. This is faith in the reality of the world, but one that is based reasonably on what seems to be the best available evidence.

Scientists also operate by a faith that reality is intelligible and that they have the ability to understand the intelligibility of reality. This is a faith in both the coherence of reality and in themselves, their methods, and their powers of observation, analysis, and criticism. But this double faith also seems quite reasonable in that it is a very effective faith. Science does indeed seem to have achieved a great deal of highly reliable knowledge about how reality operates. Faith and reason can be closely intertwined in science.

The question for a religious believer is whether faith and reason should also be interconnected in religion. Should religious faith also be reasonable, or can it legitimately be unreasonable or even anti-reasonable? In this chapter we will first have to sort out some of the things that this might mean by looking at ways in which religious thinkers have tried to establish the reasonableness of religion. When we have looked at various ways this can be done, it will be easier to judge whether indeed you think that it *should* be done.

In general, any process of reflecting rationally on religious faith by those who believe in it is called theology. When rational reflection on a religious tradition is done from a non-religious viewpoint, it is then often called philosophy of religion. (But religious believers sometimes take a philosophical viewpoint about their own beliefs, so the use of labels here gets confusing.)

THEOLOGY

The Primitive and Archaic Traditions

No one knows how many thousands of years human beings have had religious symbols, rituals, and stories. Graves that are twenty-five thousand years old have been found with stone implements buried next to the bones, as though to provide tools for the dead in a next life. This is a clue that for those twenty-five thousand years, perhaps, human beings have been conscious of the mysteries of life and have tried to make sense of them and deal with them.

Through most of those years people have eagerly thought about the many numinous beings and powers. They have wondered about the names and characteristics of the spirits, about techniques for controlling mana and divining the future. They have celebrated the reality of the powers and spirits in ritual; they have told the stories of the numinous in countless folk tales and myths. Over and over again, religious beliefs have made sense of an otherwise mysterious reality.

But a new stage in religiousness came into power in human history in the axial age, when some people went beyond the beliefs they had used up to this point to make sense of reality, and tried to make sense of the beliefs themselves. Everywhere there had been people who had questioned one belief or another, who had doubted the power of a certain magic stone or the presence of a particular spirit; but these were not the thorough kinds of doubts and questions and analysis about beliefs that finally appeared when historic religion began. At that point some people raised very basic questions about why anyone should believe anything at all.

Historic Religion Produces Theology

Historic culture, in general, is a stage in human development in which the culture begins to produce individuals who seek a logically coherent and systematically unified way of understanding all aspects of reality at once. That is obviously an extremely ambitious goal. But it is also an implicit faith that reality ultimately makes sense, that in the end it really does all hang together and that the human mind can discover how it does. This faith took the human adventure of development and self-discovery in a new direction.

This faith in the ultimate intelligibility of reality manifests itself in three major ways. The first is philosophy. That is a name first given by ancient Greeks to their "love of wisdom" which expressed itself in the all-embracing theories about the whole universe proposed by people like Plato and Aristotle. The Stoics and the Epicureans added their versions. Similar schools of thought arose during comparable centuries in China and India.

The second way that faith in the ultimate intelligibility of reality manifests itself is in science. This was originally not distinct from philosophy. If you are searching to make sense of everything at once, you cannot easily divide your knowledge into separate packages called philosophy and science, because all knowledge must fit together in the end. But in recent centuries we have come to think of science as a distinct set of fields of study. It shares with philosophy the faith that we should treat reality as intelligible and keep on learning ever more how things fit together, though the scientists tend to settle for one thing at a time rather than take on the whole universe of all possible knowledge at once, the way philosophy has often tried to do.

The third way that faith in the ultimate intelligibility of things has manifested itself is in the body of religious reflection called theology. This is the work done by those who believe in a religious tradition to show the intelligibility and reasonableness of the beliefs and rituals and moral codes and so on, in relation to each other and to all other things. At least this is what theology meant to people in historic cultures. (In modern times some theologians have given up on this and, like Tertullian, are willing to separate religious belief from rationality, especially as it exists in science. We will see more about this in the last chapter.)

What theology has done, as is true also for philosophy and science, is to look at all of existence and try to capture it in one master story, one thoroughgoing and usually abstract analysis, that includes the final and overall truth, meaning, and meaningfulness of everything. In the process of doing this, they measured all the partial folk tales and myths against each other to see which could fit together and which could not. They threw out those that did not fit well with each other or with other kinds of evidence and logic. The ones that did all fit together in a single coherent story were translated into a more abstract language so that the logical unity and reasonableness of this story could be presented with precision.

From the beginning of this project one of the most troublesome, though also creative, aspects is that there have often been many conflicting master stories. This has been true even within a single cultural tradition. The Taoists of China did not see the same overall unity as the Confucianists; the Hindus of India disagreed with the Buddhists; in the West, Jews, Christians, and Muslims have variant stories. The contrasts among the religions of China, India, and the West are even greater. It is clear that it is possible to come up with one all-embracing interpretation of life and reality, one in which all the beliefs, rituals, symbols, etc., fit together in a coherent package, but still not be able to show that that interpretation is the right one; because in the next town or across the ocean is another all-embracing interpretation that is quite different.

Today many people are used to allowing everyone to believe what she or he chooses, so people do not always worry very much about the fact that the Hindu interpretation of life conflicts with the Taoist one, and that both conflict with the Christian one. But historic religions have tended to take themselves rather seriously. This makes sense if ultimate salvation is at stake, especially if that salvation consists in something like getting to heaven and avoiding hell or avoiding endless rebirth into suffering. Moreover, if one of the historic universalizing traditions is true, that implies that the others are false, at least in some way.

In defense of their own beliefs, people will sometimes try to show that other religions are false. In contemporary times there are those who attack all religious beliefs. If you personally have faith in some religious tradition, sooner or later someone will raise questions about your beliefs. If someone attacks your religion by saying that it is unreasonable or contrary to the evidence, you may want to have a way of responding. Theology has usually tried to provide help in that respect.

Theology, in sum, is a name for rational reflection about religious beliefs and all the other religious symbols, with two goals in mind. The first is to develop and maintain an overall inner rational consistency among the aspects of the present form of the religious tradition. The second is to show that belief in those basic aspects is sufficiently wise or reasonable that even outsiders should respect that religious tradition. To say it even more briefly: theology is the attempt to establish 1) the coherence and 2) the truth of a religious tradition.

SYSTEMATIC OR DOCTRINAL THEOLOGY

Faith Seeking Understanding

Systematic theology is the name often given to the kind of theology that first presupposes that the religious beliefs of its traditions are true, and then seeks to deepen the understanding of their truth by analyzing, comparing, and integrating them with one another. This establishes the inner coherence of the beliefs. Because systematic theology takes for granted the truth and value of the religious tradition and its doctrines, it is "faith seeking understanding," a classic Christian expression used by St. Augustine of Hippo in the early 5th century and echoed by St. Anselm of Canterbury in the late 11th century.

The task of systematic theology is a very difficult one. There is always some degree of uncertainty about the message of the tradition. People interpret scriptures differently, and the doctrines are not always clear and simple. This is inevitable. Religion brushes up against the fringes of infinite mystery. It always has to struggle hard to deal with that mystery.

The particular task of systematic theology is to expose the full meaning of the religious beliefs and other symbols including their overall interrelationships. This means that sacred theology has to first clarify the beliefs and then show how all of them fit together in one coherent interpretation of all of life and reality. If this can be done well, it provides an indirect argument in favor of the truth of those beliefs. It is hard to make sense out of life in an overall, coherent way. Any belief system that manages to do so is bound to seem rather insightful and reasonable. Yet, it is also very difficult to do, precisely because the project is to achieve a total coherence of ideas in relation to an infinite mystery. That is an enormous task, as some examples here can illustrate.

An Example: God and Evil, the Problem of Theodicy

A dramatic example of this search for overall logical coherence is the Western analysis of the problem of evil. We have seen that

Zoroastrian thought may have been held back from a full monotheism by its inability to account for the existence of evil in a world created by an all-powerful and all-good God. One Zoroastrian answer was to diminish the divine power of Ahura Mazda. Evil exists, they sometimes explained, because Ahura Mazda, the Wise Lord, cannot easily and quickly conquer Ahriman, Father of Lies. As was mentioned earlier, any theological explanation of the presence of evil in a world made by an omnipotent and all-good God is now called a "theodicy," a word invented by philosopher Gottfried Leibniz about 1710.

The great Western monotheisms have had a difficult time on this topic. In the West, belief in God has included the claims that God is all-powerful, all-good, and all-knowing. The basic theological problem of evil is to show how these three attributes of God are logically compatible with the existence of human suffering. Traditional theology has not been able to say that suffering exists because God lacks the power to eliminate it. That would be contrary to traditional belief in God's omnipotence. Some have suggested that suffering is an illusion; what we call suffering is not really suffering: pain is an illusion, or we exaggerate our difficulties to ourselves. Western religious tradition has rejected this idea, though. We humans do suffer, tradition says. And most of us would insist from direct experience that at least some suffering is real.

If suffering is real but God is omnipotent, that would seem to mean that God could eliminate suffering, but does not. No theologian has seriously entertained the idea that God is callous, indifferent, or evil. God is all-good, the traditional doctrines assert. Nor could suffering exist because God overlooks it for a while, until someone's prayers call attention to it, because God is all-knowing, the traditions affirm. The all-good God must allow suffering, therefore, for some good reason. An explanation of what that reason is would constitute a successful theodicy.

That reason might be found in another belief, that we humans were born with the power of free choice, able to choose good or evil. Without this conscious freedom we would not be human. Without it we could not freely choose good or choose to love. Freedom is so valuable, one theodicy says, that God finds its sometimes evil consequences worth the price. God allows suffering, therefore, as the occasional by-product of creating free beings. It is this human freedom, not God, that is the cause of hatred and murder and war and other forms of suffering.

The problem of evil is not so easily solved, though. Much suffering has been caused not by human freedom but by the forces of nature, by drought, flood, earthquake, and disease. Children are killed and crippled by events that no human choice could have prevented or avoided. There are theological responses to this also. One of them is the traditional Christian belief in original sin, based on an interpretation of the book of Genesis in the Hebrew Scriptures.

At the beginning of things, God created the universe and placed humankind at its peak. Then the whole universe was orderly and good. But the original man and woman used their freedom to choose to sin, thereby disrupting the right order of things, perhaps so drastically that the earth itself became unbalanced. Eventually, though, at the end of the world, God will make all things right again. Then all evil will be destroyed and perfect justice will prevail. Anyone who suffered on earth without deserving it will be repaid with happiness and glory. Anyone who did evil without suffering for it will be repaid with punishment. The suffering of millions of people has been caused by original sin, but it will all make sense in the end. This is a fairly comprehensive theodicy.

Even this traditional answer has sometimes seemed awkward, though. An all-knowing, all-powerful, and all-good God might just have found a way to prevent the suffering of millions down through the ages for sins they did not commit. But everyone has committed personal sins also, the tradition replied to this objection. So everyone has also personally earned suffering. Yet, those who say this have been hard-pressed to explain the suffering of infants, who presumably have not deserved their suffering.

Other ideas have proved helpful at this point. One is that God sends suffering at times even when it is undeserved, as a means of training and testing people, to allow them to become stronger and learn how to deserve even greater rewards. If this all seems a little harsh on little children who suffer, there is the final answer that Job arrived at, that suffering is a mystery.

The story of Job in the Hebrew Scriptures is one of the great treasures of Western tradition. It is a very human story of a good man who suffered much. His initial response to the loss of his children, his wealth, and his health, is a well-known response. "The Lord gives, the Lord takes away. Blessed be the name of the Lord." But relentless questioning by his friends finally moved him to challenge the heavens. "Make sense of this to me," Job cried out to God. God responded, "Were you there, Job, when I laid the foundations of the earth and made the creatures of the deep? Can you possibly understand? Accept that the divine ways are a mystery, Job." In response Job accepted, even though he did not understand, and trusted in God.

That brief telling does not do justice to the complexities of the story of Job. The theology written about the problem of evil since the time of the story (perhaps 400 B.C.) is even more complex. We do not have to solve the problem of evil here, fortunately. But it is a good example of how great a task historic theology has taken on in its attempt to show the reasonableness, the logical coherence, of the system of beliefs.

Polytheism has an easier time of it. It does not suppose there is any final unity of reality, so it does not have to figure out how everything relates to everything else in its portrayal of that reality. But if historic religion fails to do this, it will be attacked as inadequate or internally contradictory. It will lose plausibility for the inquiring mind. By default the religious tradition will appear internally incoherent and, therefore, somewhat unreasonable.

Making the Implausible Into the Plausible

Some beliefs present a special problem in that they might not by themselves seem reasonably plausible at all. Yet as part of a larger coherent system they can gain plausibility. Most Westerners, for example, find it hard to see how people in India could believe that the universe is not truly real. The Hindu finds this belief plausible partly because it is part of sacred tradition and partly because the Hindu is used to the idea as part of the cultural context. But the unreality of the world is plausible also because it is a belief that fits coherently with other ideas. The Hindu faces the problem of evil: Why do we suffer? Is there a way to overcome suffering? To believe that our worldly existence is maya, an insubstantial shadow, puts suffering in its place by portraying it as part of the passing insubstantiality of worldly existence. The belief in the unreality of the universe thereby helps to make a kind of sense, a coherent explanation of the human condition.

Among the various beliefs of Western religions, the Christian belief in the incarnation of God in Jesus of Nazareth is one that Muslims and Jews find highly implausible. How can the absolutely infinite and eternal God possibly become human, finite, and time-bound, in any way whatsoever? One classic attempt of Christian theology to explain this is that of Anselm, archbishop of Canterbury, in his late 11th-century work, *Cur Deus Homo?* (Why Did God Become Human?).

Anselm wanted to establish that it was very reasonable to believe that God had become incarnate in Jesus. As befits a theologian of a historic religion, he sought a universal and unifying coherence among all his beliefs. Anselm's Christian tradition told him that Jesus was both fully human and also truly divine. Western beliefs shared by Christians, Jews, and Muslims alike said that humankind was sinful to some degree, and that God was all-good and all-just. Anselm decided that he could show how these beliefs made the incarnation a reasonable belief. Here is how he argued.

A sin against God is an offense of infinite seriousness because God is infinitely good. When the parents of the human race freely sinned against God they incurred a debt to repay God for their offense. But the debt would have to be repayed by an act of infinite worth to compensate for the infinite seriousness of the sin. But humankind was both finite and now also sinful and flawed. Only God who was infinite and perfect could make repayment of infinite worth. Yet reparation would have to be made by a human being because it was a human debt. Thus, Anselm concluded, only a person who was both God and human could make reparation for human sin. God's infinite justice demanded that reparation be made. And God's perfect goodness required that humankind be able to be reconciled to God. It made good sense, Anselm concluded, that God's justice and goodness would lead God to do the one thing that could overcome the infinite offense of sin. That was to become incarnate. This, Anselm went on, is why the suffering and death of Jesus saves humankind. By this sacrifice a repayment is made by a human being, a repayment of infinite worth because the human being is also God incarnate.

Since the 11th century, Anselm's explanation of the value of the suffering and death of Jesus has become accepted by many Western Christians. Anselm took the belief in the suffering of a God incarnate, a belief offensive to many monotheists, and explained it in such a way as to make it seem more plausible or reasonable. In actual fact, Anselm's arguments have probably appeared reasonable only to Christians who already accepted belief in an incarnation. But those who were Christians could say after Anselm that their belief in the incarnation and in the value of Jesus' suffering and death was not foolish belief, but reasonable belief.

We have seen that systematic theology integrates and justifies beliefs by working within a belief context, by accepting certain basic beliefs as already true. From the earliest times of historic religion, however, another challenge to belief has existed: How do the believers know that their basic beliefs are true? How could Anselm know he was correct to believe in God in the first place, for example? Confronted by doubters, those who have believed have tried to do another kind of theologizing, one that has sometimes been called "religious philosophy" or "philosophy of religion." Here we will call it by another of its names, "natural theology."

NATURAL THEOLOGY

By Reason Alone

Natural theology tries to rely only on the natural human powers of reasoning and not at all on prior beliefs or doctrines. In practice, natural theology usually ends up confirming many traditional beliefs. Every human mind is inclined to see as reasonable what is already customary. Religion is no exception. In principle, however, natural theology defends itself against doubts or attacks by using reasoning alone. It cannot support its conclusions by quoting a sacred authority or text. It assigns itself the job of making sense to people on the basis of reasoning and experience, not on the basis of beliefs already accepted.

Natural theology has been very influential in Western civilization. Beginning with the ancient Greeks of the axial age, Western thinkers have tried to uncover the ultimate secrets of the universe by reason, to discover the universal power, patterns, and stuff of things by reflection and logical analysis. We have seen one such attempt in the example of Aristotle's argument concluding that there is an Unmoved Mover, a perfect self-thinking thought that accounts for all the motion in the whole universe. Similarly, by rational analysis alone, Socrates and Plato concluded that the human soul is immortal. These are but two instances of a much larger tradition of philosophical reflection. As it happened, the thought of those ancient Greeks spread around the Mediterranean world until Jew, Christian, and Muslim began to see in such thought the possibility of proving by reason much of what they also believed by faith. The most common instance of this is in the proofs for the existence of God.

Proving God's Existence by Human Reason

There are three major kinds of proofs. They are called the argument from design, the ontological argument, and the cosmological argument. The names are not important. The last two have lost much of their original meaning. But philosophers still use them, so we might as well also.

The Argument from Design

The word "argument" is a little misleading; it is not a two-sided dispute, but a presentation of reasons why there must be a supreme and universal Designer of the universe. Probably the most popular argument for the existence of God, this begins with observations about the orderliness of nature.

There is an extraordinarily complex set of interrelated patterns to nature. The ecological patterns of even a small pond in the middle of summer are complex enough to overwhelm the capability of even a major computer to keep track of them and analyze them. Likewise, the workings of the eye and hand in coordination is a marvelously intricate and balanced interplay. The eye catches the light rays of those certain wave lengths we call visible as they reflect on the surface of a baseball in swift curving flight. Signals from the eye guide the movements of body, shoulder, hand, and fingers in precise coordination to capture the ball in flight in a smooth motion. Life forms, planets in orbit, the evolution of the stars in accordance with basic laws of nature all seem to show a detailed pattern that could not be accidental or random. Order such as this could only be the result of an ordering Power. Both Taoist and Western monotheists agree on this.

Western theology carries the argument a step further than the Taoist and says that the Power that orders the entire universe must be a conscious and intelligent Being, not a mere Force. It is the order of things that makes them intelligible. Without order there is only irregularity and unpredictability, only chaos and nonsense. But the awesome fact is that the universe is the opposite. It is as though the universe were consciously planned and intelligently ordered. No unliving and unthinking Force or Power could account for such great intelligibility. Therefore, there must be an intelligent orderer such as Westerners call "God."

This very popular line of reasoning is, unfortunately, greatly disputed. Astronomers, evolutionary biologists, and other scientists have theories about the universe that appear to be able to explain the ordered patterns of the universe as the result of a few mechanical laws of nature operating aimlessly over billions of years. We will hear more about these scientific thoughts in a subsequent chapter. Such scientific doubts have made other arguments in favor of God's existence more significant.

The Argument by Definition and Logic

A second argument is fascinating for its utterly logical simplicity. It was first developed by Anselm of Canterbury (1033–1109) and came to be known as the "ontological" argument. There is a neat modern form of it synthesized by the contemporary philosopher Charles Hartshorne. In its most condensed form it goes something like this:

A.   Just by definition, "God" is the label for the Most Perfect Being: M.P.B. (that than which nothing greater can be conceived: that which cannot be second to anything in any way, the totally unsurpassable Being).

B.   Concerning the existence of M.P.B., there are four and only four logical possibilities. One of them must be true because there are no other possibilities.

    1. The M.P.B. is logically impossible, i.e., is a self-
       contradictory notion, like a square circle.

    2. The M.P.B. is possible, but does not exist.

    3. The M.P.B. does exist, but could cease to exist.

    4. The M.P.B. exists necessarily, could not not-exist.

C.   Statement 1 must be rejected. There is nothing self-contradictory in the idea of a M.P.B. (Hartshorne has written whole books in support of this.)

D.   Statements 2 and 3 must be rejected because each statement is intrinsically self-contradictory: a being that does not exist or could cease to exist is surpassable and therefore is not a M.P.B. The possibility of not existing is incompatible logically with the definition of Most Perfect as given in this argument.

E.   Therefore, Statement 4 must logically be true, because one and only one of the four statements must be true, and 1, 2, and 3 are all false.

This argument does not appear to have the logical simplicity promised; it looks rather complicated instead. But it does not require a great deal of information about the world. It does not depend upon evidence about evolution or cosmic order. It simply argues that a Being that is called Most Perfect must be defined as one that necessarily exists (cannot not be), otherwise it is not truly a definition of a most perfect Being.

Critics of this argument, however, claim that Anselm and Hartshorne have only shown how to define a word in a self-consistent way. That is not the same thing as showing that there is a reality that fits the definition. Thus many philosophical theologians rely on a further argument.

The Argument for an Uncaused Cause

One of those who rejected Anselm's ontological argument was the 13th-century theologian, Thomas Aquinas (1225?–1274), perhaps the most brilliant of all the great medieval Christian theologians. He offered five basic arguments. The first three of these converge on a line of argumentation partly borrowed from Aristotle. Often called the cosmological argument, it claims that the fundamental facts of the cosmos, its motion, order, and actuality, can only be accounted for finally if there is an ultimate explanation of the kind that people know as God. Here is a somewhat modern and condensed version of the underlying ideas.

A. Every event that takes place has a cause or set of causes that accounts for it. This means that every event is intelligible, explainable by what caused it.

B. Every event depends on what caused it. Those causes depend on whatever caused them. These further causes are dependent on still other causes, and so on endlessly. Everything is contingent on something else. This means there is no *ultimate* intelligibility or explanation for events.

C. It does not make sense to suppose that the overwhelming intelligibility of things (as in A above) can come out of ultimate unintelligibility (as in B above).

D. Therefore, it is reasonable to assume that the conclusion of B is not correct. It is reasonable to assume instead that there must be an ultimate reality that causes everything else and thereby explains why everything else exists.

E. For this to be the truly ultimate explanation, it cannot require any cause that explains it. It would therefore have to be the sole reality that is uncaused: the Uncaused Cause of all things. This is what all people call "God," says Aquinas.

This rather abstract and bare-bones summary contains a lot of ideas. It asserts that reality is intelligible, a good common-sense approach. We find it practical to assume that events do follow from their causes, that red dye makes red cloth and not blue, that loud bangs are produced by some cause and not by nothing at all, and so on. Science operates quite successfully on the premise that reality is intelligible in this way. But it is hard to prove that. There is still enough mystery, always there, to give some reason for the Zen Buddhist to recommend listening to the sound of one hand clapping instead of trying to figure out everything. Yet it is part of the basic faith of many, especially those raised in a Western tradition, that reality is intelligible after all.

The Philosophers' God

The trickiest thing about the cosmological argument is that it claims only that the ultimate explanation known as God does exist. It does not claim that people can fully understand that explanation. To put it another way, the cosmological argument concludes that there must be an ultimate Uncaused Cause of all else. It does not say that we human beings can really comprehend what an Uncaused Cause is like. Just the opposite is the case. Aquinas argued something like this:

An Uncaused Cause is a cause which, just by being defined as uncaused, does not have or need anything that explains its existence or what it is like. Nothing accounts for it in any way. If anything could even possibly account for its existing or its way of existing, it too would be contingent in some way on an outside cause. Then it would no longer be the final answer to things. So, by definition, it must be the unique exception to the rule that everything is explained by its causes. The Uncaused Cause is self-explanatory. It necessarily exists. It is self-causing, if you like.

Therefore, the reasoning continues, the Uncaused Cause must be absolutely infinite. Any finite reality is this and not that (red and not blue, living and not dead, and so on). Every finite reality, therefore, could become other than it is (could turn blue and die). So a person can demand further explanation of *why* it is still red and living or *why* it has turned blue and died. The state of finite things is contingent, dependent on causes, in need of further explanation. Inasmuch as the Uncaused Cause by definition cannot depend on anything or require anything to explain it at all, it must apparently not be finite in any way at all.

This conclusion implies further that the Uncaused Cause is changeless. To change, a thing must first not be what it is to change into. It cannot turn blue if it is already blue. It must first be *not*-blue. But to be *not* something involves a finiteness, an aspect of non-being or limitedness. Furthermore, a changeless reality is outside of time, because time is just the process of change. The word "eternal" stands for timelessness. As was said, this is not a mere everlastingness through all time. It is eternity outside time without any before, during, or after.

There are other logical implications, Aquinas thought, of the fact that God is the infinite and eternal Uncaused Cause. There can only be one Uncaused Cause. There cannot be two absolutely infinite realities, because then each would not be what the other was, and would therefore be limited. The Uncaused Cause must always be totally simple (without any inner differentiations) because otherwise there would be internal limits differentiating one aspect from another.

As is apparent by now, the Uncaused Cause is incomprehensible. The attributes of infinity, immutability, eternity, unity, and simplicity are all really negative words: no limit, no change, no time, and so on. They are not really descriptions of the Uncaused Cause so much as they are admissions that this cause must lie beyond the limits of what human minds can comprehend.

This clearly is a philosopher's God, the absolutely infinite and incomprehensible Uncaused Cause. It is also, however, the God of many natural theologians, those who try to argue that belief in God is not just a willful leap or a wishful loyalty, but is a reasonable option for an intelligent and reflective person. The problem is that the conclusion of all this intelligent reflection is very abstract and distant. To use a better word yet, the conclusion is Mystery.

When human beings seek ultimate intelligibility, final all-encompassing answers, they have set themselves on the path to the infinite. It is no wonder they find that the ultimate is Mystery. Yet, to drawback from the ultimate is to settle for the finite powers again, a god or other limited forces, in order to express or explain the realities of life. There is no easy choice here.

The God of Natural Theology as Personal

If natural theology stopped at saying that the Uncaused Cause is the eternal and infinite incomprehensible One, it might fit the Brahmanistic views of Shankara, but not those of Western theology. The natural theology described here comes out of the Judaeo-Christian-Islamic traditions. In these traditions the Uncaused Cause is a God that is also in some sense a personal God. As Chapter Three indicated, the word "personal" can have unusual meaning when applied to God. Natural theology tries to explain why the word can be used at all and what it must mean in this case.

God is infinite, the argument goes. Existing without limit, God is therefore totally perfect, the limitless fullness of being. Out of this infinite fullness, God has somehow produced a world (without any change in God, however that may be possible). In this world there are various limited perfections. A limited perfection is something good that is real, but in a limited way. Whatever is good and real is a result of God's unlimited perfection. So whatever perfections exist in the world must somehow exist first "in" God in some way (a way incomprehensible to us).

The greatest perfections we know are those of reflective consciousness and moral freedom, the theologians go on to say. Reflective consciousness is an open-ended capability of absorbing things into the mind, an openness to the infinity of being. Similarly, moral freedom is an endless capacity to perceive the potential for good, to be continuously open to ever greater good. As consciousness and freedom are the most open to the infinite, they must be the best clues to the infinite perfection of God. Consciousness and freedom are the core attributes of personness as we know it. We are therefore closest to speaking accurately when we say that God is somehow personal. or at least that God is the fullness of what we know as personness in our limited way.

Symbols of the Divine

The Western natural theology that leads to the infinite incomprehensible Ultimate parallels the Eastern beliefs in the infinity and incomprehensibility of the Ultimate. Theologians, philosophers, and mystics all find this to be where the human quest leads them: into endless mystery. With the exception of some branches of Buddhism, however, it is not a mystery of endless emptiness, but a mystery known to be fullness and perfection, a numinous reality whose existence affords salvation of some kind.

Natural theology leads to the double conclusion that the Ultimate is Mystery, but it is simultaneously somehow the fullness of being and perfection. That is why symbols for the divine are both necessary and legitimate. Symbols are necessary because the divine or ultimate exceeds human grasp. Only symbols can represent it. Symbols are legitimate because there is a divine reality there to be symbolized. Whatever a culture understands to be the most real and most perfect of all finite things is a symbol for the infinite fullness of being and perfection. Personness, the flow of nature, or ritual power are the primary symbols in the great historic religions (and for some Buddhists, silence or emptiness).

Many of the great religious traditions say that in whatever existence follows our final death, we will all be mystics, contemplating the eternity of the ultimate or being dissolved into it. Until then, say the theologians, those who are not yet mystics will have to relate to the divine or ultimate reality by finite representations of this ultimate—by symbols. So religion must formulate its doctrines and rituals and moral codes and forms of community all as symbolic ways to guide life and mind in the direction of the divine Mystery.

FAITH AND REASON

The Danger of Reason

Religious people are often uneasy about theology. Faith and reason do not marry and live happily ever after. On the face of it, all the reasoning done by theologians seems to support faith by showing it to be quite reasonable. If the symbols of faith all fit together in a coherent unity, and if basic beliefs can be supported by rational arguments, this strengthens the religious tradition's claim to be a good and valid interpretation of life and its mysteries. By being so reasonable, though, the enterprise of theology suggests that reasonableness is a requirement religion should live up to; it accustoms people to expect that all the religious beliefs be reasonable. Many believers reject this idea.

When Anselm set out to show how reasonable it is to believe that God exists or that God became incarnate in Jesus and died for human sins, he discovered many critics. Faith is precisely faith and not reason, the critics said, and they accused Anselm of subjecting the ideas of sacred scriptures and holy tradition to rational analysis by a mere human mind. They cautioned Anselm to spend more time in humble prayer accepting God's truths, and less time relying on weak human thought to understand the mysteries of faith. Tertullian would have agreed heartily.

The critics were correct in recognizing the issue: Should religious beliefs have to live up to the criterion of reasonableness? Does the believing heart have to submit to the inquiring mind? Few people will say that they will believe in something that is logically incoherent and unreasonable. Yet, once the mind begins to analyze and argue in order to show the coherence and reasonableness of a tradition, there is no easy way to halt the questionings and critical analyses at a safe place. There are various ideas about how faith and reason should mingle.

Faith Without Reasoning

The most straightforward way to eliminate the problems caused by rational analysis of religious beliefs is to avoid such analysis. This may never be fully possible, but there are some close approximations.

There is first of all, extrinsic or artificial faith. This position is not really faith at all, although it is often called by that name. It could be a taboo compulsion to uphold certain doctrines, even though the doctrines mean little or nothing to the person. For example, a person can be taught as a child that belief in the existence of God is something that God demands of people; God will punish anyone who fails to believe. Out of sheer fear of punishment, then, a person may grow up feeling it necessary to believe that God exists, and might feel a taboo kind of motivation to defend belief in God even if he or she does not understand or value the belief at all. This kind of faith can be an empty dedication to certain words, whether the words mean anything to the person or not. It is an extrinsic or artificial sort of faith. It is a kind of legalism of belief.

The same could be true of someone who clings to certain beliefs out of a feeling that that is the only way to maintain acceptance by the community, to preserve an identification with the group. This kind of motivation is more likely to lead a person to understand the beliefs in order to talk about them with others in the community group and thus strengthen acceptance. This kind of faith is liable even to be a rather intense external support for to the doctrines the group shares. In this case it is really the group-belonging and not the doctrines and other symbols that are important. A person who fails to achieve acceptance by a group may readily begin to look about for other groups and other beliefs. In all of this the reasonableness of the beliefs is irrelevant; in fact, even the beliefs are irrelevant.

There is also an intrinsic type of faith without reasoning. Faith can exist without theological reflection, without rational process of integration and justification of the beliefs, in a way that nonetheless does respect the beliefs and other symbols for their own sake. Two things are needed: that a person accept the religious symbols as true, and that these symbols matter to the person. This is a strong and living faith, even if it is not a reasoned faith.

The most common sort of intrinsic and unreasoned faith is the everyday faith that most people simply inherit from their family and culture. For brevity, we can call it unchallenged faith. People receive their religious interpretation of life mainly from their social context, not from hours of personal theological analysis. This faith often goes unchallenged by doubters, outsiders, or theological critics, so the person experiences little need to show its coherence and plausibility. The tradition that is received and held this way may be a very complex set of symbols—beliefs, moral codes, rituals, and so forth—yet the faith involvement of the religious person can be the simple one of just living out the interpretation of reality provided by those symbols, without doubts or rational analysis. Living the faith can be simple as long as it is unchallenged.

Closely related to unchallenged faith is blind faith, which also does not rely on rational justification. This is a challenged faith, but a stubborn one. Though it may have once been unchallenged, eventually challenge arose. The skeptic, the person of another tradition, the theologian raising logical questions can each intrude upon the peaceful flow of unchallenged faith. Then those who care little about their religious tradition will stir slightly, mildly piqued by minor doubts. But those who are highly involved in the life perspective that their religious tradition gives them will be provoked to a stronger stand. Some will plunge into rational analysis in defense of their tradition. But others will reject reason and take a more stubborn stand, affirming blindly that their beliefs are true, regardless of reason and the critics. That is blind faith.

Skeptical onlookers can find many uncomplimentary reasons for blind faith. They will be quick to recognize the human need for security that makes us cling to the traditions that give us our sense of worthy identity, our meaningful belonging, our ability to overcome the powers of estrangement. Ignorance and irrationality are prices we are all ready to pay in order to remain secure in the face of threatening challenges. There may be more reasonableness or logic in blind faith, however, than is at first apparent.

There are a couple of kinds of logic to blind faith. The first is a reasoned argument to avoid the need to reason much about faith, strange as that sounds. The human quest to understand the mysteries of existence eventually ends up in the conviction that the ultimate reality is Mystery, the infinite and incomprehensible. Therefore, a person should expect that the various beliefs and other symbols of a religious tradition go beyond what reason can handle. If the truths of faith are non-reasonable, perhaps that is a sign that they are closer to the infinite Mystery which is beyond reason. This is exactly Tertullian's position. Blind faith might therefore be truer faith than reasoned faith.

Perhaps the only valid way to know the Infinite may be by the power of the Infinite itself. It has been a common idea in Christian tradition, in fact, that faith can never come from the human mind or human effort, but instead is a gift of God. God reveals truths beyond human reasoning and simultaneously provides the mind with the inner conviction that these are indeed true. It is not human reasoning, therefore, but the grace of God that empowers people to know the truth about God. Blind faith is therefore correct to trust in God, this logic says, in spite of any human reason that challenges it.

There is a second and different kind of logic at work in blind faith, a more hidden logic. This is the logic of practicality. The average religious believer lives for years by a religious interpretation of life's meaning and structure in the face of the various threatening mysteries of life, its suffering, confusion, and injustice. The religious interpretation makes sense of it all, offering a theodicy to explain the pains of life, and promising some form of salvation. Estrangement is under control; identity and belonging and values are clear and strong. Somehow the whole religious interpretation of life works well for the believer, even if that person cannot give a good theological or philosophical or scientific analysis to justify that interpretation. The believer can ask whether it is truly reasonable to abandon a faith perspective that makes such effectively helpful practical sense out of life. The person of blind faith cannot often articulate this argument in a reasoned way, but may feel it in a hidden way nonetheless. It would be foolish to give up a faith that guides and enlightens and encourages a person just because of all the rationalistic doubts raised by others. That, at least, is the second and hidden logic of blind faith. It may be the kind of faith that the scientist-philosopher Blaise Pascal (1623-1662) spoke of when he said, "The heart has its reasons which reason does not know."

Faith as a Reasonable Commitment

The existence of a logic or two, even in blind faith, is a clue that we have a hard time divorcing our lives utterly from reason. After all, to do so, we would have to divorce ourselves from our own inner nature as the peculiar beings with reflective consciousness. Ignorance and irrationality are a partial loss of our own humanity, which is a very high price to pay for the sake of religious faith.

We have seen the two major forms of using the priceless power of reason: systematic theology and natural theology. In the past they have often represented immensely ambitious attempts to achieve perfect logical coherence and intellectually compelling arguments in favor of certain beliefs. Historic religions reflect the ambition of historic post-axial culture to make ideal, coherent sense out of everything at once.

In modern times a more modest goal has become attractive. Instead of seeking perfect logic and fully compelling arguments, many theologians today are happy to achieve a position of reasonableness. They maintain the basic faith that life is intelligible and worthwhile. They assume that the same ultimate God is the source of all the universe, consciously reflective human beings included, so that the intelligibility of the universe and the intelligence of our minds should fit together. The reasonableness they expect of their faith, however, is not quite the perfect logic that historic religions have usually sought.

The theologians of modern culture are highly conscious that there is no compelling rational *proof* that the world is real and not maya, that the Mystery is divine and not everlasting chaos, that life really and finally is intelligible in spite of all the uncertainties that hover about us. No interpretation of life, including a religious one, can be shown to be absolutely reasonable and guaranteed to be true.

As a result, many people now cautiously withhold belief from all religious interpretations and settle for an agnosticism that seeks only to make do as we go along. But such pragmatic caution edges close to denying that there is any basic value or direction to life at all that we can rely on. (We will see more about agnostic pragmatism in a later chapter.) If a person still seeks some clear and basic direction to life, but also agrees that no one can finally prove the truth of one interpretation over another, one religion or philosophy in preference to all others, there is still a way to be reasonable about it.

In general, it is possible to make a reasonable commitment to a religious interpretation of human existence in the universe, even though that interpretation is not provable. A person can reflect thoughtfully on the human condition, on life's possibilities and limitations. As actually lived, life can be set side by side with a religious interpretation for conscious and explicit comparison and correlation. As in the case with the hidden logic of blind faith, there is a kind of practical test, but now done deliberately and reflectively.

The test is to ask whether the religious interpretation really makes some overall sense of who we are and what the meaning of our lives might be. Is it at least compatible with scientific understandings of the world? Does it offer an understanding of where we come from and where we are going, an understanding that is at least reasonably possible, even if not provable? Does it produce a moral vision that helps instead of hurting? Can it be lived, celebrated in ritual, symbolized effectively, all in a way that fits life's experiences and gives extra strength to life? If it can do all this, then it can be reasonable for a person to consciously choose it as his or her religious faith.

This process of thought has been call "theology of correlation" by theologian Paul Tillich (1886–1965). We can correlate our knowledge of the world, our experiences of life, and our understanding of the basic questions about life's meaning, with the interpretation of life offered by a religious tradition. When we find that this match-up produces a coherent and intelligible vision that in practice resolves our feelings of estrangement, then it can be reasonable to accept the religious symbols expressing that vision as our own faith. The act of faith for Tillich is therefore a choice, an act of making a reasonable commitment to a religious vision. It can be difficult to go through such a process of reflection. But it offers a way to reconcile faith and reason.

The Tensions of the Human Quest

Faith and reason are part of the human quest to see life as coherent and meaningful. Sometimes they can work in harmony, but there is an underlying tension that is unavoidable in the long run.

A particular faith perspective gives security to our lives by providing a way to deal with threatening mysteries. It gives the security of identity and belonging and the hope of overcoming all estrangement. It is reasonable to seek such security, at least in the hope it can be found and maintained.

But what is the basic choice or commitment that a person wants to make: to personal security or to reasonableness? Is it legitimate to give up being reasonable entirely in order to preserve the security that religious faith can provide? Which is a person more committed to, maintaining a reasoned honesty about reality as well as possible, or maintaining a sense of security even if that involves some self-deception or illusions?

We human beings are still on the great adventure of becoming ourselves. We grow in knowledge through search and questioning, exercising our capacity for reflective consciousness in new ways.

Each time we do this, we run the risk of breaking some symbol that has been our guide to life's meaning so far. The tension exists every time we begin to doubt some traditional belief. Even to continue to be fervently religious can place us in the tension between security and questioning, if the religiousness itself seems to call us to some new interpretation of beliefs. In the presence of Mystery, the religious symbols that interpret existence are always in tension between security and adventure, between past and future.

Summary

This chapter has been about theology and faith. Theology is conscious and reasoned reflection on religious beliefs and other symbols. Faith is a name for the act of commitment to the reality symbolized by a given religious perspective. Theology attempts to show the reasonableness of a set of religious symbols, both in terms of their logical coherence with one another and also in terms of the individual rational plausibility of the basic beliefs. A person's act of faith might or might not be a reasonable one, however. Some people care little for rationality in religious matters; others care a great deal.

END OF PART III

The heritage of human cultural development and of our own individual development provides us with a mixture of beliefs and other symbols, some of them primitive in style, others archaic, and still others historic. The interplay among these styles and symbols can be very complex, yet there are some general dominating themes each style tends to impose on the overall pattern of religiousness. Each style is an overall guide to life, in its turn influencing the specific guides that are morality, leaders, texts, rituals, reason, and faith. There is one more dominating style that guides people's religiousness. That is the modern style. The next part describes modern religiousness.

FOR FURTHER REFLECTION

1. To what extent do you think it is good for people to be non-rational and unreasoning about their religious beliefs and practices?

2. What would be the most important purpose be for reasoning about one's own beliefs and religious practices? To support them? To understand them more deeply? To disprove the claims of others?

3. How much should religious people be consciously reflective about the overall coherence of all beliefs with each other and with other human experiences? Why?

4. We usually say that people have a right to believe whatever they want. What limits would you set to this right, if any? Not to practice human sacrifice? Not to contradict science?

5. Which in fact is closest to how you would describe your own faith: blind faith or reasoned faith? Which do you think is better and why?

SUGGESTED READINGS

Henri Frankfort, *et al.*, *Before Philosophy*, 1949; on myth as pre-theological thought.

Paul Tillich, *Dynamics of Faith*, 1957; on faith as ultimate concern.

Thomas Aquinas, *Summa Theologica*, Part I, Question 2, Article 3; the five arguments for God's existence.

Anselm of of Canterbury, *Basic Writings*, 1962; see "Cur Deus Homo?" (Why Did God Became Man?).

Mortimer Adler, *How to Think about God*, 1980; a somewhat philosophical approach.

Brenna R. Hill, Paul Knitter, William Madges, *Faith, Religion, and Theology*, 1990; on the nature of and differences between these three.

PART IV

MODERN
RELIGIOUSNESS

Different people mean different things by the word "modern." For most of us, it means whatever has happened in our own lifetimes. Historians say that the modern era in Western civilization began about 400 years ago because it was then that a number of ideas that are still influential today began to grow rather strong in Western culture.

During these last 400 years, a new form of religiousness has slowly developed as part of the overall cultural transformation that makes up "modernity." Some aspects of it grew comfortably from within traditional religion. Other aspects of modern religiousness originated outside the religious tradition, often first in opposition to religious belief or practice. These outside influences ended up changing religion, though, to the point that ideas that were once considered unreligious or even antireligious eventually came to be part of some people's religion.

It is difficult at times to be clear on what is "modern" in religion because many religious groups that exist in contemporary times are not themselves very modern in their type of religiousness. Even religious movements inspired by modern perspectives are not entirely modern. All religious groups are made up of human beings; we are all inheritors of primitive, archaic, and historic modes of thought, both from our overall cultural history and from our individual development from infancy to childhood to adolescence to our always incomplete maturity. Even though we may hold some of the modern ideas that will be described soon, we also may believe in spirits, be influenced by some taboo morality, think of some rituals or symbols as semi-magical, and so forth.

The complexity of all this will be laid out in more orderly form as we go along. Nevertheless, it can also help now to provide a simple guide to identifying what is meant by the modern stage of religious development. There are three major aspects of it.

One aspect is the elimination of the great gulf between earthly imperfection and divine perfection that historic religiousness often emphasized. Modernness has not wiped out the distinction entirely, but it has changed it. Most Christians, for example, were once taught to think of this earth as a fallen and corrupt place, infected by sin and death, doomed to pass away at the apocalyptic end of the world. Now the modern emphasis has crept into Christian thought that this world and its comforts and challenges, its loves and joys, are also divine gifts, worthy and even holy enough for us to rejoice in religiously.

The second aspect of modern religiousness is its appreciation of freedom, variety, and change. This is a fairly radical idea for religion. Religion traditionally has provided stability and security in the face of threatening change and anxious uncertainty. Modern religiousness, however, is not just tolerant of variety and freedom; it actively supports them in various ways and to various degrees. It includes a sense that no religious doctrine is the final word on any subject. It defines ideal human "personness" in a way that emphasizes individual choices, with all the uncertainty and instability this might risk.

The third aspect is skepticism about miracles and the supernatural. The development of science and scientific attitudes has led many people to be wary of ever claiming that miracles happen. Many a modern religious person will even prefer to define religion in such a way that the notion of miracles is omitted completely. This includes a general reluctance to speak of the supernatural, of revelation as miraculous, of divine healings, or of any other sort of specific divine interventions into the events of nature and history. God's activity is portrayed instead as a more general ongoing supportiveness and presence.

This may or may not sound very religious. There is certainly no common agreement among Westerners about what religiousness should be like in these contemporary times. What we can do is go back to the approximate beginnings of modern thought and sort out some of the events and ideas to better understand and evaluate modern religiousness. For convenience we can start at about 1600, the time of Galileo.

Science and Secularity

The Modern Era Begins

Adherents of historic religion tend to believe in a perfect existence that lies beyond this earthly reality. By contrast with the mind's image of perfection, concrete earthly conditions appear to them as dismal and fallen, unworthy of our concern except as a passage we must endure and live righteously in on our way to perfect happiness. Modern thought, however, begins with a new confidence that somehow or other our earthly life has intrinsic importance and is worth taking very seriously, worth our enthusiasm and dedication for its own sake.

This modern turn to the world has its roots in the Renaissance in Europe (and before that in the great rebirth of historic thought in the 11th and 12th centuries). For a variety of reasons, some only guessed at, Renaissance Europe experienced a great surge of energy and optimism about life in this world. The new art, architecture, and music exhibited a fascination with worldly life and beauty. Great exploratory expeditions sailed from European ports to discover new continents and new wealth. Mechanical inventions multiplied; mathematical methods improved.

All of these were an early part of the great cultural development that led to the modern era. All of them together contributed eventually to a different perspective on human existence, on mystery, and on hopes for the future. This meant that there would also develop a new sense of what religiousness is, a new sense of what the deepest mysteries of existence are and how we are to discover meaning and hope in them rather than threat and confusion.

This shift toward a new way of understanding existence did not occur overnight. It is a shift that is still just beginning in the lives of many people around the world, including those in the supposedly modern cultures. To understand what this shift is, the best place to begin is with the most controversial of its early forms, the beginning of modern science.

EARLY MODERN SCIENCE

From about 1600 to 1800 in Europe and America, there developed a pattern of thought that soberly celebrated the complex orderliness of the universe. The eventual effect of this was to ban miracles, spirits, and omens from the daily life of those who firmly believed that this universe was a fully orderly place. These believers identified themselves by various names: natural philosophers, enlightened ones, free thinkers, deists. Many of these we would now call scientists, though that word was not invented until the 19th century. They had their beginning in the time of Galileo.

Galileo and the Beginnings of Modern Science

Galileo Galilei (1564-1642) died after more than fifty years of prodigious work in science. He is popularly remembered for his support of Copernicus's argument in favor of the theory of the ancient Greek Aristarchus, who claimed that the earth went around the sun. But Galileo did more than support the Copernican theory of the solar system; he promoted much of the basic methodology that came to be known as science.

Before Galileo, science was a part of philosophy. It tried to explain not merely what patterns existed in nature, but also their ultimate purposes. As we have seen a number of times, the human mind tends to presume that things make sense. The animist and polytheist assume that many events are caused by spirits and gods who have some humanlike motive for intervening in life. Those who believe in a personal universal power such as God say that all events are under God's control, so that all things that happen do so in accord with God's purpose. To understand reality thoroughly, then, it would be necessary to explain why God made them happen that way, for what purpose.

One theologian of Galileo's time, for example, is said to have contradicted Galileo's claim that the planet Jupiter had moons. Because no one on earth could see the moons without a very good telescope, he contended, there was no purpose for God to put moons around Jupiter. They could not be guides for the navigator as the stars were. They could not move people to admire God's talent as a creator since they were invisible to most people. Therefore they could not exist. One clever person responded that since Galileo's telescope showed that the moons did exist, there must be intelligent life on Jupiter, beings who used the moons for navigation on Jupiter's oceans. This person obviously agreed that it was indeed important to show the purpose for the existence of the moons.

In his many investigations of the pendulum, of motion, of centers of gravity, and so forth, Galileo had long been taking a different approach. Forget about figuring out what purpose there is behind the events of nature, he insisted. Concentrate instead on finding out with mathematical accuracy just how things act, just what the reliable patterns of physical nature really are. That is enough. Galileo summed it up as treating all physical reality as matter-in-motion: lifeless stuff, following patterns that could be described coldly and clearly by mathematical formula.

Science today no longer asks why God puts the seeds on the outside of strawberries, or why God gave Mars two moons, or why God created mosquitoes. When science asks today why something happens, it does not seek to know the ultimate purpose of each thing, but only how reality is structured so as to have caused given events to happen. Before Galileo it was hard to do science without mentioning God and God's purposes frequently. Since Galileo's time we have become accustomed to leaving God and other numinous powers out of scientific theories.

This is true of both kinds of physical events, the regular and the irregular. The unusual or irregular event is one such as lightning striking a house, a comet appearing in the sky, or a disease suddenly afflicting a healthy person. From the most primitive times to today, people have found it plausible to say that such irregular events are the work of numinous powers. Up until Galileo's times, everyone was certain that each comet was sent individually by God to warn people of a calamity to come. Every lightning bolt was God's punishment. Every sickness was caused by a demon. Many people today still speak of every flood or tornado as something God sent or permitted for some divine purpose. But under the influence of the new science that Galileo helped to establish, we are no longer so sure. We usually think irregular events in nature are actually manifestations of basic and highly regular patterns. Our scientific explanations of diseases can omit any mention of God. Also dead and gone are the spirits that once lived in the trees, the rivers, or the clouds.

Religious believers often combine their belief in scientific explanations with at least a vague sense that it is God also who is at work in the events of nature. A meteorologist may pray as though it were God who guides the tornado, even though she also believes that tornadoes follow a course laid down by atmospheric conditions, natural causes. But when she studies what is known about tornadoes, she would be surprised to find any reference to God in her textbooks as part of the explanation of how tornadoes form, why they are so powerful, what paths they tend to take, and so on.

Scientists find they can also describe all the regular aspects of nature without any mention of numinous reality. These are the various reliable patterns of nature, ranging from the extremely regular forces such as gravity and electromagnetism to the fairly regular patterns such as the movement of the tides and the chemical reactions of an acid with a base. A famous meeting between an emperor and an astronomer illustrates how science has come to describe such patterns without reference to God.

The French astronomer Pierre Laplace (1749-1827) had developed a theory of how the solar system might have slowly evolved into its present form. The Emperor Napoleon invited Laplace to describe this theory to him. Laplace elaborately explained the mathematics of gravity and mass and motion, perhaps losing Napoleon in the details. But Napoleon did notice that Laplace had not mentioned any part God played in the whole process. Legend has it that Napoleon challenged Laplace on this: What about God? Laplace supposedly replied, "I have no need of that hypothesis."

These words do not deny God's existence or power; they just state what science has come to take for granted: the patterns of nature have a regularity of their own. There is no need to slip some mention of God into a description of nature's patterns in order to explain how they operate and what events they cause.

This was not entirely new. The science of Aristotle's day—as well as the science of late medieval theologians—proposed that nature followed regular patterns that operated without extra divine intervention. But after Galileo's time the sheer number of events that could be explained as part of the patterns of nature constantly increased. Therefore, the number of things that seemed instead to be the product of divine intervention—miracles—constantly decreased, to the point where miracles no longer seemed plausible. In general, the active presence of God in the particular events of life because less directly evident to people.

Deism

By the middle of the 18th century, the century known in Europe as the Enlightenment, many scientists and science-minded people had come to share a kind of natural theology known as deism. This was a new religiousness that accompanied many other new and radical ideas such as belief in democracy and free speech.

Deism divided all of reality into two distinct realms: the spiritual and the physical. Galileo had earlier recommended treating the physical as matter-in-motion, as nonliving stuff that acted always in accordance with basic mathematical patterns that were built into the nature of physical reality. By the time Isaac Newton (1642-1727) died, there had been a century and a half of success after success in science by the use of Galileo's method of treating physical reality in this way. Deists felt entirely reasonable, then, in agreeing with this approach.

The success of science also encouraged the belief that the physical universe was entirely intelligible, and intelligible in mathematical or mechanical terms. "The force of gravity is equal to the product of the masses (and a constant), and inversely proportional to the square of the distance between those masses." That is a scientific statement. Gone from science were claims such as "God made gravity to hold the universe together." Gone also were older ideas that said, "Rocks fall because they seek a natural state of rest." Rocks do not "seek" anything, the new science said. Language that suggests any life or consciousness in raw matter is simply inaccurate, most deists believed.

The mathematical order of things awed the new scientists. Where once there had seemed to be countless unpredictable happenings caused by demons, saints, angels, or God's intervention, now there was order. Now there was dependable regularity built into physical matter. Every irregularity in nature turned out to be caused by an intersection of regular natural laws in a way that could be predicted by the mind that knew the laws of nature. This led the new scientists to new ideas about God's power and activity.

First of all, there was common agreement that the orderliness of nature, its thoroughgoing mathematical intelligibility, could not possibly be an accident. It must have been designed. The older argument for God's existence known as the argument from design took on new power. The Designer, it seemed clear, must have been a perfect intelligence capable of designing and creating a whole universe of such detailed orderliness that in spite of its enormous complexity it could run on its own by its own built-in constant laws of nature. In one famous image, God was compared to a master clockmaker who designed and created an intricate timepiece, wound it up, and then let it tick away on its own.

The same deists who were sure that God the Designer must exist promoted a second idea: this Designer did not intervene in the orderly operation of the clockwork universe. There were no miracles, in other words (though some deists made an exception for the miracles of the Bible). Robert Boyle (1627-1691), the English scientist and acquaintance of Newton, said it this way: God is not a puppet master pulling strings from behind the scenes.

Over and over, things like comets and lightning that had once been thought to be miracles, interventions by God into nature and history, turned out to be the effects of natural causes. Furthermore, the basic goal of science is to discover a natural explanation for events. To believe in supernatural miracles seemed like an obstacle to the search for scientific explanations. Finally, a logical argument was added: to believe that God intervenes in nature is to suggest that God did a sloppy job when God first designed or created the universe. People once believed God had to work to keep the planets moving in their orbits or to make the fertile rains fall each spring, as though God had made a rickety universe that required tending. We know better now, the new scientists said. We know the almighty and perfect God did a perfect job in creating. Now it is just up to people to understand that creation.

The new scientist was thereby also learning to trust the power of human reasoning. God made the world intelligible and made the human mind intelligent, able to understand the world's intelligibility. Science was what God made people for, they thought. By the end of the 18th century, many people began to assume that there were natural laws of human behavior in addition to the natural laws of physical nature. Eventually the new sciences of economics and sociology and psychology gradually developed, seeking to understand the regular laws of human life in order to tell us how to live wisely and happily.

Therefore it seemed that there would be no need to ask for God's help in life, to hope for miracles or to expect divine guidance. In the beginning God made all things quite orderly. Since then, from the first sabbath onward, God has rested. Meanwhile, we can trust that this world is a good place to live. All we need to do is to understand it thoroughly and then set to work to make it all better for us humans.

There would still be a lingering source of trouble in this magnificently ordered universe. The human person is not merely a physical and emotional being subject to the laws of nature, the deists said. The person is also a spiritual being, with a soul that has the power of free choice. The spiritual aspect of our humanness is not controlled by the natural laws of the physical universe. It can cause disorder, confusion, and evil. But if God made people free, God nonetheless would not allow freedom to wreck the overall order of things, the deists argued. God must have provided some way of regulating the human use of freedom. In light of this, a traditional Western belief seemed quite logical, that is, that God must eventually punish those who use their freedom to cause the evil disorders of life. So God is not completely at rest, but is watching us. After our deaths God will pass judgment on us and reward or punish us in accordance with the choices we have made.

Those are the ideas that constituted deism. It was called a "natural religion," one based on natural theology rather than revelation. The God of deism was the Designer God and the Judge, the God who created the world at the beginning and who will judge all people in the end but who does not intervene in the meantime. The deists believed that they especially did not need God's intervention because they had now discovered the wonderful power of human rationality. Traditional religion stressed the importance of obedience to religious scriptures and authority. The deists believed that the use of human reason was the highest authority. This and the disbelief in miracles set the deists in opposition to the traditional religious groups, although they were still explicitly religious in their own way. Before long, however, some science-minded people began to abandon this untraditional but real religiousness in favor of a non-religious position. Evolutionary thought was a major contributor to this shift.

EVOLUTION AND AGNOSTICISM

Evolutionary Theory

The deists lived in a universe they saw as static; no significant changes were expected in its basic structure. A few thousand years earlier, God had placed the sun in the center, with the earth and other planets around it and the stars in their appointed places in the sky. But by the 17th century the astronomers began to guess that perhaps the universe had evolved. Laplace's 18th-century theory said that the universe was a changing process, that the sun and planets had slowly formed over very many thousands of years out of some heavenly gasses or matter.

By the 18th century geologists began to be confident that the earth had evolved physically also. The Bible had seemed to indicate that the earth was created no more than 6000 years ago. The only major geological changes in the biblical record were catastrophes caused by God's intervention, such as the great flood which only Noah and his family had survived. (That seemed to account for the strange phenomenon of seashell fossils up on mountain tops.) By studying the numerous layers of different kinds of rock formations, however, geologists became convinced that only a slow process of change taking place over many millions of years could account for the appearance of those layers.

It was not long before many people began theorizing that maybe not only heaven and earth had evolved, but life also. It was very difficult to construct a suitable theory about this. There were many attempts, each with its own problems and limitations. Finally, Charles Darwin (1809-1882) captured the attention of the scientific community with a theory that has turned out to be amazingly fruitful. He published this as *The Origin of Species* in 1859. For thirty years Darwin had gathered bits and pieces of information about fossils, seashells, and mountainsides, about similarities between species and about odd animals in strange places in the world. But evidence is not really evidence until someone sees how it fits into a theory. The mangled match on the patio floor is not evidence to the detective until he realizes the murder might have been committed by a left-handed former cigarette smoker who chews matchsticks.

Darwin provided a theory borrowed from economics. Nature was like a capitalist economy, said Darwin (harking back to Adam Smith [1723-1790] and Thomas Malthus [1766-1834]). There were two main factors at work. The first was that there are random variations among members of a species. The offspring are not all exactly alike. The second factor is what Darwin called natural selection. The most successful variant forms grow and produce others like themselves; the unsuccessful die and wither. Philosopher Herbert Spencer (1820-1903) summed it up as "survival of the fittest."

There was a variety of responses to this theory. Many religious authorities rejected it completely, as they rejected other theories that seemed to contradict the Bible. Some deists traded in their static deism for an evolutionary deism, proclaiming that the evolutionary pattern followed a God-given natural law, that of the survival of the fittest. How ingenious of God, they said, to have built into nature an evolutionary process. These evolutionary deists, along with traditional religious people of various beliefs, at least agreed that there still was a Creator God. Not everyone else did.

Atheists and Agnostics

Atheism is a name for the belief that there definitely is no God. Agnosticism is a name for the conviction that no one can know whether there is a God or not. In practice, both the atheist and the agnostic get along without God, but the true atheist is close to saying that the mystery we humans face is ultimately just a meaningless emptiness. The agnostic just says that the mystery is a mystery.

When the new science had begun to cast doubt on some aspects of traditional religion, many turned to the nontraditional religion of deism, but others simply turned away from religion altogether and became atheists. With miracles eliminated, church authority weakened, and the accuracy of the Bible in doubt, the reasoned arguments of natural theology still favored by the deists were no longer as convincing to everyone as they had been.

Darwin's evolutionary theory gave an additional boost to atheism in a number of ways. One was Darwin's claim, published only in 1871, that humans had descended from apes. This made many persons doubt there was a soul or any place for the soul, such as heaven or hell. It made God less necessary, no longer needed as a hypothesis to account for human existence, nor even as a Judge for the soul in an afterlife.

Of great importance was the fact that the theory said evolution operated by random variation. The evolutionary process, as Darwin described it, was a very long, aimless one. Each generation begets dozens of offspring. Randomly, each offspring is a little different from its parent, and that difference, also by random chance, occasionally is of use in the offspring's struggle to survive. As a result of this double randomness, that particular offspring is more likely (not guaranteed) to grow up, breed, and pass on that lucky variation. As long as that variation helps for survival, it will tend to become more common. Many billions of such random variations over more than the last 3.5 billion years of life on earth, according to current estimates, have given rise to the present species.

All theories that stressed the factor of randomness in the evolutionary process made it seem less reasonable to accept the traditional belief that the universe was guided by a God who intervened to guide things, or even the deist belief that God was a master designer. Those who were already inclined to be atheistic saw evolutionary theory as additional support for their atheism. The theory also helped produce the new word, agnosticism.

One of Darwin's main supporters was Thomas Huxley (1825-1895). In the heat of arguments about God's existence, he was asked whether he was a theist or atheist. In order to have a label for his position, he invented the word "agnostic." It literally means "one who does not know" or "not-knower." Huxley heard those who argued that an evolutionary process that resulted in humankind could not be purely accidental, but must have been planned by God. He also heard those who said the randomness of evolution proved there was no God. As a scientific-minded person, he could see no way in which either of these claims could ever be tested scientifically. He therefore came to what seemed to him to be the most rational conclusion: no one can know whether God does or does not exist.

Agnosticism and Social Darwinism

Agnostics usually claim they arrive at their position by reasoning. It is intellectually sound, they say, to acknowledge that the ultimate state of things is simply unknowable. But we humans do not live by intellect alone. It is easier to be an agnostic or atheist if there is also no practical and emotional need for a God. The 19th-century agnostics could feel comfortable in a godless universe because they believed human beings could do quite well without one. A movement known as social Darwinism is a good example of this kind of agnostic optimism. Herbert Spencer was its best-known advocate.

It is reasonable to believe, said the social Darwinists, that the pattern of evolution will continue as social evolution. Human reasoning is a product of life's evolution, they said, and is itself evolving. With reasoning as a tool for survival, those who use it best will survive best. Those ideas that would best promote survival are ideas that promote better health, international peace, and economic prosperity. Therefore, these ideas would steadily increase in influence until one day humankind would enjoy health, peace, and prosperity everywhere. Thus does society evolve. (Karl Marx offered his own version of this kind of belief.)

Because social evolution was doing all this by itself, there was no need to rely on God's help to improve things. People would be saved from hunger and war not by divine help, but by the natural process of evolution. The millennium was coming but not because of ancestors, gods, or God. This time of joy and peace and love would arrive, liberating people from their estrangement, because this was the pattern of evolutionary progress.

SECULAR EVOLUTIONARY HUMANISMS

A Substitute for Religion
From 19th-century thought until today, there have been visions of salvation that are like this agnostic evolutionary optimism. They are most often called secular evolutionary humanisms, or just "secular humanism." There are various forms of them (we will look at two), but they have some characteristics in common.

First, they are secular, which means that they are thoroughly this-worldly. They do not believe in any numinous powers, not spirits, gods, or God (although they sometimes believe in a God-substitute, as we will see). They are also this-worldly in that they do not believe in any life after death. We humans are born into nature and history, live our lives and die, they say. Our meaning, value, and purpose must be found within the limits of these earthly lives and our effect on the lives of the generations to come.

Second, an evolutionary view holds that reality is in a constant process of development. There is ongoing change which is not merely repetitious, but is a process of improvement, at least in the long run. That includes human culture, its social conditions, morality, economics, politics, and so forth.

Third, humanism is a viewpoint that maintains that the quality of human life is the most basic value there is, to be sought in all else. A humanism is a basic-value morality that proposes that a humane, loving, free, and creative existence for all people is the most important goal there is. (Note that there can be *religious* humanisms as well as secular ones.)

A look at secular evolutionary humanisms can help to understand modern religiousness because these humanisms are actually modern substitutes for religion. Secular evolutionary humanisms incorporate the notions that modern religiousness accepts: a renewed appreciation of this-worldly existence, an emphasis on growth and freedom, and a disbelief in the supernatural including miracles. This can be seen in the 19th-century belief system of Karl Marx (1818-1883) and in the 20th-century belief system of Julian Huxley (1887–1975, Thomas Huxley's grandson). Each is a quasi-religious vision of salvation.

Marxism

The most famous secular belief system in the world today is Marxism. People who are antagonistic to the socialist or communist ideas associated with the name Karl Marx would not call Marx's thought progressive. That implies improvement. For many Marxism is just the opposite. Yet to Marx himself and to millions of later Marxists, Marxist theory was truly a progressive one. We can more easily see why Marxists have believed this if we look at a rather simplified version of basic Marxist theory. (In passing we might note here that Lenin changed Marx's theory somewhat. Communism in modern Russia, China, and some other places is not quite what Marx predicted or wanted.)

Karl Marx felt great sympathy for the suffering of humankind. He knew well that people have endured sickness, loneliness, hatred, oppression, and hunger throughout history, but he believed that history had been following a certain developmental pattern that was now producing a series of events leading to an ideal earthly life, a secular millennium. History, to him, was a kind of pattern of events operating by its own inner laws. At times, Marx treated the flow of history almost as a Taoist treats the Yang-Yin pattern. One major difference between Taoism and Marxism is that the Taoist does not believe that there can be strong and useful progress in culture, politics, or economics, but Marxism does. To Marx, social and political, and, above all, economic developments were precisely the main manifestations of the progressive power of history.

Marx was highly impressed with industry. Late 18th-century and 19th-century techniques for using energy from steam engines held the promise of a transformed human existence. Coal power (and water, oil, gas, nuclear, and solar power) that was changed into usable machine-driving energy could accomplish something unseen and unheard of prior to this time: it could produce enough food, clothing, and shelter for everyone. In fact, Marx claimed, industrial power could even create such incredible luxuries as leisure time for most people, education for everyone, the ability to travel and learn about others. Everyone might be able to live life more freely and comfortably than even kings once could. Marx has turned out to be at least partially correct about this. In highly industrialized countries this has become generally true. The average North American citizen now lives better than King Henry VIII of England or even Queen Victoria.

There is something that Marx considered more important than material goods. Adequate material possessions were only a base for supporting the higher values of freedom and equality. Marx believed that in the past ages of desperate scarcity humankind had become accustomed to valuing possessions and wealth as a means for survival. It was because of this, Marx thought, that people had learned to measure their own worth in terms of the quality of their clothes, the size of their home, their social class, instead of by what should be the true measure of worth: compassion and concern for one's neighbors. The ideal society would reverse this and give primacy to justice and compassion. (Piaget and Kohlberg would say, contrary to Marx, that the desire for outward status and possessions is just a normal—if regrettable—stage in growing up; Hindu tradition agrees.)

Marx was wrong about how the human society was to evolve. He thought the industrial nations, unlike Ruissia and China, which were mainly pre-industrial, would experience violent revolutions. This would lead to the overthrow of capitalism and the establishment of ideal socialist states. Regardless of Marx's errors of prediction, this general vision of the perfect society has been an inspiring one, shared by many who are not Marxists. It is a vision of a society of material abundance. More important, it would be a free and equal society in which everyone would work together in harmony, sharing the products of their work. It would be a thoroughly democratic state with equal justice, rights, and power for everyone.

With such a vision it is not hard to see why Marxism has been popular in the world. It is true that it does not offer an afterlife. Nor did Marx believe there was a God such as Jews, Christians, and Muslims believe in. Moreover, Marxism has not proved correct or even wise in its effect on many nations in the world. Nevertheless it has been an appealing vision because it promises salvation from hunger and hatred, from oppression and futility. To the person who dedicates his or her life to the advancement of Marxism, it offers a sense of being important, of contributing to a grand and glorious humane world. Moreover, it encourages hope by claiming that the flow of history is like an all-embracing pattern driving cultural developments toward a perfect earthly realm.

Marxism is often considered anti-religious because of its opposition to belief in God, in divine help, or in heaven. Marx described religion as the opium of the masses, numbing their pain by promising pie in the sky in the great by-and-by. Marxism sees religion as a force supporting the traditional economic and political powers that oppress people. Yet Marxism functions as a kind of quasi-religion. It offers an equivalent for God in its belief that history can be trusted to act as a kind of ultimate power influencing everything to move toward the ideal state in which many forms of estrangement will be overcome. One person's atheism is sometimes another person's religion. Marx proposed his vision as one worthy of a faith commitment.

Huxley's Earthly Religion

Karl Marx is probably the most famous of the secular evolutionary humanists, but many view Marxist thought with suspicion. So it is good to give at least one other example, that of the evolutionary philosophy of Julian Huxley as proposed in his book, *Religion Without Revelation*, published in 1928 and in revised form in 1956. As the title of the book suggests, Huxley did not believe in any supernatural revelations from God. In fact, he was rather thoroughly secular, rejecting belief in miracles and heaven and hell, and taking a strongly agnostic position about the existence of any other-worldly power or being.

Nonetheless, this secular viewpoint is also a religious viewpoint, according to Huxley. He defined religion as a unifying perspective on reality that expresses people's deepest convictions about the ultimate nature and purpose of life. Huxley's unifying perspective treats evolution somewhat as Marx treated history, as a force or pattern within the universe tending in a predetermined direction. For Huxley, therefore, the pattern of evolution is a minor sort of God-equivalent, not all-powerful but nonetheless universal in its influence and transcending the limits of all smaller powers and forces. Huxley also offered salvation through cooperation with evolution, a this-worldly salvation of an ideal human future.

Huxley's vision proposed a theory of purposeful cosmic evolution. A contemporary version would go something like this. At the beginnings of the present universe, the primal energy divided into various forms including the many subatomic particles. Because the particles are different from one another, they could organize into complex atoms. Because there are different kinds of atoms they can react to one another in complex ways, causing chemical reactions and new organized bondings. These molecules interact and become organized into amino acids, proteins, early life forms, and eventually into living cells. The incredibly complex organized living cells develop in different ways and eventually interact to form multicelled organisms. The complexity of interactions between cells increases and the multicellular organisms become complex plants, animals, and eventually humans. In particular, the extraordinarily complex interactions of the various nervous system cells produce the human ability to interact consciously with the environment and with one another. Because of the complex organization of the consciousness system in each individual, people are able to interact with one another to create social structure, farming, politics, literature, and so forth.

Throughout this long process of cosmic evolution, Huxley says, there is a pattern. Whatever exists differentiates, i.e., takes different forms. The different forms can then unite in something more complex. This is a higher level of organization. There is further differentiation among these more complex forms. They then unite in even more complexly organized ways. Differentiation, complexity, and organization are constantly on the increase. The first major aspect of the pattern of cosmic evolution can be summed up, therefore, as the law of increasingly complex organization.

As complex organization increases, it also produces ever higher levels of consciousness. This is the second law of cosmic evolution. The highest form of consciousness produced by this evolutionary process so far is human consciousness. And it has already differentiated into different sets of ideas, languages, tools, institutions, roles, rules, values, visions, poetry, religion. These now interact in complex ways to constitute the different cultures of the world. These cultures are more complex levels of organized consciousness. A world culture in which all the prior cultures retain their identity but interact positively with one another would be an even higher level of more complex organization and consciousness. All of this is part of the same single cosmic evolutionary process.

We humans are part of cosmic evolution, not only in our biology but also in our ideas; not only physiologically but psychologically, socially, and culturally. There is but one evolutionary process and it encompasses all aspects of the universe from the birth and development of stars to the birth and development of cultures; one pattern runs through it all. There are many moments of apparent randomness, Huxley acknowledges. The potential for chaos in history and nature is evident. This make it all the more awesome that cosmic evolution has occurred as it has, effectively making use of the possibilities of greater diversity, complex organization, consciousness, and the complex interactions of the consciousness in culture.

Most striking of all is Huxley's idea that we humans are now cosmic evolution become conscious of itself. We are not merely aware of evolution; we are evolution's highest self-expression so far. Now that we are cosmic evolution's most conscious form we have great power in our hands. We might fail to make use of our power, Huxley acknowledges, but he is basically optimistic. We can increase our consciousness of evolution, of ourselves, and of our potentials. This increase, itself a more complex consciousness, will be our path into a secular sort of salvation. As we become enthused with evolutionary potential and dedicate ourselves to it, we can create a future society of peace and prosperity, of humane and loving existence. Huxley saw this as a vision worthy of a faith commitment. It was his secular religion.

The Hidden Forms of Salvation

Secular evolutionary humanisms offer millenniarist visions of salvation of a this-worldly kind. There is a future utopian lifestyle on earth that will someday be available, they assure us. Some secular humanisms are more modest in their aspirations than Marx's or Huxley's. Some settle for getting by as we go along, believing that even small gradual improvement is a good deal when compared to the fearsome alternatives of nuclear war, mass hunger, or the spread of totalitarianism. In general, though, it is the future of the world, the improvements to come, that constitute salvation, even if we do not yet recognize this. This is salvation of the kind discussed in Chapter Five: an ideal place to be.

There are other, but hidden, kinds of salvation that go with allegiance to some secular evolutionary humanism. These are the same salvations, also often hidden, that go with belonging to any large movement. These are forms of belonging and identity, as described in Chapters Six and Seven.

A vision like Marx's or Huxley's offers a picture of the universe, an interpretation of nature and history, that tries to tell us the meaning of life. It can offer a high moral challenge, inviting us to rise above short-term pleasures and pursuits in order to make our life more meaningful. It challenges us to give our time and energy to the well-being of future generations. If we were dissatisfied with the achievements of life, yet also dubious about any afterlife or numinous powers, we might experience a restlessness, a longing for some deeper and lasting purpose. Marx, Huxley, and others offer us that; they tell us that children now being born need not starve, because of us; that the oppressed of the world can find freedom, with our help.

Even then, our enthusiasm might waver. A solitary person can do so little. Is it really worth all the effort? Marx and Huxley offer more at this point. They tell us that our efforts are not merely small human attempts to deal with one more problem. Rather, they are contributions to the great pattern of history or evolution. These efforts we exert are like helping a God bring about the millennium; they identify us not just with the morally right, but also with the ultimately victorious inner drive of nature and history. This is a meaningful form of belonging. In this we can also find a lasting value for our life; we achieve a sense of worthwhile identity. No wonder Marxist thought has had a strong appeal to many people. It and other such visions are very much like religions in their appeal, offering a share in lasting truth and deep purpose. They offer salvation in the face of troublesome mysteries.

The End of Easy Optimism

From Galileo to Marx and Huxley there grew a confidence in the intelligibility of the universe, and in the capacity of the human mind to grasp that intelligibility and live by it. This world increasingly appeared to be a potential utopia. More and more, human society was considered something perfectible. As a result, secular humanisms began to replace traditional religiousness in a few people's minds. But then came the shattering experience of World War I.

People were too rational to kill each other for a few miles of earth or for national pride, the optimists thought. Yet, for a few miles and for pride millions died. Technology would bring only health and wealth, the optimists believed. But mustard gas and improved armaments contributed to the slaughter. People had outgrown blind patriotism and military pride, optimists believed. But for the glory of the homeland people were eager to spill the blood of their neighbors. Two hundred years of "enlightenment" were not enough to eliminate war. In some ways the development of scientific rationality made it even worse.

Thoughts such as these released other doubts and confusion. Old beliefs had been breaking down for a few centuries now. Many people were uncertain about religion, about the social and economic order, about all the new ideas and inventions, about changing morals. The twentieth century was going to prove to be a very difficult one. The next chapter will describe one of the greatest difficulties for religion, atheistic skepticism.

Summary

Traditional historic Christianity had relied on divine revelation and church authority as the source of true understanding. From Galileo on, science-minded people began to trust human investigation and reasoning more. An early result was deism, which promised a religion based on reason, celebrating a watchmaker God who did not intervene in history. Evolutionary thought then moved further from traditional religion by suggesting that the process of evolution was too random to have been planned or guided by a God, but was orderly or purposeful enough to provide hope for an ever-better worldly existence, even one without any God.

When the 20th century began, World War I clouded many people's hopes for human progress even while skepticism about religion was still common. That is the topic of the next chapter.

FOR FURTHER REFLECTION

1. How do you distinguish miracles from nonmiraculous events? Explain why it seems reasonable or not reasonable to you to believe that miracles do happen.

2. Describe any ways in which scientific ideas about laws of nature and evolution have an effect on your religious beliefs. Should they?

3. Which position seems most reasonable to you: atheism, agnosticism, or theism (belief in a God)? Do you decide this entirely on the basis of reasonableness? Explain.

4. Does the description of Marxist thought make it sound appealing? Is Marxism an adequate substitute for religion? Why? Why not?

5. Julian Huxley perceives a great cosmic pattern behind the cosmic events of the universe. Could this be evidence that there must be a Designer-God? Explain.

6. Are you optimistic about how we human beings will handle issues of war and peace, of economic justice, of the environment through our growing knowledge and our moral commitment?

SUGGESTED READINGS

Charles P. Henderson, *God and Science*, 1986; individual chapters on Darwin, Marx, and others.

J.A. Leo Lemay, ed., *Deism, Masonry, and the Enlightenment*, 1987; various essays.

Allen Wheelis, *The End of the Modern Age*, 1971; the impact of science on our sense of reality.

John Herman Randall, *The Making of the Modern Mind*, 1926.

Michael D. Nicklanovich, *From Cell to Philosopher*, 1973; survey of evolutionary theory and religious reactions.

Karl Marx, *The Communist Manifesto*, 1964.

Julian Huxley, *Religion Without Revelation*, 1956.

Paul Kurz, *In Defense of Secular Humanism*, 1983; by one of North America's leading humanists.

Life Without Religion

Skeptical Humanisms

Throughout history, people have perceived mysteries in life and have had faith nonetheless that life is coherent, intelligible, and meaningful on the deepest level that they could conceive of in their own time. The primitive person took it for granted that various stories could explain the pieces of life. Archaic people, who believed in larger powers at work in reality, were less sure life could be fully happy, but they usually lived with some confidence that their myths explained the structure and events of life. Historic religions have had the grand faith that there is an ultimate and unified intelligibility and value beneath or beyond all the seeming chaos or evil in life.

In the 20th century, however, a skeptical interpretation about life's intelligibility and value has gained a significant number of adherents. A variety of factors, including the end of 19th-century optimism, have persuaded many people that there is no *ultimate* intelligibility and value to human existence, or at least none that anyone can be sure of.

Only a few people are this skeptical, most of them confined to the industrialized nations of the West, but they tend to be influential because most of them are rather well educated. Knowledge of history, of philosophy, of various religious traditions, and of the methods of science can make people doubt things they once took for granted. Although most well-educated people seem to have retained some kind of religious belief, this chapter is mainly about the skeptics rather than about the religious believers.

EARLY ATTACKS ON TRADITIONAL RELIGION

Behind modern skepticism about religion there is more than intellectual doubt about the truth of religious belief. There is also the conviction that religion is all too easily a harmful element in human life. Religion, the skeptics often say, is not merely mistaken, but dangerous.

The history of religion and science in the West is a story of frequent tension between traditional religious authority seeking to maintain the power of the theological system, and the new philosophical science promoting ideas that threaten both the system and the authority behind it. Year after year, decade after decade, century after century, there were religious leaders who opposed parts of the new science and even oppressed those who favored it. The story of Galileo's forced recantation is a well-known instance. The Copernican astronomy that Galileo favored cast doubt on the literal truth of the Bible and on the religious authority of tradition. So religious people fought Galileo.

In many lesser instances, individual religious voices spoke out against scientific innovations. The lightning rod is an affront to God, some said, for God sends each bolt of lightning to warn people or to punish them. How dare human technology intervene! Likewise, disease is a punishment from God. The new medical technique known as vaccination against smallpox is ungodly, some claimed.

Allied with the new science was a new political philosophy that promoted equality and the free exchange of ideas. Repeatedly religious leaders opposed these innovations as threats to traditional authority and therefore to social order. Freemasons and other freethinkers often had to flee countries such as Germany or France to find refuge, often in the Netherlands, from a political oppression that church authorities supported.

Those who experienced oppression also became more sensitive to the amount of intolerance and even bigotry that was often part of religious life. For Christ's sake, Christians had persecuted Jews, Muslims, and one another for centuries. From 1618 to 1648, the Thirty Years' War had devastated the German-speaking states, as Catholic fought Protestant for political power. The Inquisitions burned heretics at the stake, often after first torturing them.

Concomitant with the rise of the new science in the midst of the Enlightenment, as though to stamp religiousness for good with the seal of superstition, were the great witch hunts of the 17th and 18th centuries. The times were troubled by changes in politics, science, religion, economics. For the new scientists this was a time of glorious learning; for the new political philosophers, a time of promise. But for many religious people it was merely a time of insecurity and doubt, so they looked for a cause of all the troubles, or at least for something on which they could focus their fears. They found it in the witches. Thousands of women and men were accused of being agents of the devil and were killed.

In the 19th century, religious people found one more horrendous blasphemy to oppose: the theories of evolution. No matter that the evidence was overwhelming that the earth must be at least a few million years old. To accept this meant shattering the secure system of religious doctrine by doubting one part of it; it meant undercutting all religious and biblical authority by suggesting that there might be points on which it was wrong. There was no need for honest reflection on the evidence; it just could not be true.

Throughout all this, another major point of contention was the significance of earthly existence. Even if Marx and Spencer and other 19th-century secular humanists had been too optimistic about earthly progress, at least they cared about the quality of earthly life and tried to promote a more humane existence for people. Many religious leaders, threatened by so much that was new, classified it all as too worldly or materialistic. They recommended instead keeping our eyes on heaven, where rust and moth do not consume. One effect of this other-worldliness, as Marx pointed out, was to distract people from useful efforts to make this world a better place for future generations.

By the 20th century, then, there was already a long list of complaints against religion. According to the most severe skeptics religion is an opponent of potentially beneficial progress in human ideas and techniques. It is authoritarian and repressive, even vengeful against its enemies. It is intolerant and even bigoted against those who disagree with it. It promotes irrationality by supporting beliefs that go against reason, thereby making it seem legitimate to be irrational. It is other-worldly, calling people away from the kind of efforts that might feed the hungry, clothe the naked, and free the oppressed. In brief, although religion promises people heaven, it makes their lives more hellish.

Not all skeptics were this harsh in their critique of religion. Some, like Freud, classified it as a mildly debilitating illusion. Others, such as the sociologists who simply noted its social function of supporting the cultural forms, spoke of it more neutrally. In general, though, the various skeptics, atheists, or agnostics had decided that religion was not only wrong but, on balance, somewhat harmful.

In the 20th century there are various forms of skepticism about religion, some of it just casual doubt; but there are at least two kinds of positive movements that are fully skeptical. They are both secular humanisms: American pragmatism and French atheistic existentialism. To understand them, it helps to begin with two other sets of ideas. One is about a new way of understanding reality; the other is about a new way of understanding what it is to be a human person.

A NEW WAY OF UNDERSTANDING REALITY

From the time of Galileo a number of philosophers had stressed that the way to know the truth was by checking out theories in a concrete way. As far back as the 13th century, Roger Bacon (1214?–1294?), a Franciscan philosopher-scientist, had urged this method. Do not simply believe what has been handed on to you. Do not even believe whatever seems logically to make most sense. Test it out. That is, of course, exactly what Galileo later did. Concrete tests gave evidence that traditional beliefs and logical-sounding ideas were sometimes wrong. The method now known as "empirical verification" was gaining acceptance. Verify claims about what the truth is by finding physical evidence of some sort. If there is no evidence that the eye can see or the ear hear or the hand touch, then you cannot claim to know what the truth of the matter is.

As we have seen, this method of verification produced wonderfully reliable results, especially when coupled with Galileo's approach to measuring matter in motion. What is measurable can stand as evidence for or against a theory; what is not measurable, such as God's purposes, can only be a matter of speculation. Using this as the basic method of approach to knowledge, the centuries following were lighted with the results of geniuses and of ordinary but persistent researchers.

Science is a method of learning about reality. Part of the method is active doubt. No matter how many learned people have accepted an idea as true, doubt it. It might be wrong. Check it out. Then when you have doubted and devised tests and have come up with a new answer all well checked out, let others doubt. Let people know what your theory is, how you tested it, and what results you got; so that the others can doubt you, doubt your theory, your tests, your results. If your theory survives new doubts and new tests, it is more probably true in some way. By this open-ended testing of truth-claims, science advances. We are accustomed to thinking of science's conclusions as certain and reliable. They seem to be, but science remains most true to itself only when it continues to doubt its own conclusions. Every claim of science is supposed to remain open to further questioning and further testing. Every truth-claim is a conditional one.

This was not fully apparent in the early days of modern science. The same scientists who became angry at the dogmatic stubbornness of religious authority developed their own dogmatic attitudes. Sometimes they were modest in their claims. Copernicus's theory was first published with an introduction that said it was only an interesting and different way of describing how the sun, planets, and stars *might* move. But the early success of the new scientific method led many people to forget about doubts and become convinced that science was going to provide people with the complete, final, fully accurate truth about everything.

By the late 19th century, this scientific dogmatism was sometimes allied with a radical reductionism. This is a reversal of Julian Huxley's position. Huxley celebrated the development of matter-energy into atoms and then compounds and then life-forms and cells and multi-celled organisms and eventually conscious processes in us and our cultures. Reductionism stands this on its head by emphasizing that culture and consciousness are, after all, only the product of brain activity, that brains are only organized cells, that cells are only chemical processes, and that chemicals are just atoms. The reductionist attitude is one that tells us not to get too impressed with consciousness and life because they are just variant forms of matter-energy.

This thoroughgoing reductionism was done in the name of science as a way of excluding religion and philosophical speculation from the scientific project of understanding reality. In the 19th century various philosophers had argued that science would have to believe in souls or in some cosmic Spirit in order to explain life and consciousness. Some scientists believed that these ideas were unscientific and would impede the progress of science. So they responded by reducing life and consciousness to nonliving and nonconscious atomic and chemical activity. This left no room for souls or a cosmic Spirit. These reductionistic scientists were probably correct in their basic scientific ideas, but the unfortunate implication of their emphasis was that the human spirit which is manifested in noble thoughts, great moral concerns, and awesome works of art, is nothing more significant than chemical processes.

Another aspect of some early science was the conviction that all human problems could be solved by the application of scientific reasoning. The confidence that science could provide the final, fully accurate truth, especially through a reductionist analysis of everything down to the basics, fit nicely with the evolutionary hopes for a steady progress into a glorious future. Dogmatism, reductionism, and optimism were a potent combination in some early science.

But the 20th century administered shock treatments to shake science into a different frame of mind. Even as World War I edged over the horizon, spreading doubt about human reasonableness and the beneficence of science, new ideas jolted scientists out of dogmatic attitudes. Newton had drawn a basic picture of the universe as stable and predictable. Evolutionary theory removed a little of the stability, but many physicists at the turn of the century thought the universe's laws were now settled, once and for all.

Then came the new physics, like that of Albert Einstein (1879-1955). Suddenly, the whole universe had been taken apart and put back together in a new kind of unity. Newton had been accurate enough about middle-sized events in the universe, but in order to include such extreme happenings as light or energy particles at the small end, and the interrelation of time, space, and energy at the other end, a new set of theories was needed. The ones provided by Einstein said strange things. If you travel in space, for example, at extremely high speeds compared to your friends back home, when you return they will have aged more than you. Physicist Werner Heisenberg (1901–1976) declared that although the universe had once seemed fully predictable and therefore fully intelligible, it turned out that on the subatomic level reality was unpredictable.

In subsequent years there were enough new, odd ways of looking at the universe to get scientists accustomed to treating their own theories more skeptically. As far back as 1790, the philosopher Immanuel Kant (1724-1804) had carefully pointed out that the way we see the world, even in our most reasonable and well-tested interpretations, are still interpretations to some extent. This doubt-filled approach to knowledge was actually recommended by ancient Greek philosophers called "skeptics" some 2000 years ago. But it is only modern times that have accepted this recommendation and found a very positive use for it in science.

It was especially in the 20th century that science found out for itself that Kant and the ancient skeptics were on to something. The theoretical scientists of today are accustomed to the idea that when they describe electrons and gravity and the furthermost edges of the universe and black holes in space, they are not relaying the simple truth. Instead they are providing good working models of how things might well be, based on the available evidence. Science provides models, tentative maps, of reality.

Imagine a map of the Amazon jungles of Brazil that is based on reports from a few explorers, sightings from a dozen hot air balloons, and some examination of debris taken from the river at its mouth. Many highly reliable claims could be made about the jungle on the basis of this evidence, but the overall map might have to undergo serious changes as new evidence came in. Scientific theories are like such a changeable map.

Scientific theories are also like sets of instructions telling a person how to get certain results. Treat light as though it were collections of tiny particles, say the instructions, each particle having a certain minimum size. If that is true, then you should be able to get certain results. And you do. The problem is that if you treat light not as particles but as waves of energy, you could get a different sort of results. And you do. What is light, then: particles or waves? The scientists are accustomed to saying that the particle-model is a useful one to predict some results, and the wave-model is useful for predicting others; but it is not possible to say which is more "true."

Out of the 20th-century experience of scientific theories as maps and models has come a reinforcement of the early scientific experience: a person should accept only what is well tested. But now there is the additional awareness that even a well-tested theory is still a working model that must always be left open to some doubt. This is not an expectation that science will always be changing its conclusions, but rather the conviction that scientists must always be prepared to accept changes in their conclusions if someone devises a better interpretation of the evidence.

The scientific method is fiercely dedicated to critical honesty, but honesty can be unsettling. Dishonesty can be more comforting. Every once in a while dishonesty shows up in a scientific work. A cancer researcher fakes certain results in the skin condition of laboratory mice because he is certain he is on the right track and needs impressive results to get the grant money to continue. A noted psychologist invents data about identical twins raised in different environments, in order to support his firm belief that intelligence is inherited. In addition to dishonesty, unconscious bias also leads scientists to overlook or misread data that would lead to an uncomfortable conclusion. All sorts of odd ideas about differences between the sexes or various races have been popular among scientists.

Yet it is characteristic of modern science to recognize the dangers of dishonesty and unconscious bias. As a counterbalance, science follows a hard regimen of collective honesty. Every truth-claim must be published publicly with the evidence. Any person, friend or foe of a theory, has a right to challenge it and test it again. All theories must stand up to ongoing testing, doubt, critical analysis, regardless of who likes the theory or who does not, regardless of the impact of changes in theory on social, economic, political, and even religious beliefs.

This concern to build honesty into the method of science is done partly for a practical reason. Even excellent theories are not necessarily the final truth. To achieve real success at discovering what is probably true, science admits this and is open to change, as well as open to the challenges and testing that produce the change. Science works well because it forces itself to be more honest than people are usually inclined to be.

Honest science also promotes human well-being. The knowledge produced by critical honesty has created better medicines and more food. Scientific questioning has broken traditional beliefs that supported harmful superstitions such as belief in witches. The methodical honesty of science has broken many prejudiced claims about religions, races, cultures, and the sexes. The honesty of science, however unsettling in its unending willingness to doubt, is morally constructive.

As a result, there is a new way of understanding reality. Or to say it more accurately, there is a new way of understanding what understanding is, a new way of knowing what knowing is. It is not receiving the truth from authoritative sources, as tradition-bound societies think. Nor is it just a matter of taking a very good look at the evidence, as early science tended to think when it first doubted tradition. Nor is it a matter of arriving at wonderfully logical interpretations of reality. One more thing is needed: *doubt* about your evidence and your brilliant interpretation, so you test them again.

It is a matter of looking at and interpreting what you see, but then also testing your interpretation and your perception of the evidence by any and all means available. And even then you must remember that your well-tested interpretation is not the final truth. It may be so well tested and so useful that it would be irrational to reject it or to treat it as no better than a guess. It may be so well tested that for ordinary practical purposes you are correct to treat it as though it were the simple truth. In principle, though, it is still a model of reality, a good interpretation of reality, but not the final truth.

Another way to say the same thing is that scientific theories are also symbols. Like religious symbols, they too re-present reality. They are especially well-tested symbols that have had to compete in the scientific marketplace for acceptance. They have shown their power at re-presenting reality in such a way that people can use them as a reliable and productive guide on how to deal with reality. But they are not absolute truth.

Scientific theories are symbols that are produced by human beings. They are human interpretations of reality. The constant element in science is not the scientific conclusions called theories, models, maps, or symbols. It is instead the ongoing human activity of interpreting reality and then testing the interpretation in an endless pursuit of ever better understanding. It is a human person who has the never-ending job of interpreting reality and testing the interpretation. It is, therefore, the person who is always responsible to be honest and open to change in understanding things. This is a basis for a new understanding of what a person, a self, is.

A NEW WAY OF UNDERSTANDING THE SELF

From the late 18th-century writings of Kant to the experience of modern science, the conviction has grown that we are responsible for our interpretation of reality. How we think of the world and ourselves, how we think of what it all ultimately means, and how we actually live and believe because of this is all very much in our own human hands.

A way to illustrate this is to imagine that you suddenly had an overwhelming spiritual vision and saw an image of God or heard God's voice, so to speak, telling you the truth about life and how to live. What would your response be? A normal human response (if this situation can be called normal at all) would be to accept gratefully this guidance from on high and follow it. But there is an alternative response.

The human person has some capacity to step back from such a religious experience and, as with all experiences, treat the instructions from God and the experience of God both as something to be questioned, as a scientist might question certain test results and their meaning. A person might not want to do this or be in the habit of doing it, but a person is capable of doing it. Was that really God? How do I know? How honest am I being in examining this? Even if it was God, should I just agree? Or should I make my own analysis of how wise or good or useful these ideas are? These questions represent the human ability to take personal responsibility for the ideas and values we live by.

A word often used to represent this human potential is "autonomy," the power of conscious self-ruling. There are many ways we are not consciously self-ruled but instead are ruled by various forces. Our biological characteristics determine some of our behavior; our social conditioning has a very strong influence on us. In moral behavior we normally tend to be heteronomous, i.e., ruled by another, rather than autonomous. The taboo moralist obeys others who can reward or punish. The acceptance moralist obeys group standards. A universal laws moralist looks for the ultimate objective set of standards to follow. These are all instances of heteronomous morality.

It is not enough, however, that a person obey inner rules rather than external rules or standards in order to be called fully autonomous. The inner rules must also be those the person has consciously chosen on the basis of his or her own *consciously evaluated* morality. A person who just follows inner habits or conditioning is not autonomous, but is under the control of the habits or the psychological and sociological conditioning. A person who has consciously reflected on what makes things good or bad, and has then decided that this personal judgment of what is basically good or bad must rule, is an autonomous person. This person would sit in judgment even on God's instructions, therefore, and ask whether those instructions lived up to the person's own best moral standard.

This means that a fully autonomous person is a person who accepts full responsibility for his or her own moral standards and decisions. This is a person who believes it is not enough to obey orders or be loyal to the group or live up to supposedly objective external standards for their own sake. The autonomous person may well obey social rules, be very loyal, and honor high standards, but only because these fit with his or her best moral vision.

There is a socially very dangerous form of autonomy, that of the taboo moralist who has found how to avoid punishment and simply chooses to grab all the pleasures available no matter who gets hurt. The modern people who recommend autonomy actually have in mind not this dangerous one but the one built on a basic value morality. This kind of autonomy would listen to God's voice and then ask whether agreeing with God would promote human well-being. On the basis of compassion and concern for fellow humans, this type of autonomous person would be responsible to accept or reject God's instructions, a religious tradition, various civil laws, a group's standards, or any other guides to life.

This sort of responsible autonomy is also sometimes called "authentic existence," a shorthand expression for "authentically mature human existence." Children cannot take autonomous responsibility for their own lives. They are dominated by emotional drives, societal conditioning, and short-term practical judgments on how to get along. Only adults have a chance at coming into the kind of reflective self-possession that enables them to choose the very foundation of their moral orientation through careful, conscious reflection.

As we mature, the distinctively human capacity for conscious reflection on our lives becomes stronger. We develop an increasing ability to take personal responsibility for our ideas, biases, values, and behavior. The more we do this, the more we are doing the thing that sets us apart from other animals. Those who favor such autonomy can therefore claim that it is an exercise of real humanness, that autonomous freedom constitutes authentic human existence.

This idea of authentic existence presents a challenge because we humans often try to escape from our own peculiarly human capacity to be responsible for our own values and decisions. Psychologist Erich Fromm (1900–1980) summed it up nicely in a title of a book, *Escape from Freedom*. We all tend to say we want to have freedom, yet real freedom can make us nervous. Do we really want to carry individual personal responsibility for every one of our decisions? It would often be more comfortable to be able to let someone else make the decisions and be responsible for the consequences. There is security in obedience and conformity. Even if that should produce bigotry, intolerance, persecutions, and war, at least someone else is to blame. (There is evidently danger in a lack of autonomy as well as in autonomy.)

The emphasis on authentic existence, on personally responsible autonomy, is dangerous, as was said, when interpreted by a taboo moralist, whose only understanding of morality is what feels good. This emphasis is meaningless to the acceptance moralist, who needs to have group rules to follow. The emphasis on autonomy will not make sense to a universal laws moralist, who is convinced that there are objectively and universally valid rules that everyone has to obey in order to be correct.

Those who favor responsible autonomy, though, are convinced that Kant and science have shown us that all our interpretations of reality, including even our ideas about morality, are interpretations, models, symbols. Alternative interpretations and models and symbols are available. Because we have the capacity to reflect on these interpretations and evaluate them in an ongoing way, we have the capacity to be responsible for them. To refuse to reflect and choose is to be responsible for avoiding personal responsibility. Dangerous and difficult as it is, therefore, authentic human responsibility is an ideal that has gained a great deal of support.

That, in turn, has meant that there is a new emphasis on the way modern culture understands what it is to be a self. The "authentic human existence" of the modern person would not sound authentically human to other cultures: primitive cultures seek to do what the ancestors established; archaic cultures obey the gods of their people; historic cultures know that ideal human life is one of submission to the single, universally correct way of things. Modern culture is not sure of the final truth or the single truth or the universal truth, so it defines the ideal person as one who accepts individual responsibility for the interpretation of reality that person lives by, including responsibility for how that interpretation affects others.

Modern culture has thereby become more explicitly conscious that human life is lived in the presence of mystery, that all our beliefs, values, traditions, and lifestyles are encompassed by a larger field of mystery, even by an infinitely receding horizon of mystery. There are religious interpretations of life based on this awareness. Chapter Fourteen will describe some of them; but there are also non-religious interpretations. Here are two of them.

TWO SKEPTICAL PHILOSOPHIES

Contemporary skepticism, which grew out of earlier attacks on religion, includes the new scientific understanding of knowing and the new understanding of the human person as autonomous. It also accepts the basic view of the universe suggested by the astronomers' big bang theory and the evolutionary theory of life as random variations. We can see all this in two philosophies about life: American pragmatism and French atheistic existentialism.

American Pragmatism

American pragmatism is the approach found in the writings of John Dewey (1859-1952) among others. It is a school of thought that is generally agnostic, cautious about making unsubstantiated claims. The universe is a vast and somewhat confusing place, the pragmatists say. We have learned a lot about it. We have a lot to learn. We will never know all there is to know. The most honest and reasonable thing to do is to learn what we can as we can, and make the best use of it we can.

The pragmatists' view is suspicious of religious belief. The history of humankind is a history of unsubstantiated beliefs, they say, many of them religious. Adherence to these beliefs has usually prevented the growth of genuine well-tested knowledge and has bred intolerance and hatred. It is good to be wary of such beliefs. Even the belief systems of a Karl Marx or Julian Huxley claim more than can be verified rationally. There is no adequate evidence for the existence of any ultimate Power, neither God nor history nor evolution turned into minor God-equivalents. The pragmatists conclude that there is little profit in trying to argue out all the ultimate questions about the origin, pattern, or purpose to everything. There is no need to take such questions too seriously.

It is reasonable to act as though there is no God, to live as practical atheists without being dogmatic in our denial of God's existence.

There is, nevertheless, a faith we can all live by, says Dewey, a common dedication to our human needs for material sustenance and ethical ideals, a dedication to be as honest and cooperative as we can in order to achieve what we can for our fellow human beings. We live in a changing universe, open to progress; we are free beings, open to development. Let us learn to cherish the openness of things and selves in order to improve life.

This faith is a form of secular evolutionary humanism, but its emphasis is much more practical-minded than the quasi-religions of Marx and Huxley. Dewey was willing to live with a great deal of uncertainty about the basic thrust of history or the ultimate answers to life's direction. Make do as you go along, Dewey said; much can be achieved this way if we just try to be honest, reasonable, and deeply concerned with the well-being of human life on this planet.

This has been the major contemporary atheism or agnosticism in America. Groups such as the American Humanist Association or the Ethical Culture Society reflect many of the same views. There is another and more radical contemporary atheism, however, that takes ultimate questions with great seriousness. That is the perspective associated with the French existentialist, Jean-Paul Sartre (1905-1984).

Atheistic Existentialism

The pragmatist turns away from the ultimate mystery in order to pay attention to practical possibilities of improving the human condition. The atheistic existentialist, on the contrary, keeps an eye fixed resolutely on the unendingness of mystery as an awesome but important reality. The fact of infinite mystery reveals to the existentialist the strange situation of the human person.

Central to existentialism is the concern to define who we humans are, both immediately and ultimately. Even on the everyday level, says Jean-Paul Sartre, we humans are terribly odd. We are self-consciousness beings, able to take our lives into our own hands to some extent through our conscious decisions. This is the power of free self-determination. It is human autonomy. That means that in contrast to all other living beings, we "ex-ist," meaning that we stand out. We stand apart from the unfree and unthinking patterns of inanimate nature. We stand out from all the animals, who have a limited kind of conscious awareness but not the self-consciousness that would allow them to decide about themselves and their lives. We are different. We ex-ist.

Our identity is in our own hands, Sartre says. We can look ourselves over and see how we act and think. We can measure our acts and thoughts by various rules, standards, values, or goals. We are responsible for how well we measure up to our standards, and even for choosing the standards. All this is a terrible burden because we are beings with a capacity for the infinite. Our capacity to question and reflect and then question again makes it impossible for us to arrive at the final and complete truth. That is true also in moral matters. And yet we must do our best to choose standards of morality and truth, of how to live and treat each other. The great blessing of our freedom is therefore also a difficult burden.

There is no preset limit to how far our minds can range in our quest for the answers to life. When we begin to seek the purpose of our existence, that which makes it truly worthwhile and will tell us how to live, we are on an exploration without apparent end, because we can raise the ultimate questions. Perhaps ultimately all is mindless randomness, as some scientific theories suggest.

The historic religious traditions have answers for those who worry about such things. Our ultimate purpose is to belong to the infinite, the Tao, or Brahman, or God. By learning the Tao of nature or the path of contemplation or the mystical way, we conform to the eternal fullness, these traditions say.

But Sartre sees a great threat to our humanness in these traditions. Our human selfhood lies in our self-possession as consciously free ex-istents. To hand ourselves over to some ultimate path, or Being, or Power, he claims, is to give up responsibility for ourselves; it is to dream of finally laying down the burden of having to choose for ourselves the identity, belonging, thoughts, and actions that together make up our life stories.

Perhaps Sartre might have been able to accept the idea of handing over one's life to the infinite Mystery by only a basic trust that it is fullness and not emptiness. This trust is sufficiently general that it could give confidence that life is ultimately worthwhile, without taking away individual responsibility for each decision made in a lifetime. But Sartre feared that the religious impulse is always to sacrifice responsible autonomy on the altar of security. Faced with endless options about who to be, how to live, and where to find a sense of certainty, we are all too eager to submit to the specific beliefs, roles, rules, and rituals of a religious tradition. So Sartre believed.

What Sartre proposed as a philosophy of life for the being that ex-ists is a life of courageous affirmation of selfhood in a universe where selfhood is ultimately meaningless. To Sartre, it was clear that the processes of this enormous universe are indeed mindless and purposeless. He was surprised that anyone could find a purposeful direction buried within the evolutionary process, which has been a long and messy one, built on the bones of countless species that failed and died. It has scattered countless bodies killed by starvation, flood, disease. For the last 50,000 years of human existence, war and torture and suffering have been the rule, so much so that it all seems natural. If there is some God behind this process, Sartre concludes, it must be a grossly evil or incompetent one to set in motion all that misery and chaos.

To Sartre, sheer reasonableness requires that we must all accept the possibility that in the end nothing really means anything. Life, then, is absurd. Since we need not merely meaning but ultimate meaning to satisfy the endless reach of our consciousness, the ultimate meaninglessness of the universe stands over against us as a crushing emptiness. In a sense, it becomes irrational ultimately to live for anything.

Yet Sartre, like other atheists (most less extreme in their atheism) did find something to live for: his own existence as an authentic self, a self-conscious self, willing to be responsible for his own life. To Sartre, this emphatically includes responsibility to value authentic existence wherever it is or might be. So Sartre tried to live by a deep moral concern for the selfhood and freedom of every person. He proposed a basic value morality of unrestricted concern for authentic human existence. For this reason, he called his own existentialism a humanism.

Sartre's atheism faces ultimate mystery with the same serious attentiveness that historic and modern religions often do. But Sartre claimed that concern for authentic selfhood requires the honest courage to accept what he saw as the most probable scientific model of the universe, one that portrays the universe as aimless and human life as ultimately lacking in any cosmic purpose. This is atheistic existentialism's challenge to religion.

It is a very fundamental challenge. Any religion that focuses its attention on asserting that miracles do happen, that there is a divine guide and helper, or that there is life after death, may be a very satisfying religion, but it does not yet meet the full challenge of atheistic existentialism.

The Deepest Challenge to Religion

Imagine that you live in a universe where there is a high god, filled with loving concern for all people (a sort of all-good super-Zeus). This would be a god who can work miracles, reveal the right path of life, bring people to a paradise after death. As comforting as this sounds, the atheistic existentialist has the same sort of questions about it as a Hindu or Buddhist might about a paradise: What is the *ultimate* meaning? Perhaps the high god and all people are trapped together in an ultimately meaningless reality. Whether a person's life ends in death after seventy years or endures everlastingly in some sort of paradise with a high god, what is the value of it? The question of *ultimacy* is present again.

Then add to this the further modern concerns that arise. First of all, there are the scientific theories which suggest that the best evidence points to a model of the universe as an aimless series of events without meaning. Secondly, there is still the modern awareness of our need for ultimate meaning because of our existence as the self-conscious, and therefore free being. To respond to this adequately, religion must somehow be able to see the possibility of truly ultimate intelligibility and value to human existence. The basic faith that humankind has lived by from the earliest times, at least implicitly, has finally been challenged in modern times: Does it all ultimately make sense? Is it all ultimately worthwhile?

A modern religion, whatever else it does or does not say about such things as miracles, divine guidance, and life after death, also has to look at the universe and human existence and be able to show how a reasonable and honest person, willing to take responsibility for his or her own life, can find good reason to affirm that the mysteries we all face are signs not of ultimate meaninglessness, but of a divinely numinous Ultimate, which somehow is the meaning of everything.

The language becomes abstract and difficult when we talk about these things because it is talk about the Ultimate. It is talk about what the civilizations of the world have found to be the infinite and incomprehensible God or Tao or Brahman. For the atheistic existentialist, it is not merely difficult to talk about any such Ultimate; it is difficult to show that a reasonable person could believe in it. That is a challenge modern religion faces. Chapter Fourteen will describe the response of modern religion.

Summary

In recent centuries religion has been severely criticized. At the same time agnostic or atheistic alternative religions have grown stronger. The developments of science have convinced many that modern scientific honesty, self-criticism, and openness to change constitute the only legitimate kind of knowledge. This has also produced a great emphasis on the responsibility of the individual person not to follow traditional authority unthinkingly, but to be responsibly self-determining. Scientific honesty and responsible autonomy are two ideas that inspire modern unreligious humanisms, such as American pragmatism and atheistic existentialism.

The ultimate mysteries of life still exist, however, and the attitudes of agnosticism or atheism toward them can be much less than satisfying. Modern religion has tried to provide a religious humanism as an alternative. That is the topic of the next chapter.

FOR FURTHER REFLECTION

1. Do the criticisms of religion made early in this chapter seem accurate and fair to you? Why? Why not?

2. Give any reasons you can think of why a religious person could not be fully dedicated to human progress in this world.

3. Find examples in your own life of beliefs you hold that seem very reliable to you but which, like scientific knowledge, are open to change if the evidence demands it. Which of them, if any, are religious beliefs?

4. Do you share the belief that ideal adult authentic existence is a willingness to take full personal responsibility for one's own values and choices? Explain.

5. Is it possible to be an autonomous self, committed to the idea that all knowledge is tentative, and also be deeply religious? Explain.

6. If Sartre is wrong about the absurdity of life, explain what you think is the ultimate purpose of human existence.

SUGGESTED READINGS

Franklin L. Baumer, *Religion and the Rise of Skepticism*, 1960.

Gregory Baum, *Religion and Alienation*, 1975; sociological critiques of religion and a religious response.

Thomas Kuhn, *The Structure of Scientific Revolutions*, 1970; a frequently used description of science as based on models or paradigms.

Charles Davis, *Temptations of Religion*, 1973; descriptions by a religious thinker of how religion can go wrong.

John Dewey, *A Common Faith*, 1934.

Jean-Paul Sartre, "Existentialism Is a Humanism," in Walter Kaufman, *Existentialism from Dostoevsky to Sartre*, 1956, pp. 287-311.

Gordon Stein, ed., *An Anthology of Atheism and Rationalism*, 1980; a variety of atheists argue their case.

In the Presence of Mystery

Modern Religion

Long ago the development of agriculture produced a cultural revolution in many societies, leading them into a new complexity of social organization and thought patterns. Primitive religion gave way to archaic religion, which absorbed the primitive beliefs into its more complicated and hierarchical views. Then came the axial age, and all the primitive and archaic beliefs had to meet a new test imposed by a strikingly ambitious mode of human consciousness. These beliefs now had to fit within the all-encompassing, integrated interpretations of reality proposed by historic thought, as humankind sought a perfect and eternal unity, a mysterious wholeness behind all the complexities of existence. Today, after twenty-four centuries of culture influenced by historic modes of thought, another mode of interpreting reality has been growing strong, one that includes but redefines the various symbols from past historic, archaic, and primitive stages of thought. That is modern culture and its religiousness.

THE MODERN CHALLENGES TO RELIGION

Modern religiousness is still being hammered into shape in a long process that is only a few centuries old and, as is true of any cultural development, will never finally be complete. The most formative impacts have come from four strong challenges posed by modern thought: the new scientific world-views, secularity, an appreciation of autonomous selfhood, and the idea that all knowledge is tentative.

The Challenge of Scientific World-Views

The universe is a vast and strange reality, as we have seen in various ways. It is billions of years old, with a hundred billion galaxies of hundreds of billions of stars each, exploding outward to either an eventual cosmic death or a collapse into another great explosion. The wondrous process of life on this single minute planet may have been a random process, mindless and meaningless. The overall story of human life has had great evil, pain, and despair in it.

There seems to be little hard evidence that there is a divine Being who guides the universe in a coherent way or who has some ultimately meaningful purpose for it. The atheistic existentialists claim that the evidence points mainly in the direction of an ultimate meaninglessness to all things. There also seems to be very little reliable evidence, such as we would ordinarily demand for scientific conclusions, that there is a God who intervenes in nature or in human lives to do miracles, to provide a kind of supernatural help or guidance beyond what the ordinary processes of nature already accomplish. In fact, the scientific approach to reality works well precisely because it does not accept this kind of explanation for any event.

The challenge of the modern scientific world-view to religion is this: can a reasonable person maintain belief in a divine or numinous dimension to our existence in the face of scientific theories, evidence, and methods? Modern religion says yes, but it has had to do more than just say yes; it has work out a reasonable justification for this bold "yes."

The Challenge of Secularity

The atheistic and agnostic secular humanists have abandoned reliance on divine help. They have also turned their hopes away from heaven or any other life beyond this limited earthly one. These seventy to ninety years are ours and nothing more, say the secular humanists. It is up to us to choose how to use them well. We are on our own.

Because of that, the secular humanist claims, we ought to devote all our energies toward the needs and potentials of our fellow human beings. We ought to work to eliminate oppression, poverty, hatred, and war. We ought to learn to love one another as best we can in ever more effective ways.

The traditional religions usually meant well, the secular humanist continues. The religions have usually preached love of neighbor and performed great works of charity, but they also distracted themselves from full attention to this by devoting many resources to churches and monasteries, resources that might otherwise have helped to develop agriculture to feed people, or helped to promote psychological research that could free people to be more humane toward one another. The religions have diminished the intensity of worldly efforts for human growth by relying on a divine help that is at least extremely unreliable, if it exists at all. They have led people to accept unjust conditions, oppressive governments, bigotry and war, all on the grounds that such worldly events ultimately do not count because heaven or nirvana or such is our true home.

Altogether, then, the challenge of secularity to religion is this: can a morally concerned person devote time and energy to religion when there is so much to be done out of concern for our fellow human beings? Modern religion says yes to this also, but it has had to show how religiousness does not have to diminish the well-being of others in this world, but can actually sustain and promote it.

The Challenge of Autonomous Selfhood

Modern culture fought its way into learning the potential of individual freedom. The early scientists, then the deists and Freemasons and eventually many others, came to appreciate the value of free thought and the free speech to express it. They came to believe that it was not merely true, as Western religions had long said, that every single person was of infinite value; it was also true that every single person ought to be able to live in accordance with his or her value as a free and equal person. Out of all of this came the ideal of responsible autonomy as authentic human existence.

All along the way, religious leaders and believers alike were in the forefront of those who opposed freedom. The traditional religious beliefs did say that every person had to follow his or her conscience in making decisions, but they also insisted that the only correct decisions were those in accord with the Bible, with church tradition, and with the established authorities of both state and church. Those who freely went against what was correct must be made to be quiet or to be punished or both.

The model of behavior celebrated by modern thought praises the self-determining, responsible individual. The model of behavior urged by the more traditional religious thought praises the person who humbly submits to God's truth as it is found in scriptures or in religious teaching. The religious ideal has been one that usually approves only of the person who uses individual freedom to submit obediently to the one truth of God.

The challenge that the modern notion of personhood poses to religion is this: can religion truly promote the growth of each person toward authentic selfhood, one that is a responsible freedom exercised in a free society? Modern religion says yes also to this, but it has had to show how promoting this autonomous selfhood is religious rather than somehow foreign to true religiousness.

The Challenge of the Tentativeness of Knowledge

The fourth and final way modern thought has struck at traditional religion has been by shattering the idea that we can ever possess the final and correct understanding of reality. The experience of modern science fortified what many philosophers had been pointing out, that all human understanding is a way of interpreting reality, as hypothesis, theory, map, and model. It is often very reasonable and very useful knowledge, but there is always the possibility that some other different map or model might be a better tool for understanding how things probably are.

The notion of the tentativeness of knowledge has reinforced other modern values. If knowledge is always imperfect, then continuous research, reflection, and imagination are needed to explore endless possibilities. For this there must be freedom. Every person must be free to ride even the wildest horse of imagination in case it can lead us all into better terrain.

This means, in turn, that there will be a plurality of positions on any topic, whether in science, history, economics—or religion. Pluralism is now a fact in contemporary cultures; there is no longer a single accepted system of thought, moral code, or religious tradition. To the modern mind, pluralism is not merely a fact but a positive value. A plurality of interpretations is necessary to allow for the growth of ever better ones through free interplay and competition among them. This will also best serve the secular desire to improve the human condition through the growth of knowledge.

The tentativeness of knowledge makes the ideal of autonomous selfhood more important. If the truth about reality is obscure, uncertain, or changeable, then no person can rest content with tradition. Everyone must be prepared to look over new ideas, evaluate them in some way, and accept those that seem to be both more reasonable and valuable, even if this means discarding or changing older ideas.

Religion has not often been the friend of tentativeness, pluralism, and changeability. Religion serves to provide security in the face of life's threats; it is a haven from insecurity and confusion. Religious people have frequently insisted that their beliefs offer security precisely because they are not tentative models of reality, but instead are the clear and firm God-given, unchanging truth. Religion trusts its doctrines to be true.

Here the challenge to religion is whether there can be a religiousness that accepts the idea that its symbols and beliefs are tentative interpretations, symbols of ultimate truth, rather than rocklike, unchangeable doctrines. Can there be a religiousness that sustains people in their needs, but is still open to changes in belief and to a free competition of religious symbols in a pluralistic context of autonomous people? Modern religion says yes to this also, but it has to explain how.

Before looking at modern religion in some detail, it is good to remember that most religion today is not very modern. That is not necessarily a criticism. There is great value in tradition, and "modern" is not a synonym for "good." But in those areas of the world where modern ideas and values have flourished religious beliefs have been affected. There is a somewhat modern form of Hindu thought, for example, such as that of the Indian philosopher Sarvepali Radhakrishnan (1888–1975). Reform Judaism, which originated in 19th-century Germany, is quite modern. Most of the examples to follow here will be taken, however, from contemporary Christianity. But first to put modern religiousness in context, here are some contemporary unmodern alternatives.

RELIGIOUS BELIEFS TODAY

Traditional Faith with Accommodations

The religiousness that is still dominant now can probably be described best as that unchallenged traditional faith discussed at the end of Chapter Eleven. It is a faith that thinks of itself as comfortably traditional. It is historic in its central doctrines about God and salvation, but it may include a number of archaic elements.

It is also a faith that has accommodated itself to modern culture by adding some modern adaptations to traditional beliefs. Though it still firmly believes in God, it expects fewer miraculous interventions than past generations once did. Though it still hopes for life after death, it is willing to invest more energy in this-worldly social concerns about poverty and injustice. Though it believes that each person is a child of God, it also believes that we have been produced by an evolutionary process. Though it believes in the importance of God's work for all humankind, it is willing to make this a matter of personal belief and individual free choice rather than follow the tradition that says everyone should belong to the one true religion.

This traditional faith is often not conscious of how much accommodation to modern ideas it has made. This-worldly emphasis on justice, acceptance of evolution, and the rights of individuals to publicly disagree on religious matters were once radical ideas, considered to be very misleading or dangerous. There are conservative religious groups today that are not so ready to accommodate such ideas.

Fundamentalism

The most unaccommodating religious style is the one that has come to be known as fundamentalism. As Chapter Nine indicated, the name came from a conservative movement among American Protestants in the early 20th century. Against the growing force of modern thought in religion, known then as liberalism, a set of twelve volumes entitled *The Fundamentals* was set forth explaining and defending traditional Christian faith. The viewpoint was thoroughly unmodern and even anti-modern, rejecting all four of the main points of the modern challenge.

Fundamentalism rejects the idea that the basic religious beliefs might be only tentative formulations, useful but never fully adequate symbols. The doctrines of the Bible are God's eternal and unchangeable truths, given once and for all, says fundamentalism.

There is no purpose to human autonomy, according to fundamentalism, except to make the one valid choice of obedience to God's will and adherence to God's truth. We humans are too sinful to rely on our reason, to be self-determining. In fact, it is a sinful pride that inclines us ever to do so.

Involvement in this world is dangerous and misguided, insists fundamentalism. The secular world of history is a contest between good and evil. Those who follow God should help others in all kindness and charity, it is true, but they should not expect that justice and love can ever reign on this planet through human involvement in social causes. Only God's power, to come in full force some day, will finally defeat the powers of evil and establish a righteous kingdom.

Fundamentalism also rejects modern science's conclusions whenever they conflict with the fundamentalist's interpretation of God's truth. This is not a vast, 12-billion-year-old evolving universe lacking any clear plan or goal, but a more recent product of God's creative activity. It is under the ongoing general guidance of God and is directed specifically by God through many miraculous interventions. Fundamentalists tend to be creationists, believing that God made the earth, all the basic kinds of living things, as well as the first parents of all humans, about 6000 years ago. Some creationists have tried to claim that their interpretation of this is scientifically respectable, but the scientific community has been consistent and clear in rejecting that position.

Sects and Cults

Modern thought creates insecurity and confusion. The modern emphasis on tentative truth, on a need to be autonomously self-directing, on dedicated involvement in even the frustrating confusions of this world, and on the scientific method with its demand for honesty and self-criticism as well as its sometimes gloomy world views, has led many religious believers to cling more tightly to the security of traditional beliefs as in fundamentalism. These same threatening aspects of modern thought may also have a lot to do with the intensification of sectarian and cultic religion.

Christian sects are somewhat fundamentalist in their attitudes. Strict in defining beliefs, strict in providing moral rules, strict in expecting people to follow the single truth, they provide clarity and security. Variant or quasi-Christian sects do the same. The Mormons follow the Book of Mormon and not the Bible as such. The Unification church reads the Divine Principle of Rev. Sun

Myung Moon, loosely based on Judaeo-Christian tradition. But by strictness of belief and morality they provide a refuge from the ambiguities of modern thought.

Cultic groups, some of them Hindu-inspired, as in the case of the Krishna Consciousness movement, accomplish the same thing. Behind saffron robes, shaved heads, bells and incense, are the same human needs and hopes and fears all people share, and the same desire to find clear answers to life in the midst of its mysteries. These cults generally reject the modern challenges to religion, finding no value in secular, scientific, autonomous life according to tentative symbols.

Traditional faith along with fundamentalism and even sects and cults are all alternatives to modern religion. Many forms of non-modern religiousness are strong today. But, finally, it is modern religion that remains to be described.

MODERN RELIGION

Religion and Scientific World-Views

This world of ours as seen through the best available theories of science has little or no room for miracles, especially by comparison with the world views of prescientific cultures. This world also can easily appear in scientific theories as a random and aimless series of processes, rather than as one filled with divine guidance or directed toward some ultimate goal or value. Modern religion has had a very difficult time responding to all this. There are three major categories of responses by modern Christian theology to science: segregation, integration, and patience.

Segregation of Science and Religion

The first position has been to segregate religion from science, to quarantine religion in order to prevent contamination by the potential of science to produce skepticism. German theologian Friedrich Schleiermacher (1768-1834) led the way as long ago as 1799 when he published *On Religion: Speeches to its Cultured Despisers.* "True" religion, he said, is not the kind that is based on miracles. In fact, it is not dependent in any way on evidence from the world, evidence such as science depends on. True religion, claimed Schleiermacher, is based on an inner intuition or feeling, a sensitivity to the utterly awesome mystery of the universe as a reality that is right there all around us, but is inexplicable. Each item in the world is dependent on something else, and all things together proclaim: we do not account for ourselves. The perceptive soul will sense deeply and thoroughly that there is a God, the Other who is the Independent upon whom every person and all reality depend utterly. This is an insight or feeling, not a scientific conclusion, said Schleiermacher.

Another German, however, philosopher Ludwig Feuerbach (1804-1872), also analyzed our inner insights and feelings, but did so in order to show how our inner feelings about God or religion can deceive us. In *The Essence of Christianity* (1841), Feuerbach claimed that the intuition of God's reality of which Schleiermacher spoke is really only an intuition of our own inner capacity for the infinite, out of which we invent the idea of God.

Feuerbach described the potential of our own minds to form ideas of infinite perfection, to create images of perfect love and total power and unrestricted knowledge. But we see ourselves as finite and imperfect. In order to find the embodiment of infinite perfection, said Feuerbach, we invent it and call it "God," and then demean ourselves before this fiction through obedience and humility. Feuerbach wanted people to recognize "God" as nothing more than a product of their own wonderful, infinite capacity and thereby take pride in themselves. He wanted people to stop being obedient to their own invention called "God," and take control of their lives back into their own hands.

Feuerbach could not prove that his theory was true. But he did sow the suspicion that maybe we invented God as a projection onto the heavens of our own inner potential for the infinite. About 70 years later, Freud would give these suspicions new energy, as Chapter Two described. All this made it difficult to appeal, as Schleiermacher had, to one's own inner intuition or feeling or conviction that God exists. After all the belief might just be a self-delusion.

A semi-modern response to all this appeared in Switzerland just after World War I. Calvinist theologian Karl Barth (1886-1968) was modernist enough to abandon belief in miracles, but traditionally orthodox enough to claim that faith in God is a gift of God, not dependent on science or inner intuition or any other merely human source. This mixed response was called Neo-orthodox.

Barth was modern in that he translated all miracles into non-miracles. He treated the Bible, for example, not as a set of writings miraculously revealed or inspired by God, but as a recording made by people of their human responses to Jesus. He spoke even of the Christian doctrine of life after death not so much as literal truth but as a symbol of a more general trust that somehow human life has ultimate meaning in spite of the fact that we all die.

Barth was not very modern, though, in his insistence on the very traditional Christian doctrine that faith in God is an inner state created in us by the action of God's grace working in us. No human power, not human reason as in science, nor human intuition and feeling as in Schleiermacher's theology, can possibly bring us to faith in God. A kind of blind faith is justified on the grounds that the God who is beyond human reason can be known only by the power of God's grace. Only God can produce faith in God, said Barth. This was the main emphasis of Neo-Orthodoxy.

Unfortunately Barth was never very clear on explaining how God can do this if God does not literally work miracles, because the action of God's grace on people seems to be a kind of miracle. Moreover, Barth's claim was open to the criticism that it is a circular argument. Barth said he believed in God because God gave him the grace to believe. But how did Barth know there even was a God to be the cause of belief in God? God had to give Barth the grace to make him believe that. The followers of Feuerbach and Freud were still suspicious. Maybe the belief in God's grace is just part of the overall fictional idea that God exists at all.

In response to all this a German scripture scholar named Rudolph Bultmann (1884–1976) proposed another way of segregating religious belief from threatening scientific world-views. He was called a Christian existentialist because he too thought that we humans "ex-ist." The best scientific evidence, Bultmann believed, makes the universe look like an aimless process with no ultimate meaning to it. Yet, we humans are the kind of being that the existentialists say we are, in need of meaning, even ultimate meaning, in order to have some direction and purpose to our lives. So we stand out as beings whose conscious awareness makes them seek ultimate values as a ground for a meaningful life in a universe where there is no ultimate value. On the surface, therefore, life does appear to be absurd.

In spite of this existentialist interpretation of the human situation, Bultmann was a Christian because of his response to the situation. What was needed, said Bultmann, was a free human decision to face down the awful implications of science and shout out loud, "Nevertheless." Nevertheless, he said, I will believe that there is Ultimate meaning and value; in spite of all the external scientific evidence I will rely on my internal courage and freedom and stand up to emptiness, stand up to death, and believe. As a Christian, Bultmann took his inspiration from the example of Jesus of Nazareth. In Bultmann's interpretation Jesus leads the way for this great and courageous "nevertheless," by his willingness to take on even a horrible death on the cross because of his dedication to God as ultimate meaning of life.

Those who live by blind faith have already partly taken Bultmann's position, though usually without all the existentialist language. But Bultmann's rather desperate response has not appealed to everyone. Those who live by unchallenged traditional faith feel no need for it. Many people are probably satisfied with just a rather general sense that science is science and religion is religion, that the two are separate and should not interfere with each other. Others, however, have found ways to integrate science and religion.

Integration of Science and Religion

The deists had united science and religion by replacing traditional sacred sources such as Bible and church with human reason and using that reason to produce a religious view of God as Great Watchmaker-Creator. When evolutionary thought filled the intellectual air, German philosopher G. W. F. Hegel (1770-1831) set out a massively complex theory in 1807 that the universe of science was not aimless and dead but an evolution of God, of a divine Spirit evolving into greater and greater spiritual self-awareness.

By the 20th century, some French philosophers were exploring similar ideas. An Englishman, Alfred North Whitehead (1861-1947), came to Boston and Harvard to propose a philosophy of nature that was highly religious, based nonetheless on scientific descriptions of nature. (Charles Hartshorne, mentioned in Chapter Eleven, is one of the major proponents and developers of Whitehead's position.)

A French paleontologist and Jesuit priest, Pierre Teilhard de Chardin (1881-1955), offered a science-based religious interpretation of the universe that is an easier example to explain here because it is close to the views of Julian Huxley, which we have already seen.

Teilhard (to use the usual brief way of referring to him) looked at the whole cosmic process of change and did not see aimlessness there. Like Huxley, he saw a process of complexification going on, as each stage of cosmic evolution produced variant forms, which then combined in more complexly organized unities—from particles to atoms to compounds to basic genetic material to life forms to cells to organisms to humans and their stages of social development. Like Huxley, Teilhard also saw this as a process with a direction toward higher and higher consciousness. This in turn was producing higher and higher levels of interpersonness, as human consciousness led to family life, social connectedness, global communications, and so forth.

Teilhard felt that it was scientifically legitimate to claim that there must be a force at work throughout the entire cosmos, driving it along the path toward ever more complex organization, and hence also toward ever greater consciousness, humaneness, interpersonalness. Just as a scientist argues for the existence of the invisible force called gravity to account for the observed actions of physical bodies, so Teilhard argued for the existence of an invisible cosmic force behind the directionality of evolution toward personalization. Teilhard felt it was therefore scientifically sound to claim that there must be a supreme Personness or Person that was the primary driving force of evolution. This is actually a variation of the "argument from design" for the existence of God.

In fact, Teilhard felt it was legitimate to claim that the tendency of all things to unite in ever more complex and conscious ways was a sign that love, a tendency toward union, is the ultimate force behind everything. God is love, Teilhard claimed. The goal of all cosmos evolution is a final and complete union with God, a goal that was already beginning to be realized in the growth of conscious love in the human element of the cosmos.

Teilhard tried to prove too much, perhaps. He managed to find all sorts of ways in which scientific theories could support his own Christian faith, even on many specifics concerning God and Christ and the eventual end of the world, though he had to reinterpret some traditional doctrines to make it all work. In contrast with such an ambitious attempt to show in detail how religious beliefs and scientific conclusions mesh, some have made more modest claims.

Patient Moderation Concerning Science and Religion

Some have severely divided religion from science; others have made them fit together very intimately. A third approach has been one of patience and hope. This middle ground is taken by those who do not claim to have the answers about the eventual interplay between religious beliefs and scientific theories, but who will nevertheless trust that in the long run good science and reasonable religious faith will prove compatible.

Such a position is sometimes one of a traditional faith that has adapted slowly to some aspects of modern thought. Modern religiousness also often takes the position of cautious hope in that it happily accepts science, secularity, human autonomy, and the tentativeness of knowledge. It is willing to insist that faith should be a reasonable choice of a free person concerned with the worldly conditions of all people.

On the whole, this position accepts science rather than hides from it. It accepts the scientific notion that claims about what is true or not true should not be merely a matter of individual inner experience, obedience, or commitment, but also, at least, a publicly defensible position. Science corrects its own tendencies toward prejudice, bias, or premature conviction by insisting that all people who are willing to try should be given a chance to test the evidence and study the reasoning behind any conclusions. This process of public reasoning is one that many of the patient moderates are willing to engage in about their own religious beliefs as well.

In general, it is safe to say that modern religion tries to be honestly reasonable. It trusts that somehow religious claims about life's meaning have not been invalidated by the methods or conclusions of science. A later section will say more about all this.

Religion and Secularity

Schleiermacher, Teilhard, Barth, Bultmann, and the moderates in between are all modern in their willingness to live without expectation of miracles, without specific interventions by God to control individual events or give directions on how to act. That means that this religiousness is not primarily a means to get help and guidance from God. It has a more secular purpose. The secularity that arose in recent centuries often advocated a total secularism, a denial that there is anything at all to existence except the ongoing problems of life, a denial of any numinous or divine dimension. But in the 19th and 20th centuries, modern religion has begun to see secular interest in this world as part of its own purposes.

Traditional historic Western religion insisted that people are weak and confused, in need of divine help. Modern religion has come to agree that indeed we humans do suffer under many limitations, but modern religiousness has a stronger trust that there is also much strength already present in us just as we are. Modern religiousness has a faith that our existence somehow comes from

God and that this numinous source of our being has always empowered us to do what is worthwhile. In this sense, help from God is always already present; there is little need for additional acts by God in some miraculous way. A common modern way of speaking of God, in fact, is to use a model God as one who calls and empowers rather than one who intervenes.

As the Infinite, God is a symbol of all that has yet to be done, of the more that is always possible. Meditation on God is reflection on goodness to be achieved. God is the one who calls and empowers people to do all of value that can be done. In the modern style of thought this is a symbolic way of speaking to represent a human trust that the divine reality is somehow there behind our efforts to live life for one another, even if we cannot know just how that divine presence works. This trust is a basis for taking charge of human life in this world to make it better as much as is possible.

Where traditional historic religion has viewed this world as fallen, a source of sin, unable to be improved (unless it is first destroyed), Anglican bishop John A. T. Robinson (1919-1983) summed up a contrary, rather modern religious appreciation of this world in his small book, *Honest to God* (1963). The world is not ungodly, but God's presence, said Robinson. God is not "up there" or "out there," Robinson declared, not a figure in the sky as though divine realities were removed from worldly ones. Rather, the infinite divine Mystery is the ground and source of all creation, especially the ground and source of personness. So to find the presence of the mystery of God, look to what exists around us, to creation and especially to other persons. It is not "out there" but within things that God is to be found.

To Robinson, these are not just traditional pious thoughts about the presence of God in all things. They have implications for how to be religious. What Robinson recommends is a secular religiousness, a "worldly holiness," as he calls it. This means a deep and consistent involvement in all that touches on persons in the world. Concretely, it means that concern for political freedom, social equality, psychological well-being, physical health, and all the other aspects of human life, are ways of involvement in the presence of God.

This is especially secular because Robinson and others like him do not say much about a life after death as salvation. The salvation they are mainly concerned about is a worldly one. It is a continuous healing of the world's wounds, a constant attention to the needs of personness as being of ultimate value here and now.

Striking examples of this secular religiousness are the various Christian liberation theologies, as they are called. Black liberation theology is a theology that interprets human existence in terms of the experience of oppression. To understand and feel what it is to be oppressed is the foundation of an approach to life that works for a transformation of earthly conditions, material, political, economic, social, and psychological; an approach that sees this work as the basic meaning of the idea of building God's "kingdom" on earth. It is a response to God as to a call to change the conditions of our lives.

Likewise, women's liberation theology brings to consciousness the reality of domination through power, of a division of people into the higher and lower, then rejects these as a model for human existence. Equality, cooperation, and mutual supportiveness are the ideals of feminist theology, not just as useful virtues but as the key images for interpreting where life's ultimate values and meaning lie.

Similarly, the Catholic social-political liberation theologians of Latin America claim that the most immediately imperative religious project is not that of getting to heaven at some future time but of transforming earthly conditions as much as possible now in an ongoing way. Trusting that God will take care of the ultimate destiny of their lives, these liberation theologians respond to God as the God of the poor and oppressed, of those who live their humanness under stifling conditions of domination. The domination itself and all the social, economic, and political structures that support it are the "sin" that these religious liberationists attack.

A final secular interest of modern religion is ecology. Traditional Christianity had a number of ideas that went contrary to a concern to preserve the earth. Apocalyptic-minded Christians even today have said that God will destroy the earth before long, so that attempts to preserve the earth are foolish. Christians who look to heaven as the only true home may also loose interest in caring for the planet. And the scriptures tell its readers to subdue the earth. They do not explicitly say to cooperate with it. But some modern Christians claim that the most basic belief should be that this universe is God's creation, to be cherished and respected. These Christians take it as their God-given responsibility to care for the earth, preparing it to be a better place for the generations still to come. This is a somewhat secular, i.e., this-worldly, orientation.

Religion and Autonomous Selfhood

Modern thought values individual freedom very highly, emphasizing that the capacity for self-determination means that each person is *responsible* for all of his or her values and for his or her choices. Traditional religion in the West has also held each person responsible for her or his choices. But there is nonetheless a difference between modern and traditional views. That difference lies in the amount of confidence placed in human ability to do what is good.

Traditional Christianity describes us humans as fallen, weak of will, and confused of mind. We are fallen people in a fallen world, unable to reason clearly, whose autonomy leads to sin, whose secular involvement is a mistake, and whose science is not to be trusted when it conflicts with revealed truth.

The modern evaluation of the person, on the other hand, trusts that our capacity for autonomy is to be trusted and encouraged for the sake of making constructive and creative decisions for improving worldly existence, sometimes with confidence in science as the best way available to judge what is probably the truth.

All of this can be very unreligious, even anti-religious, as in many forms of secular humanism. But a number of contemporary theologians perceive a religiousness that lies within such secular humanness and that is intrinsic to science, secularity, and a concern for autonomy. Various persons have recently supported this idea in similar ways: Bernard Lonergan (1904–1984), Karl Rahner (1904–1984), Schubert Ogden (b. 1928), and others. The names are not important here; a general presentation of the basic idea will do. To have a handy label, we can call it the implicit-faith position.

The main theme is that there is a genuine religiousness that is part of any trust in human responsible autonomy, although it may be a hidden or implicit religiousness. When persons take on their shoulders the burden of using their own efforts in science, for example, to determine what is true, or the burden of making their own decisions about love and loyalty to one another as the most basic value of their lives, they are making implicit acts of faith that there is ultimate meaning and value in human life.

Whenever a scientific inquirer pursues knowledge through the human method of investigating and theorizing and testing, that inquirer is showing faith in the fact that, first of all, reality is intelligible. This is a reasonable faith; it works well in practice. But it is also a kind of faith in the world. That inquirer, secondly, is making an act of faith in her or his own intelligence and responsibility. This also is a reasonable faith. The human scientific enterprise has worked fairly well in learning more and more. We have some reason to trust our powers of understanding and commitment to truth, in spite of our many failures.

Most important, there is a fundamental faith at work that it is really worthwhile being a knower, being a person in pursuit of understanding. Atheistic existentialism challenges religion to show that ultimately anything makes sense. Without answering that challenge directly, even seemingly non-religious people pursue knowledge through science as though it really were worthwhile. They thereby act as though they had an implicit faith that it really does make sense to be a human person, using the person's power to learn and to develop new knowledge. This is an implicit act of faith in the ultimate value of being a knower.

The same implicit faith appears when we love one another or give deep loyalty to others or bring our children into this world. We thereby act as though we trust that life makes sense. This manifests an implicit faith that our selfhood, our consciousness, our ability to learn and choose and love are ultimately meaningful. All this can be a faith in the value of autonomous selfhood because it is precisely our ability to learn and choose, to think for ourselves and make responsible choices, that is autonomy.

This faith in ourselves is not ultimately valid if in fact the ultimate truth about life is that it is a meaningless accident in an aimless universe. Our selfhood is ultimately valid if it somehow rests upon a source or ground of ultimate meaning and value. Belief in God as Personal is a belief that personhood is grounded in Personhood. The Hebrew Scriptures expressed this by saying that every person is made "in the image and likeness of God." In this belief every person is therefore a symbol, a re-presentation, of the Ultimate. A belief, therefore, in the ultimate value of autonomous selfhood is an implicit faith that there is indeed something like God as the ultimate truth.

Notice that in this implicit faith a person does not believe in God on the basis of an outside authority instructing the person to do so. Belief in a personal God is instead based on a prior act of self-affirmation. Theism thus becomes a reasonable way to spell out and affirm a person's basic faith in the ultimate worth of being a person. This implicit-faith position supports the idea of faith as a reasonable commitment.

The Christian theologians who argue this way go a step further and claim that the vision of a human person, Jesus of Nazareth, as the presence of the mystery of God helps to express and maintain this faith in personness. Similarly, for the Jewish religious philosopher Martin Buber (1878–1965), every time we encounter someone else on a personal level, as a "thou," to use Buber's language, we encounter the presence of God. In these implicit-faith theologies the modern emphasis on individual and free personness is not found to be unreligious, but intrinsically religious.

Religion and Tentative Knowledge

Fundamentalists strive to maintain a strict adherence to what they see as the single truth delivered by God. Even those of a more accommodating but traditional faith attach a high degree of certitude and permanence to their religious beliefs. In contrast, a result of modern reflection on science and history has been the conclusion that all our ideas have changed and will change again, even our religious beliefs.

There are religious thinkers who have found that their faith could get along quite well with the idea that all knowledge, even religious belief, is tentative. They have found that they can be modern in their religiousness by emphasizing an idea that is actually rather traditional, that is that God is a name for the Ultimate Reality that lies beyond human comprehension. The infinite Mystery of God can never be captured by any name, category, or belief that the human mind can comprehend. Many religious beliefs may be valid symbols of the infinite Mystery, but every such valid belief is also inadequate. Every legitimate idea about God is a clue to the full reality of God, but is not the simple truth. Therefore, all ways of speaking of God are open to improvement. Alternative ways may also be legitimate.

Religious traditions usually ignore the limitations of the beliefs and practices. It is more comfortable to feel secure with firm and clear doctrines than to stand before Mystery. But the actual history of the traditions exhibits many changes. Rituals, moral codes, leadership roles, interpretations of sacred sources, ideas of salvation: these have all undergone changes. The changes might be rare in some cases, but if even one unexpected change is legitimate, then many more may eventually turn out to be also.

Religious tradition has made available some core symbols. It may be that some of these in particular remain basically unchanged, generation after generation. A thousand years from now people will likely still be praying "I believe in God..." or "There is no God but God..." or "Hear, O Israel, the Lord your God is one." Yet, the ways in which these words will be understood by future generations are never fully predictable. There is a degree of tenta-tiveness. Historic religion has usually been committed to many specific doctrines and rules as the universally valid truths for all people, everywhere, at all times. The elaborate systems of theolo-gy such as those constructed by an Anselm or an Aquinas are tes-timonies to this. Modern religion, on the other hand, tends to commit itself not so much to the many specific beliefs and practic-es as to an underlying, more general faith in the ultimate meaning and value of being a person in the universe.

Modern religious faith is focused on the ultimate meaning and value of being a person, a real, concrete, world-developing per-son, free and capable of responsibility, conscious and able to grow in understanding. It is a faith that scientific honesty is not ungod-ly, that secular concern is not a distraction from God, that self-affirmation is not a sin of pride, and that openness to change in re-ligious forms is not an abandonment of religion.

THE FUTURE OF RELIGION

Religion will continue to exist. As conscious beings, we will al-ways face mystery. Our basic faith in the intelligibility and value of our existence will shine through all our doubts and confusion, and we will give that faith concrete expression in various beliefs and practices that tradition makes available to us.

Religion will continue to take many forms. This is true partly because there are many traditions, each with its own symbols. It is also true because even if there were but one religious tradition in the world with one set of symbols, different people would still in-terpret them in different ways.

Each of us has some primitive-style memories and feelings and thoughts, a sense of meeting and sharing in something mysterious and even numinous. Each of us has some archaic inclinations to see reality as an arena of conflicting finite powers, some of them numinous perhaps. Each of us has some exposure to the historic style, the universalizing impulse to believe in an overall unity, a single truth, the one right way to be and to act, perhaps expressed as a belief in one God. And each of us has been touched by mod-ernness in some ways.

Historic religion did not eliminate primitive or archaic ideas. It transformed them by taking them under its universalizing um-brella. Modern religion will certainly not eliminate or replace primitive, archaic, or historic thought. What it will probably do is exert a continuing influence on the great historical syntheses by relativizing them.

The absolute doctrines of historic thought will be tempered by the modern sense of tentativeness. The historic passion for perfection beyond this world will be diluted by an involvement in the far less than perfect ambiguities of this world. A patience with science and an enthusiasm for its method of honesty will counterbalance the historic desire to affirm final answers once and for all. A modern appreciation of autonomy will guard against the historic temptation to make all people follow the one true path.

A constant temptation modern religiousness faces is to become impatient with other styles of religiousness and to try to abandon them. This would be foolish. The other styles, primitive, archaic, and historic, are part of the life of each of us. It is unwise to try to ignore part of one's own life story. The other styles are also an endless source of riches. Without all the symbols, moral codes, and belief structures of the past, modern religiousness would be an attitude without specific expression, an orientation without concrete form.

Modern religion faces the danger of increasing vagueness of belief and values and direction in life. Where historic religion offers clear and precise beliefs, where archaic-style religion provides inspiring myths to symbolize the meaning of life, modern religion is open to so many stories and to so many interpretations of beliefs that it can lose all focus. It needs to have strong stories and clear doctrines as symbols of its basic faith. Modern religiousness will be vital to the extent that it learns how to cherish and draw upon the rich resources of historic and archaic traditions.

The future of religion will be what it has always been, troubled and confused as well as joyful and invigorating, destructive as well as life-giving. But it will be there because we are the religious animal, the being whose consciousness leads us into mysteries, and whose faith in the meaningfulness of life leads us to perceive a kind of divinity in that mystery.

Summary

This chapter has reviewed the main challenges of modern thought to religion, and the responses of modern religion. Most religion today is not all that modern. Fundamentalism rejects the modern orientation entirely. Much of traditional faith has accommodated itself to modernness in some ways. There is, however, a religiousness that is rather thoroughly modern in that it has come to terms with scientific world-views, has a secular orientation, promotes responsible autonomy, and lives by an openness to new ideas and changes. Modern thought in religion will never replace earlier forms, but it will continue to influence them as well as draw upon their heritage.

FOR FURTHER REFLECTION

1. Which of the challenges of modern thought to religion are worth taking most seriously: the challenges of science, secularity, autonomy, or tentativeness of belief? Why?

2. Is it legitimate and possible to maintain traditional faith in these modern times? Why? Why not?

3. To what extent does your religious faith rest mainly on inner experience or choice rather than on external evidence?

4. Identify the main themes of the three kinds of liberation movements and explain why they should or should not be taken seriously by religion.

5. Are other people worth loving because God says so, or because they are of intrinsic value? Explain.

6. How useful is a religion that cannot guarantee the stable permanence of its beliefs and moral rules and so forth?

7. How much more must a religion do for people beyond affirming its basic faith that there is ultimate value in being a person in the world? Explain.

SUGGESTED READINGS

Roger A. Johnson, *et al.*, *Critical Issues in Modern Religion*, 2nd ed., 1990; an excellent introduction to many issues in this chapter.

Rudolph Otto, *The Idea of the Holy*, 1958; chapters 1-3 present an influential Schleiermacher-style interpretation of religion.

Ronald Gregor Smith, *Secular Christianity*, 1966.

John A. T. Robinson, *Honest to God*, 1963; chapter 5 "Worldly Holiness."

Paul Tillich, *Shaking the Foundations*, 1948; ch. 7 "The Depth of Existence."

Karl Rahner, *Theological Investigations*, Vol XX, 1981; chapter 13, The inexhaustible transcendence of God and our concern for the future.

John Haught, *Religion and Self-Acceptance*, 1980; an implicit-faith response to most of the challenges to religion.

Yvonne Yazbeck Haddad and Ellison Banks Findley, eds., *Women, Religion, and Social Change*, 1985; a collection of essays on women and religion in various cultures and times.

Robert Ellwood, *The History and Future of Faith*, 1988; chapter 8 offers three alternative scenarios on the future of religion in the secularized world.

Epilogue

This has been an interpretation of the story of religion, an attempt to make sense of human religiousness. There are dangers in any such attempt.

One danger is that of forcing all religiousness into categories we can make sense of. There are elements of religiousness, just as there are elements of art and values, that elude our nicely sensible categories. Some degree of mystery exists within all aspects of humanness, including human religiousness.

A second danger is to take the categories by which religion is analyzed here, categories such as primitive, archaic, historic, and modern, too literally. All such categories are artificial approximations. They provide reference points like lines of latitude and longitude on a map. The real contours of land and flow of weather patterns do not fit neatly into such lines. And in the case of the story of religiousness, we are still in the early days of map-making with much to learn.

The map here portrays religion in history as a process whereby we human beings come to terms with the mysteries of life, which our peculiar consciousness unendingly reveal to us. It is a map of religion and culture evolving together. This map may have led you a little further along the path that generations before you have taken towards a greater sense of mystery and a concomitant greater sense of selfhood. But no map can substitute for the actual, wonderfully confusing process of living.

In spite of all the possible dangers and confusion, the attempt to understand our religiousness is well worthwhile. The adventure of human existence continues. The religious dimension—our orientation to the endless Mystery—is at the heart of that adventure.

Index

(Also see Table of Contents subheadings)